DATE DUE

3-2-07	

GAYLORD   PRINTED IN U.S.A.

DOCKRILL

PEACE WITHOUT...

Peace without Promise

Peace without Promise

Britain and the Peace Conferences, 1919-23

Michael L. Dockrill
and
J. Douglas Goold

ARCHON BOOKS

Hamden, Connecticut

First published 1981 in England by
Batsford Academic and Educational Ltd
and in the U.S.A. as an Archon Book
an imprint of
The Shoe String Press Inc.
995 Sherman Avenue
Hamden, Connecticut 06514

ISBN 0-208-01909-X

Made and Printed in Great Britain

Library of Congress Cataloging in Publication Data

Dockrill, M. L.
  Peace without promise.

  Bibliography: p.
  Includes index.
  1. European War, 1914-1918.–Peace. 2. European War,
1914-1918–Great Britain. 3. Great Britain–Foreign relations–
1910-1936. 4. European War, 1914-1918–Territorial questions.
5. Europe–History–1918-1945. 6. Near East–History–
20th century. I. Goold, J. Douglas, joint author. II. Title.
D645.D58   1981   940.3'141   80-28121
ISBN 0-208-01909-X (Shoe String Press)

To the memory of
Cedric Lowe

CONTENTS

Abbreviations	9
Preface	10
Maps	12
Chapter 1 Britain Prepares for Peace	17
Chapter 2 The German Settlement	31
The Rhineland	34
The Saar	38
Belgium	39
German disarmament	43
Reparations	45
The League of Nations	56
The German colonies	64
Aftermath, June 1919	69
Epilogue	80
Chapter 3 The East European Settlement	87
Bulgaria	93
Rumania and Hungary	101
Yugoslavia and Italy	105
Czechoslovakia	110
Austria	111
Poland	113
The Baltic provinces	118
Russia	121
The Hungarian settlement	125
Fiume	127

Chapter 4   The Dissolution of the Ottoman Empire:
   the Middle East, 1919-1920   131
   Introduction and background, 1914-18   131
   Britain's position and policies at the end of the
      war   143
   Emir Faisal's claims at the Peace Conference   150
   The Zionist's claims   158
   The King-Crane Commission   162
   The British withdrawal and French occupation
      of Syria, Armenia and Cilicia   164
   Faisal's secret agreement with the French, and
      Anglo-French negotiations, December 1919   169
   The Syrian Coup   172
   San Remo   173

Chapter 5   The Dissolution of the Ottoman Empire:
   Turkey 1919-1923   181
   Introduction and background   181
   The conflicting aims of the Greeks and the
      Italians   186
   The decision to land Greek troups at Smyrna,
      May 1919   190
   The problems of the Greeks and Italians in
      Anatolia, June-December 1919   199
   The rise of Mustapha Kemal   202
   Anglo-French conversations on the future of
      Turkey, December 1919   204
   The Treaty of Sèvres, 10 August 1920   207
   The Greek advance and the fall of Venizelos,
      June-December 1920   214
   The London Conference and its failure,
      February-March 1921   216
   The continuation of the war   219
   Anglo-French acrimony and the postponement
      of allied mediation, October 1921-January
      1922   221
   The desperate position of the Greeks, and the
      final attempt at allied mediation   223
   Montagu's resignation, March 1922   225

Lloyd George and the Greeks, January-August 1922   226

The Chanak crisis, September-October 1922   228

The Conference of Lausanne, 20 November-July 1923   236

Conclusion   253

Notes   259

Bibliography   275

Index   281

ABBREVIATIONS

CAB   Cabinet Papers
DBFP Documents on British Foreign Policy 1919-39 First Series
FO   Foreign Office
FRUS Foreign Relations of the United States; Paris Peace Conference, 1919
HJ   Historical Journal
IO   India Office
JCH   Journal of Contemporary History
JMH   Journal of Modern History
WO   War Office

PREFACE

Peace Without Promise examines Great Britain's policy towards the entire peace settlement after the First World War. That settlement remains to this day the most important since the Congress of Vienna remoulded Europe after the destruction of the Napoleonic Wars. The work utilizes the most recent unpublished archival materials. It is also alone in considering in a single volume all the peace treaties, and the negotiations leading up to them, that Britain signed from 1919 to 1923 with her wartime enemies: Germany, Austria, Hungary, Bulgaria and the Ottoman Empire.

Any attempt to deal with this settlement is fraught with awesome problems. The source material and published literature is vast. The controversy surrounding the treaties was gathering momentum even before they were completed. In the case of the Treaty of Versailles, that controversy profoundly influenced the politics of the interwar years, and even beyond. Because the peace involves such an enormous number of important and complex issues, and affected virtually all parts of the globe, some questions have necessarily had to be omitted or dealt with only briefly, in keeping with the strictly limited space available.

We are grateful to the Controller of Her Majesty's Stationery Office for permission to quote from unpublished Crown Copyright material held at the Public Record Office and from Crown Copyright records in the India Office Political Department papers, to the Department of Manuscripts of the British Museum for the authority to reproduce material in the Balfour papers, to Lord Scarsdale and the Kedleston Trust for permission to transcribe unpublished Copyright material in the Curzon Papers at the India Office Library, to Mr A. J. P. Taylor and the Trustees of the Beaverbrook Foundation and to the Clerk of Records at the House of Lords for approval to quote from unpublished material in the David Lloyd George papers held at the House of Lords, to the Marquess of Lothian for permission to quote from the private papers of Philip Kerr at the Scottish Record Office and to the Cambridge University Press for authorization to reproduce material in the Hardinge papers. We are most grateful for the assistance we received from the librarians and archivists at the above institutions.

We would also like to thank the Canada Council for their generous assistance, which enabled us to complete the massive undertaking of researching the huge collection of the Paris Peace Conference (the Foreign Office 608 series) at the Public Record Office more expeditiously than would otherwise have been possible. We are highly conscious of the helpful advice and support generously given to us throughout by Dr Zara Steiner of New Hall, Cambridge, and by Professor F. H. Hinsley, Master of St John's College, Cambridge, although of course the views the authors express in this volume are entirely our own. Our thanks are also due to Mrs Sylvia Smither who was faced with the formidable task of typing our much amended manuscripts. Finally this book is dedicated to the memory of the late Professor Cedric Lowe of the University of Edmonton, Alberta, Canada, who was an associate and close friend of both authors, and who died tragically in a motor accident in 1975.

M. L. DOCKRILL AND J. DOUGLAS GOOLD
London and Edmonton   1980

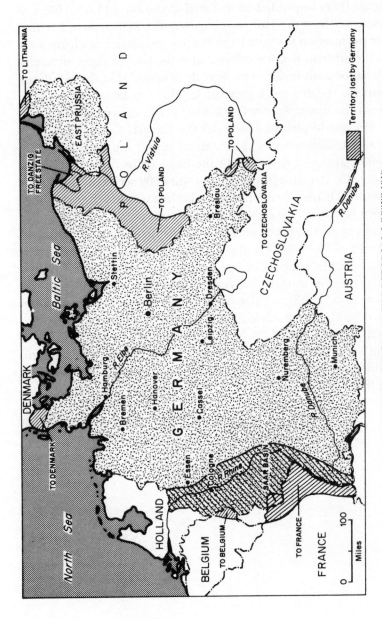

I GERMANY'S EUROPEAN TERRITORIAL LOSSES 1919

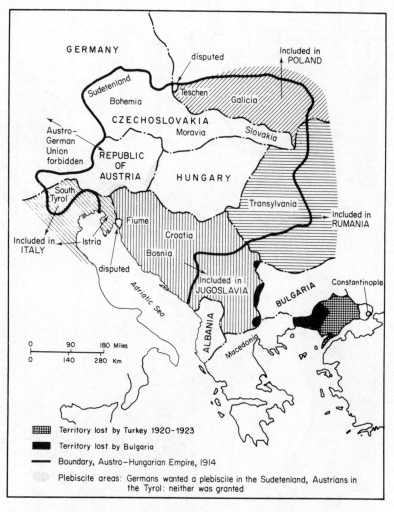

II THE PEACE SETTLEMENT: CENTRAL AND SOUTH-EASTERN EUROPE
1919-1923

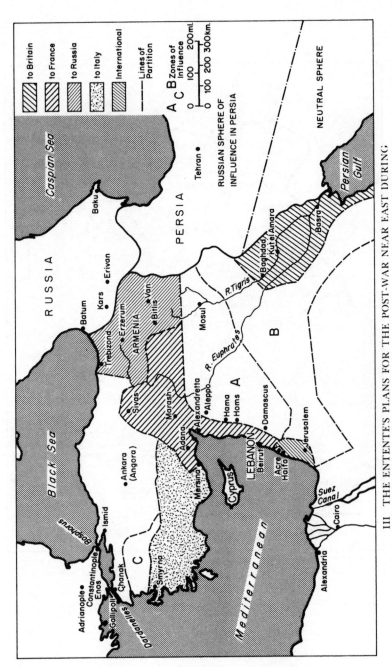

III THE ENTENTE'S PLANS FOR THE POST-WAR NEAR EAST DURING THE FIRST WORLD WAR

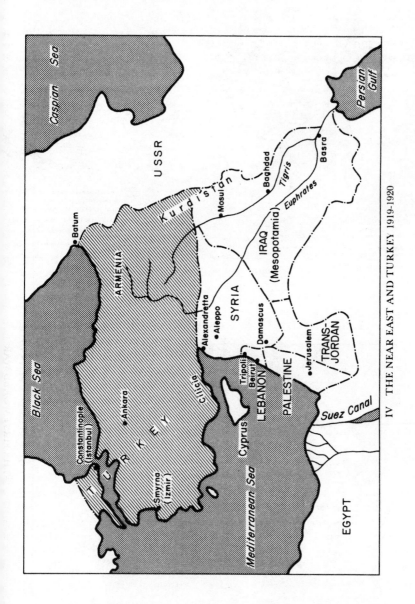

IV THE NEAR EAST AND TURKEY 1919-1920

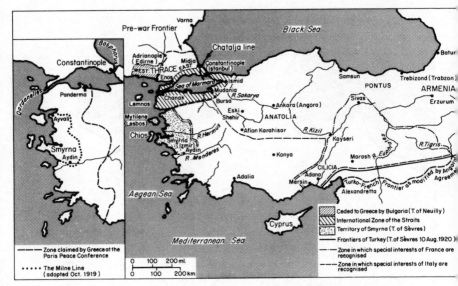

V THE DIVISION OF TURKEY PROPER 1919-1920

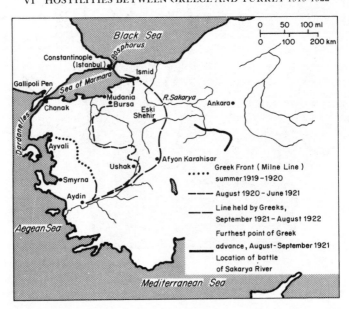

VI HOSTILITIES BETWEEN GREECE AND TURKEY 1919-1922

CHAPTER ONE

BRITAIN PREPARES FOR PEACE

During the early years of the war, the British Government did not prepare any comprehensive war aims programme.[1] In public the Asquith administration emphasized that the war had been forced on Britain by Germany's ruthless violation of Belgian neutrality, and that Britain's intervention was in accordance with her traditional concern for the rights of small nations and the sanctity of international treaties. At the end of July 1914 the Foreign Secretary, Sir Edward Grey, insisted in the cabinet that Britain had to become involved in order to preserve French independence and to maintain the balance of power. However, it was on the evils of Prussian militarism that government spokesmen concentrated once Britain had entered the war.

Although there was hardly any alteration in this public stance, the British government was forced, once the early expectations of a rapid allied victory were confounded, to expand its commitments in order to attract new allies and to maintain the loyalty of the existing ones. Thus the secret treaties with Italy in 1915 and with Rumania in 1916 promised these countries generous territorial compensation at the expense of the Habsburg empire. Added to these were the secret agreements with France and Italy, pledging British support for their aspirations in the Ottoman empire,[2] and with Japan in 1917, when she was assured of British support for her demand for Germany's rights in Shantung. When the Russian Bolsheviks published some of these agreements at the end of 1917, the British government was placed in an embarrassing position, since the agreements conflicted with President Wilson's post-war programme and with sections of Entente public opinion which supported a peace without selfish territorial gains.

The advent of David Lloyd George as the Prime Minister in a predominantly Unionist coalition on 6 December 1916 did not at first end the government's reluctance to encourage public discussion of war aims. In fact the reverse was the case since most of the Unionist ministers were out of sympathy with 'idealistic' peace talk. A German peace offer and an American proposal for a negotiated peace were brushed aside. Indeed, when the United States declared war on Germany in April 1917, the pressure for public statements on war aims diminished, because President Wilson discouraged them. Since it would be difficult to formulate a common Entente programme Wilson felt that such public discussion would only lead to disagreements within the allied camp, and inhibit the conclusion of a separate peace with one or more of Germany's allies.

Towards the end of 1917, however, the British government's attitude began to change. There was a ground-swell of liberal and radical opinion, identifying itself with Wilsonian idealism, in favour of a British declaration in support of an 'idealistic' peace. With almost nothing to show for the carnage on the Western Front, and increasing war weariness at home, an initiative which could steel the masses for the sacrifices which lay ahead and undermine the will of the enemy populations appeared attractive. In A.J.P.Taylor's words, 'the great purpose of war aims became increasingly to satisfy allied opinion in the Allied countries and in the United States'.[3]

Lloyd George's hand was forced by the negotiations between the Central Powers and the Bolsheviks at Brest-Litovsk, negotiations which were based (in principle, but not, as it turned out in practice) on national self-determination. The British Prime Minister wanted both to warn the Bolsheviks against concluding a separate peace with Germany, and to convince the British working class that the Entente was committed to a just peace.

On 5 January 1918 Lloyd George delivered his famous war aims address to the Trades Union Congress in London. Much of it was taken from drafts prepared by General Jan Christian

Smuts, a member of the Imperial War Cabinet, and Lord Robert Cecil, the Minister of Blockade. Lloyd George assured his audience that Britain had no intention of destroying Germany or Austria-Hungary, but that the new Europe must be based on 'reason and justice' and 'on government with the consent of the governed'. Specifically Britain demanded the liberation and indemnification of Belgium, and the restoration of Serbia, Montenegro and the occupied areas of France, Rumania and Italy. The Prime Minister also called for the 'reconsideration of the great wrong' done to France in 1871 (a reference to France's loss of Alsace-Lorraine), an independent Poland, self-government for the Austro-Hungarian nationalities, the satisfaction of the legitimate claims of Italy and Rumania, and recognition of the separate nationalities of Turkey. Self-determination would be applied to Germany's former colonies. The allies could not be expected to assist a Russia whose people showed no disposition to fight for themselves, and some form of international organization would have to be established to settle future disputes and limit armaments. 'Finally,' Lloyd George contended, 'there must be reparation for injuries done in violation of international law.'[4]

His speech was followed three days later by Woodrow Wilson's enunciation of his Fourteen Points, which received much greater acclaim from Entente liberal opinion than the British Prime Minister's effort. Many of the President's points coincided with those of Lloyd George, although there had been no prior collaboration between them, and the President went further in some directions than had the British Prime Minister. He demanded 'open covenants of peace openly arrived at', 'absolute freedom of navigation upon the high seas', 'the removal . . . of economic barriers', 'the evacuation of all Russian territory', and her admission 'into the society of free nations', 'the restoration of Alsace-Lorraine to France', and the formation of 'a general association of nations . . . under specific covenants for the purpose of affording mutual guarantees of political independence and territorial integrity of great and small states alike'.[5] These were supplemented later by statements which were intended to provide a comprehensive framework for peace. The enthusiasm with which Wilson's pronouncements were greeted in the Entente forced a greater degree of harmonization between British and American peace policies than Lloyd George's ministers wanted. British dependence on American aid, however, and the government's hope for continued Anglo-American cooperation after the war, both required that Britain keep in close step with the United States.

By 1917 British policy makers had made considerable progress behind the scenes towards the elaboration of concrete post-war goals. Their scope, of course, depended on the fluctuations of the military situation but by 1918 there was a broad official consensus on the demands that Britain should put forward at the Peace Conference. The internal discussion was set in motion by Lord Hardinge, who returned to the Foreign Office as Permanent Under-Secretary in June 1916, having served as viceroy of India since 1910. Convinced that an allied victory on the Somme was imminent, and that Britain might find herself unprepared for the Peace Conference, Hardinge hurried along the work of a Foreign Office committee under Sir Louis Mallet, a former ambassador to Constantinople. This committee produced a series of proposals which postulated a Europe reorganized in accordance with the principle of nationality. Germany's world power base was to be destroyed by the seizure of her colonies and her fleet, leaving her as a medium power in Europe, with much truncated frontiers. Inevitably these goals entailed the military defeat of Germany, and the discrediting of Prussian militarism in the eyes of her people.

Lloyd George's predecessor as Prime Minister, H.H.Asquith, had also asked members of the War Committee to draw up proposals, which duly appeared towards the end of 1916. Given the different vantage points represented by the Colonial Office, the Admiralty, the India Office, the Treasury, the General Staff and other interested bodies, these naturally reflected 'the sheer diversity of views on the nature of British interests'.[6] Apart from Lord Lansdowne, a former Foreign Secretary and Minister without Portfolio in Asquith's coalition, who advocated a compromise peace on the grounds that there appeared to be little immediate prospect of Germany's defeat, and that the continuation of the war would lead to the collapse of European civilization, all proposals were based on the expectation of a British victory. The differences were mainly over the severity of the terms to be imposed on Germany. General Sir William Robertson, Chief of the Imperial General Staff, for instance, argued for the maintenance of a relatively strong Germany (which should, for example, be allowed to retain her colonies) in order to preserve the balance of power. This provoked bitter protests from other Departments, which were anxious to see Germany's colonies annexed by the British Empire, and which feared a future challenge to the Entente if Germany was allowed to keep her 1914 frontiers.

The need for Germany's defeat was adhered to throughout the latter stages of the war, despite occasional waverings from Lloyd George and others in 1918, when Germany appeared to be on the brink of victory, and when it seemed likely the war would extend into 1919 or 1920, an eventuality which would greatly increase the chances of an American-dominated peace settlement. It is unlikely that Lloyd George took much notice of the welter of recommendations from the Foreign Office and other Departments. Nevertheless in April 1917, as a result of dominions' pressure in the newly-created Imperial War Cabinet, he set up committees under two members of the War Cabinet, Lord Milner, Secretary for War (economic) and Lord Curzon, Lord President of the Council (territorial) to investigate war aims. These committees trotted out most of the demands which the Prime Minister was to make public in 1918, although the territorial committee, as befitted Curzon's obsession with Eastern questions, concentrated on the need to secure as much as possible after the war of the Middle East and Germany's colonies.

The Germans' March offensive in 1918 inhibited much further public discussion of war aims in Britain, while official circles, pessimistic about the prospect of victory, began to doubt that Britain would be able to achieve all her demands. Although the German tide was reversed by the early autumn, Entente military leaders were busily drawing up their campaign plan for 1919, in which the American army was to play a prominent part. The German Chancellor, Prince Max of Baden's appeal to President Wilson for an immediate armistice on 4 October 1918 took British policy-makers by surprise[7]: indeed, reinforced by the warnings of the Commander-in-chief in France, General Sir Douglas Haig, about German resilience, the Entente found it difficult almost to the day of the armistice (11 November 1918) to believe that Germany was not capable of resuming the war from her own frontiers. There thus appeared to be good reason for a cautious approach to the question of war aims and to the armistice terms: and the naval terms (severe as they were) were not as harsh as the Admiralty had wanted them to be. Once it was clear that Germany was incapable of resuming the war British leaders, of course, insisted on the realization of all their demands.

In preparation for this they persuaded the American Secretary of State, Robert Lansing, on 14 October 1918, to agree to transfer responsibility for the formulation of the armistice conditions to the allied military and naval advisers. They also secured Wilson's agreement to the despatch of his aide and close friend, Colonel Edward House, to Paris to discuss the application of the Fourteen Points with Lloyd George and the French and Italian Prime Ministers, Georges Clemenceau and Vittorio Orlando, before the armistice conditions were presented. Since Lloyd George was confident that the Fourteen Points could be interpreted so that they fulfilled Britain's war aims, he refused to accept the principle of the freedom of the seas, despite House's warning that failure to do so might force the United States to sign a separate peace. The President overruled House and accepted the British reservation with the proviso that the Entente should be willing to discuss the question at the Peace Conference. The matter thereafter dropped from sight. The Entente secured a further reservation from Wilson on the points dealing with 'restoration'. The allies were now to receive compensation 'for all damage caused to the civilian population of the Allies and their property by land, by sea and from the air'.[8]

With these reservations in her pocket Britain could look forward to the Peace Conference with some complacency. The months of November and December were crowded ones, with the attention of British politicians distracted by the lead-up to the general election in early December, in which the Unionists and the Lloyd George Liberals were to campaign on a joint platform. The campaign degenerated into a vicious onslaught on Germany, in which all the leaders of the coalition engaged. The slogans 'Hang the Kaiser' and 'Make Germany Pay' were the product of the release of pent-up emotions and a hatred of Germany which had been growing increasingly virulent since October and which was reflected widely in official circles. The Coalition's overwhelming victory in effect made Lloyd George almost a total prisoner of his Unionist allies.

The way was now clear for the conference. Clemenceau's official visit to London on 1 December[9] and Foch's appeal for the independence of the Rhineland under allied military protection, did not encourage British ministers to seek close Anglo-French cooperation at the conference. Lloyd George's eyes—and those of other influential figures such as A. J. Balfour, the Foreign Secretary—were fastened on the more desirable prospect of post-war collaboration with the United States. President Wilson's triumphal visit to London at the end of December seemed to confirm that there were few issues which divided Britain from America—although the more contentious were not raised. The War Cabinet agreed however that Britain should keep in close touch with France during the conference in case the strategy of cooperation with the United States should prove abortive. 'After all', as Sir Eyre Crowe put it, 'we must remember that our friend America lives a long way off. France sits at our door.'[10]

The influential Foreign Office Political Intelligence Department had already summed up these main lines of British policy in a memorandum of 18 November 1918: 'It is in our interest to work vigorously and honestly in cooperation with

America on the general lines of the programme which President Wilson has put forward, and to which we have given our adhesion.' However, Britain must guard against the possible failure of the League of Nations and therefore must not neglect her national security or national interests. The memorandum further urged that, while she had no territorial or special commercial interests to pursue in Europe and sought only a stable and peaceful continent, Britain could not afford to ignore the balance of power in Europe and the security of the coastline opposite her coasts. The establishment of independent states based on the principle of nationality would strengthen the balance of power since states

> based on the conscious existence of a common nationality will be more durable and afford a firmer support against aggression than the older form of State, which was often a merely accidental congeries of territories without internal cohesion, necessary economic unity or clearly defined geographical frontiers. In this matter our interests entirely coincide with the principle of nationality . . .

The League would protect Dutch and Belgian security, while the settlement of the Alsace-Lorraine question would end 'the territorial struggle which has for many centuries been the cause of repeated wars . . . and a condition of permanent security [will] be established.'[11]

While the Foreign Office had been active in preparing a comprehensive programme of British war aims, it had also gone to considerable trouble to organize British participation in the conference. Indeed, since 1917, Alwyn Parker, Hardinge's secretary and Foreign Office librarian, had at Hardinge's prompting been preparing a memorandum 'on the elaboration of a whole Peace Conference in being'. The results of his work were set out in a long memorandum of 10 October 1918, which was sent to Balfour. His complex proposals envisaged a preliminary conference of the victor powers, which would deal with the fundamental issues of war and peace, followed by a peace congress to settle the details, which would be expanded later to involve the neutrals in such matters as the League of Nations and the revision of international law. There would be a number of interlocking British and inter-allied committees dealing with legal, political, territorial, financial and economic questions, which would report to a grand committee of allied spokesmen. The Foreign Office Historical Section had prepared 180 peace handbooks, each written by an expert, to provide the British delegation with information about subjects which might arise in Paris, and a comprehensive war aims index containing the peace aims of the allied, enemy and neutral powers.[12]

This memorandum was not accepted in its entirety by Lloyd George as the basis for the British organization of the Peace Conference. On 21 October the War Cabinet asked General Smuts to prepare a brief for the Conference setting out the British case in summary form. By this time the War Cabinet recognized that the Allies would be able to impose their terms on Germany and, like Hardinge, envisaged a preliminary conference of the Allies, followed by an international conference to include the neutrals. Smuts, of course, recognized that the British delegation would require technical information which could only be furnished by the various government departments, with the Foreign Office supplying experts to deal with the territorial questions.

The Foreign Office was not to be at the centre of the organization of the Conference and Hardinge, who had expected to head the British secretariat, was passed over in favour of the Secretary of the War Cabinet, Maurice Hankey. This reflected the personal preference of Lloyd George, who had little time for the Foreign Office in general and for Hardinge in particular, and who found Hankey's advice more congenial. Hardinge was embittered by this decision for, although he would rank as 'Organizing Ambassador', in practice his powers would be very limited.[13] Also he was ill and this meant that the real administrative work of the Foreign Office section at Paris was concentrated in the hands of the able Assistant Under-Secretary,

Sir Eyre Crowe.

The conference was formally opened on 18 January 1919. The five great powers—Britain, France, the United States, Italy and Japan—immediately established themselves as the Council of Ten, that is the prime ministers and foreign secretaries of the four, plus two Japanese representatives. They established commissions on the League of Nations, Reparation, Responsibilities of the Authors of War, International Labour Legislation and the International Regime of Ports, Waterways and Railways. The Council of Ten failed to get down to much serious business beyond settling an unseemly dispute over the number of representatives the smaller powers should each have at the Conference. Robert Borden, the Canadian Prime Minister, complained to Lloyd George on 21 January that 'an entire week was occupied in settling procedures that might reasonably have been settled within two days'.[14] There was however plenty of activity behind the scenes, with the British delegation making contacts with its American counterpart.

Then towards the end of January the Conference began to consider territorial claims in Europe and heard the representatives of Rumania, Czechoslovakia, Yugoslavia and Greece. As a result the conference created in an *ad hoc* fashion territorial committees on various aspects of the European settlement. These spawned numerous technical sub-committees. Here the Foreign Office personnel, who had been complaining that they had little to do and whose advice on other subjects was generally ignored by Lloyd George, came into their own. Harold Nicolson, Esmé Howard, William Tyrrell, Allen Leeper, E. H. Carr, Arnold Toynbee and Eyre Crowe all played useful roles on these inter-allied committees. Finally, on 27 February, a Central Territorial Committee was created to coordinate the work of the various committees with Crowe as the British delegate. Apart from the Polish Committee's recommendations the decisions these committees made and the boundaries they drew were rarely altered by the overworked political leaders. Some Foreign Office officials, like Headlam-Morley, who was personally requested by Lloyd George to draw up a compromise on the Danzig and Saar disputes,[15] and John Maynard Keynes, the Treasury representative, who composed useful memoranda on reparations and financial questions, were able to perform important tasks, thus leaving their marks on the treaties. But in other areas—Russia, reparations, the League of Nations— the Foreign Office was ignored.

From about mid-February to mid-March Lloyd George and Woodrow Wilson returned to their capitals to deal with internal problems, leaving Balfour and Colonel House as their representatives in Paris. Clemenceau was injured in an assassination attempt on 19 February, which left Stephen Pichon, the French Foreign Minister, to represent him at the Council of Ten. These substitutes were determined not to let the conference drag its feet while their leaders were absent. On 23 February Balfour, supported by House, introduced resolutions into the Council calling on the conference to hasten the preliminary peace by settling the military and naval terms as soon as possible, and requesting the territorial committees to submit their reports by 8 March (few of them could in fact do so). When Wilson came back to Paris on 14 March he correctly suspected that House had given way too readily to the French on a number of issues, but did him less than justice in assuming that he had tried to rush through a preliminary peace which would exclude the League of Nations. These suspicions led to Wilson's abandonment of the idea of a preliminary peace and to his insistence that the conference should draw up a final, comprehensive treaty of peace with Germany to include the League Covenant.

After Wilson's return, steps were taken by the four leaders to secure a much tighter hold over the decision-making process. On 24 March the three prime ministers, Lloyd George, Clemenceau and Orlando, and the President, began to meet as an 'inner council' to try to accelerate the proceedings. They thus became the Council of Four (or Three when the Italians were absent). Their foreign ministers and the Japanese representatives formed a separate council of five to consider items of lesser priority.

At first the new regime did not work smoothly. Because the Four sat without a secretary there was considerable confusion as to what they had decided. However on 19 April Hankey, with Lloyd George's backing, became their secretary and matters improved. At the same time the Rhineland and reparations disputes threatened the very existence of the conference. Lloyd George was uneasy about the severe terms the allies were already proposing to inflict on Germany and his fears were reinforced by those of his private secretary, Philip Kerr, and Maurice Hankey, who warned him that unless these were mitigated Europe would succumb to Bolshevism. General Sir Henry Wilson, Chief of the Imperial General Staff, shared their pessimism and, as a result, Lloyd George, accompanied by Kerr, Hankey and General Wilson, spent the weekend of 22-24 March at Fontainebleau to undertake a thorough review of the peace talks.[16]

The outcome of these discussions was embodied in a memorandum based on drafts by Kerr, which was sent to the other delegations on the 25th. The 'Fontainebleau Memorandum' was designed to impress the French Prime Minister with the virtues of moderation in the terms to be imposed on Germany—otherwise the treaty would cause further wars. Lloyd George warned the French that whatever terms were imposed on Germany she would ultimately recover her strength and become a renewed threat. 'The maintenance of peace will ... depend upon there being no causes of exasperation constantly stirring up the spirit of patriotism, of justice or of fairplay.' With these sentiments as a preface Lloyd George then urged that as few Germans as possible be transferred to other states. The British Prime Minister believed that a just peace would prevent a Bolshevik takeover of Germany. He insisted that the League must be established 'as the effective guardian of international right and international liberty throughout the world' and that the powers should agree to German disarmament as a preliminary to universal limitation. He renewed the offer of an Anglo-American guarantee to France and appended a list of more specific proposals, including the rectification of the proposed Polish and Bohemian borders in Germany's favour, the retention by Germany of her Rhineland sovereignty, the return of Alsace-Lorraine and the ten year cession of the Saar coalfields to France.

Clemenceau had little patience with what he regarded as Lloyd George's pro-German sympathies. He poured scorn on the notion that Germany would be satisfied by the kind of peace Lloyd George had proposed: 'It is a pure illusion . . . [to] think that she can be appeased by a certain amelioration of her territorial conditions'. He drew attention to Germany's pre-war global ambitions, noted the Eurocentric nature of Lloyd George's proposals and suggested sarcastically that it would be better if Germany were also offered colonial, naval and commercial concessions. The French Prime Minister was not deterred then or later by threats of Bolshevism — in his opinion to deny the nationalist aspirations of the new states, as Lloyd George had suggested, would be more likely to open Central Europe to Bolshevism or to its eventual 'enslavement by a reactionary Germany'. He described Lloyd George's memorandum as composed of 'partial and temporary solutions' as far as Europe was concerned, while it entailed Britain's permanent acquisition of Germany's colonies. He characterized it as an unequal solution which would, if implemented, embitter inter-allied relations.[17]

Here Clemenceau touched on the core of the Anglo-French dichotomy. Britain seemed prepared to make concessions to Germany at other countries' expense. Her eyes were fastened on imperial considerations and, as a result, she showed little interest in France's dilemma. Here France faced the combined opposition of Britain and the United States to her plans, and the remainder of the conference witnessed the gradual acceptance by France of many of Lloyd George's desiderata. But it was a grudging acceptance and was to result in bitter disputes between the two countries over Germany in the 1920's.

CHAPTER TWO

THE GERMAN SETTLEMENT

There were deep divisions between the United States, Britain and France in their approaches to the German settlement. This was evident despite agreement that the evil of German 'militarism' must be eradicated, and that the League of Nations should guarantee Europe against a resurgence of German aggression. Woodrow Wilson was wedded to the somewhat vague principles he had enunciated in the Fourteen Points, the Four Principles, the Five Particulars and other statements he had made during the course of 1918. As a result the United States delegation was broadly committed to a settlement based on national self-determination.[1]

Germany was quickly disabused of any notion that the internal changes brought about in October and November 1918 amounted to that redemption of character for which the President had repeatedly called. From the outset the victors agreed that Germany should be excluded from their deliberations and would only be allowed written comments on the final draft treaty. Since all the defeated nations were to be treated alike, it was difficult to perceive how the peace settlement was to be governed by 'a justice that plays no favourites and knows no standards but the equal rights of the several peoples concerned'.[2]

It was a matter of intense allied speculation as to whether the new German republic was a genuine manifestation of a new spirit in the German people or merely a device to hoodwink the allies. The French were convinced that the German constitutional apparatus was a continuation of the Wilhelmine military regime in an internationally more acceptable guise, but without the Hohenzollerns. The British delegation was deluged with conflicting intelligence reports about Germany's internal developments. While Headlam-Morley was convinced that Germany was now a liberal and constitutional republic, and that the powers should take this into account in drafting the treaty, others like Crowe and Hardinge had little faith in the possibility of German redemption.

Some of Wilson's principles, such as the freedom of the seas, could after an initial fuss be fudged over or conveniently forgotten. However the President's insistence on 11 February 1918 that 'there shall be no annexations, no contributions, no punitive damages'[3] was bound to lead him into a head-on collision with France and Britain, whose demands for reparations exceeded any sum that Wilson was prepared to accept. Indeed, to the French the treaty was to serve as an insurance against the short-term revival of Germany in case Anglo-American-French war-time collaboration failed to survive the peace settlement. While it was true that the President had accepted the allied interpretation of his pledge on the restoration of invaded territories, to the effect that 'compensation will be made by Germany for all damage done to the civilian population of the Allies and their property by the aggression of Germany by land, by sea, and from the air',[4] the many ambiguities in this statement created fruitful opportunities for unedifying quarrels.

Woodrow Wilson had also demanded the evacuation and restoration of Belgium, of all French territory, of Rumania, Serbia and Montenegro, a new order in the Balkans, the evacuation of Russia, the creation of an independent Poland with 'free and secure access to the sea' and the restoration of Alsace-Lorraine to French sovereignty. In principle the allies could agree to all these, although in practice it became clear that Wilsonian concepts of even-handed justice clashed with French insistence on the strengthening of those countries that bordered Germany, even if this entailed overriding the principle of national self-determination. Similar claims of strategic necessity were advanced by Italy and the victorious Balkan states in support of their territorial demands. Added to this was the difficulty of applying national self-determination to the mixture of nationalities in central Europe.

Woodrow Wilson was suited by neither temperament nor inclination to perform the role of mediator. There could be no genuine reconciliation between the ideals paraded by the President and French evaluation of what their national interest required. As a result of the President's lack of flexibility, at first clinging stubbornly to his principles and then grudgingly allowing them either to be distorted or abandoned, he emerged as a self-rightous, peevish and narrow politician.[5] To his erstwhile supporters, like John Maynard Keynes, who had put too much faith in Wilson's power to improve the world, the President's fall from grace was total,[6] while to his many detractors he was a woolly-minded idealist with little understanding of the complexities of international politics.

Nor were the British in a better position to restrain excessive French demands, which not only conflicted with Wilsonian idealism but also threatened to undermine British hopes for a stable post-war order, based on long-run Anglo-American cooperation. In the War Cabinet the Lord Privy Seal, Andrew Bonar Law, described French demands on Germany as 'a series of pinpricks, involving every calculated humiliation',[7] while the British General Staff pointed out that 'the complete collapse of Germany. . . and her obvious inability to renew the struggle, have tempted the French to increase their claims'.[8] On the other hand, the British also had demands which were difficult to reconcile with Wilson's ideals, including complete control over Germany's former colonies, the recognition of her Middle Eastern hegemony, and a large share of reparations. Britain was already in possession of the German colonies and the German fleet, and she insisted on retaining them. At the same time her opposition to French schemes was bound to revive French suspicions of British hypocrisy, while her fluctuating allegiance to Wilsonian principles scarcely enhanced her prestige in Wilson's eyes.

The Rhineland

During its first few weeks the conference was preoccupied with settling procedural issues and with the establishment of commissions on the League of Nations, War Crimes, and Reparations. Little in the way of concrete decisions emerged. However a bitter battle was being waged outside the Council of Ten. In December 1918 Marshal Foch proposed to the British Prime Minister the establishment of autonomous regimes in the Rhineland, which should be allied to France and garrisoned by French troops. At Paris Foch continued his campaign for this plan. The British government wanted to satisfy legitimate French fears of a future resurgent Germany. Self-interest dictated such a policy, since Britain would be forced to come to France's defence were she again attacked by Germany. Also she required French support for her Middle East aspirations. Furthermore, a satisfied France might support Britain in 'the adoption of a merciful policy towards Germany',[9] but this latter desire ruled out the creation of more Alsace-Lorraines in Europe. The War Cabinet, meeting on 28 February and 4 March to discuss acceptable ways of providing for French security, ranged over such possibilities as a temporary allied occupation of the Rhine bridgeheads and a large measure of German disarmament.

The issue was also discussed at length by the military and civilian advisers to the British delegation in Paris. While British army officers were, like their Foreign Office counterparts, opposed to Foch's demands for independent or autonomous Rhenish states, they were prepared to concede to France the extension of the 1870 frontiers of Alsace-Lorraine to include the Saar and the tongue of Rhenish Prussia. In the General Staff's view, these concessions, together with an alliance between France, Holland, Belgium and Luxemburg, would provide France with an effective barrier against future German aggression. Sir Henry Wilson noted what was to be the constant dilemma for the peace-makers, that 'as in other parts of the world, ethnographical claims are in distinct opposition to those of military security and defence'.[10]

This view was, of course, anathema to the civilians in the British delegation. Headlam-Morley minuted on 16 February that 'a settlement in which political considerations are subordinated to strategical may defeat its own ends'. The demilitarization of the Rhineland, which was also proposed by the General Staff, was castigated as likely to expose south Germany to the constant danger of a French invasion. 'The conception, in fact, is a just one only on the assumption that Germany will remain a strong, vigorous and aggressive military Power, but that France will remain peaceful and unambitious; this is an assumption that it will be difficult to justify'.[11]

The British and Americans, Woodrow Wilson above all, were in agreement that 'the French schemes on this subject. . . are short sighted, selfish and quite impractical'.[12] The Anglo-American experts resolved on 21 February that French security would best be protected by the demilitarization of the left bank of the Rhine. However, if this could not be achieved, the Anglo-Americans were prepared to consider the rectification of the northern frontier of Alsace-Lorraine in France's favour. The French persisted with their Rhineland project. Clemenceau assigned to André Tardieu the task of persuading the Anglo-Americans to accept the French demands, which he embodied in a memorandum on 25 February. He followed this with a series of meetings on 11 and 12 March with Philip Kerr, acting for Lloyd George, and Dr Sidney E. Mezes of the American delegation.

Both Kerr and Mezes opposed the stationing of allied troops on Rhenish soil, although Kerr wavered about the possibility of a temporary occupation. On the 12th Kerr informed Tardieu of the British view that the reduction of the German army to 100,000 men, the demilitarization of the left bank of the Rhine and an Anglo-American guarantee to assist France if she was the victim of German aggression, would be adequate to uphold future French security. Tardieu would not budge: he told Kerr that while the offer of a guarantee was gratifying, in practice it was inadequate because of the long time lag between a German invasion and the arrival of allied troops from overseas.

'It is, in fact, impossible for France . . . to give up positive security in exchange for hopes'.[13] Kerr strongly resisted the setting up of quasi-independent Rhenish republics which, in his view, would require either a permanent allied occupation of the area or an allied guarantee or both, in order to prevent future German attempts to recover them by force.

The notion of an Anglo-American guarantee to operate in peace time was a startling innovation and it is doubtful whether, at this stage, it had been approved either by President Wilson or by Lloyd George. The British, American and French delegations were still manoeuvring for position, with Kerr and Mezes desperately trying to persuade the French to abandon their efforts to sever purely German land from the Reich: in other words, to put the clock back to 1870. The Europe of 1919 could not, in their view, be treated like the Europe of 1814. In the face of continued French intransigence Kerr could only suggest an allied agreement to occupy the Rhine bridges until the conclusion of the peace preliminaries. If the unthinkable transpired and the French managed to induce the allies to agree to the establishment of autonomous Rhenish republics, he could only hope that the peace treaty would provide for the eventual revision of the arrangement either by the League of Nations or by plebiscites.

In any case President Wilson was implacably opposed to such a blatant breach of his cherished principle of national self-determination, while Lloyd George could not agree to such an enhancement of French power. The British ambassador in Paris, Lord Derby, summed up the French dilemma in a nutshell:

The French are still in a mortal funk over Germany . . . The disparity between the populations of the two countries is a perfect nightmare to them. They are . . . determined to get a big buffer between them and Germany and I feel confident that they will sacrifice almost anything to secure our support for that.[14]

Balfour had little sympathy for France's predicament. He was .
as scornful of what he described as their 'lurid' view of the
potential threat of Germany, as he was for their 'very forcible'
but 'very one-sided' Rhineland claim. In his view German
militarism could be cured only by

> a change in the international system of the world — a change
> which French statesmen are doing nothing to promote, and
> the very possibility of which many of them regard with ill
> concealed derision. They may be right: but if they are, it is
> quite certain that no manipulation of the Rhine frontier is
> going to make France anything more than a second-rate
> Power, trembling at the nod of its great neighbour on the
> East and depending from day to day on the changes and
> chances of a shifting diplomacy and uncertain alliances.[15]

Balfour's prophecy would not have made any impression
on the French leadership, who demanded tangible guarantees
against a country which, given its relative superiority in
population and industrial resources, would sooner or later
recover from its defeat to become a renewed threat to France.
The French preferred to prevent German recovery until France
possessed an overwhelming superiority both in armaments
and allies. They therefore scornfully rejected Wilsonian
nostrums about the future world order adumbrated by individ-
uals such as Balfour. Nor were they much comforted by Balfour's
belief that future German expansionism would be directed
towards the east — the unstated corollary of this would be the
eventual emergence of an even stronger Germany.

Thus the Anglo-Americans regarded their offer of a guarantee, a much reduced German army and a temporary allied
occupation of the Rhineland bridges as alternatives to the
severance of the Rhineland from Germany, while Foch and
his supporters regarded them as welcome additions to it. Indeed
on 14 March Lloyd George persuaded a reluctant Wilson to
agree to an American treaty of guarantee for France, which, if
accepted by the Senate, would have the additional merit, from

Britain's standpoint, of tying the United States even more closely to the European settlement. In case the Senate rejected the American treaty Lloyd George ensured that the British guarantee depended on the ratification of the American one.

Clemenceau was not overtly impressed by this offer. He suspected that the United States and Britain, preoccupied with reducing their military expenditures, would be in no position to act on their pledges. He insisted that the separation of the Rhenish provinces from Germany and their occupation by allied armies for at least 30 years were the irreducible minimum requirements for French security. Privately, however, Clemenceau was wavering and on 15 April the issue was resolved: on that day he and Colonel House agreed that, in addition to the treaty of guarantee and the demilitarization of the Rhineland, allied troops would occupy the Rhineland for 15 years. There would be a phased withdrawal over the 15 years if Germany observed the terms of the treaty. On 29 April it was further agreed that the occupation might be extended if Germany showed signs of embarking on an aggressive policy.

Although this compromise was opposed by Lloyd George, who was in London when it was negotiated, Wilson's approval decided the issue. At the Council of Four on 22 April the British Prime Minister pleaded in vain for a reduction in the period of occupation, on the grounds that British public opinion would object to the stationing of British troops in the Rhineland for 15 years. The British army would be hard put to find the required effectives. There was also the question of the cost. Clemenceau, having abandoned the concept of an independent Rhineland and faced with the opposition of Foch, the French military, sections of the Chamber and President Poincaré to any further concessions, would yield no further. Lloyd George therefore acquiesced.

The Saar

The future of the Saar proved to be another stumbling-block

to the settlement of Germany's western borders. The French wanted to annex the area but, once again, the Anglo-Americans objected vociferously. On 5 February Headlam-Morley put forward a compromise whereby, as compensation for the destruction of their coalfields in Northern France, France would be given control over the Saar coalfields, but would not exercise any sovereignty over the area. This was not a solution which commended itself to the French, and weeks of trying negotiations ensued. Between 9 and 11 April, however, the Council of Four reached a compromise along the lines originally suggested by Headlam-Morley. France was to mine the coal while the League of Nations was to administer the area for 15 years, after which a plebiscite would be held to enable the inhabitants to determine their future. These arrangements were grudgingly accepted by the French.

Belgium

Whatever may have been the calculations of British statesmen in August 1914 about the balance of power, for the majority of the British people Germany's invasion of Belgium was the justification for Britain's entry into the war. In these circumstances Belgium could anticipate considerable British sympathy in 1919 for her efforts to secure the strengthening of her frontiers, to enable her to defend herself against any future German aggression until the Allies could come to her aid. To many British officials the satisfaction of Belgium's relatively modest claims was essential if the settlement in the West was to be a stable one.

These claims included the annexation by Belgium of the German owned areas of Malmédy and Moresnet and the control of the Eupen-Malmédy railway, some form of Belgian control over Luxemburg and the internationalization of the Scheldt so that warships could reach Antwerp in war-time. Furthermore she pressed for the transfer of Dutch Limburg to her sovereignty on grounds of strategic necessity, proposing that in exchange Holland should receive East Frisia from Germany. All this amounted to a complete revision of the 1839 treaties which had imposed controls on her independence. The British delegation supported these demands and wasted little sympathy on Holland's protests: after all Dutch neutrality during the war was considered to have been very useful, both economically and strategically, to Germany. The refusal of Holland to surrender the former German Emperor to the allies for trial further infuriated the British.

France's attitude towards Belgian claims was ambivalent. Her security requirements suggested the strengthening of the states on Germany's borders—hence her support for a plebiscite in German Schleswig (a plebiscite promised in the Treaty of Prague of 1867, but never held). This eventually resulted in the transfer of North Schleswig to Denmark. A Belgium freed from the restraints of the 1839 treaties might become a French ally as both shared a common aim—to extract large reparation payments from Germany. On the other hand the British believed that the French had designs of their own on Luxemburg. This country's passivity in the face of the German invasion in early August 1914 and the German character of her ruling house were the two arguments used to explain Britain's willingness to agree to a Belgian controlled Luxemburg.

The motives behind French policy in this area were difficult to discern. Certainly reports reaching Brussels early in 1919 suggested that the French military authorities in occupied Luxemburg were encouraging pro-French feelings amongst the inhabitants. Balfour asked Lloyd George to remind the French that, since they were gaining Alsace-Lorraine, the Saar and extra-European territories, they should not stand in the way of Belgium's more modest claims. Clemenceau denied that France had any ambitions in Luxemburg.

On 11 February 1919 Paul Hymans, the Belgian Foreign Minister, presented his country's case before the Council of Ten, which thereupon appointed a committee to investigate. The British representative, Headlam-Morley, fully supported the Belgian claims in the committee, although he believed that the inhabitants of Dutch Limburg and of Luxemburg should be consulted prior to their transfer. There was, however, the problem of the compensation Holland was to receive at Germany's expense for her loss of Limburg. Headlam Morley commented:

> Here we get on difficult ground. The idea of separating territory from one State and giving it territory belonging to another State merely on the ground of compensation belongs to the order of ideas which ruled at the Congress of Vienna and which have been generally repudiated: it is by its rejection of this conception that the Paris Conference is to show its superiority to Vienna.[16]

It was not going to be easy to find a moral or legal justification for this transaction.

The committee agreed in March that Belgium should receive Prussian Moresnet, Malmédy and Eupen, and part of the Dutch Limburg, with Holland receiving some German territory in compensation. Now Headlam-Morley was faced directly with the dilemma of reconciling a transfer of German territory with the principle of self-determination. 'The desires of the population themselves may be something quite different from the interpretation put on their economic and moral interests by the Allies,' he wrote. In this instance realpolitik was to prevail over idealistic considerations:

> And yet on a larger view, it must surely be acknowledged that Belgium has claims on us of a nature quite different from those of Poland and that, while Poland is — and must always remain — to a large extent outside the orbit of British influence and British interest, the future of Belgium must be a matter of the highest importance to us. If Belgium does not receive from us the support which she may justly expect, I foresee the dangers which may arise in the future.

If Britain did not support Belgium's claims her reputation

'will be greatly diminished, but our reputation is one of our greatest assets'. The danger of Belgian enmity towards Britain was that Belgium would drift into France's orbit: 'If we acquiesce in this the result of the present Conference will be that we shall have been giving up the cardinal point of British policy which has been maintained since the reign of Edward I.'

Crowe was prepared to go 'so far as to suggest that our support of French claims in the Saar valley and to a pro-French settlement on the Left-Bank-of-the Rhine question should be distinctly made conditional on Luxemburg being given to Belgium'.[17] Headlam-Morley and Crowe were supported by Hardinge and Balfour. The Foreign Secretary minuted the Prime Minister: 'This is both important and pressing . . . it would be most unjust, and in the long run most inexpedient, that France should get Alsace-Lorraine and the Saar coal and Belgium *nothing*.'[18] However the French insisted at the Council of Four in early April that there must be a plebiscite in Luxemburg to determine the wishes of the inhabitants. Despite further appeals from Balfour, Clemenceau refused to yield on this issue.

This was a purely Anglo-French dispute as Woodrow Wilson refused to become involved. No doubt the spectacle of Britain and France squabbling over the principle of self-determination had its amusing aspect. On 16 April the Council agreed that Belgium should receive Eupen, Malmedy and Moresnet, with plebiscites being held after six months. It was anticipated that by then the Belgian case would have prevailed. The Council shelved the Luxemburg issue on 25 April, amid British complaints about France's double-dealing. Balfour attempted to persuade Lloyd George to reopen the question. When Kerr informed the Foreign Secretary of the Prime Minister's view that if Luxemburg wanted to join France 'it is not our business to prevent it', Balfour washed his hands of the subject: 'I have taken a good deal of initiative in favour of Belgium . . . but I can do no more'.[19] Any lingering Belgian hope of acquiring Luxemburg disappeared entirely on 28 September 1919 when a referendum in the grand duchy produced large majorities in favour of the preservation of the dynasty, and equally large majorities in favour of economic union with France.

The Belgians were singularly unlucky since they were also unable to persuade Holland to part with the Dutch Limburg or to agree to any change in the Scheldt regime. The Conference promoted Dutch-Belgian meetings in May and June, but the Dutch refused to make any concessions. In July the Conference set up a committee of Britain, France, Belgium, Holland, the United States and Italy to consider the revision of the 1839 treaties. Belgium demanded a treaty of guarantee from the allies similar to that given by the United States and Britain to France, as well as Belgian-Dutch staff talks to plan the joint defence of Limburg in the event of a German attack. However, the Committee made no progress since the Dutch refused to consider entering into any bilateral military arrangements with Belgium, and promised only to join the League and to declare that they would consider any violation of Limburg by an aggressor as a *casus belli*.

The futile negotiations dragged on into the winter. The French tried to convince Belgium that the League would protect her independence but, since the Belgians shared the French scepticism about the likely effectiveness of that organization, they insisted on the more tangible protection of an Anglo-American guarantee. This too was a non-starter. The British cabinet firmly rejected the idea on 18 November, while the United States Senate was preoccupied with the debate over the ratification of the Versailles treaty. The British finally abandoned the entire issue, leaving France to sign a treaty of alliance with Belgium in 1920.

German Disarmament

The French demands for territorial guarantees against Germany were coupled with equally strong pressure for restrictions on the size of Germany's armed forces and for the reduction of German armaments. The great powers were at least generally agreed on the principle of German disarmament, although there were inevitably differences of opinion as to the means whereby this goal could be accomplished. Lloyd George thought that German disarmament was 'good for her as well as us',[20] while Woodrow Wilson had, in his Fourteen Points message, called for the reduction of armaments. Germany later protested that this should be a multilateral agreement and not a one-sided agreement forced on her by the conference.

On 12 February the Council of Ten set up a Military Commission under Marshal Foch. The allied service experts and their political masters agreed that Germany should be allowed no general staff, no military airforce and that her fleet should be restricted both in the size and number of ships. The scuttling of the German fleet at Scapa Flow on 21 June saved the British from the prospect of endless bickering with her allies as to its ultimate disposal. Germany was forbidden submarines and her navy was restricted to 15,000 officers and men, six battleships, six light cruisers, 12 destroyers and 12 torpedo boats. The allied experts meticulously calculated the quantity of armaments the German army was to possess, applied rigid restrictions on the productive capacity of German armaments industries, and set up allied air, naval and military commissions with the power to conduct on-site inspections.

There were two areas of allied disagreement over disarmament questions. The British and Americans were susceptible to accusations of hypocrisy in imposing unilateral disarmament on Germany, while making no promises about future allied disarmament. Then there was considerable contention over the method of recruitment for the German army. The first issue was hardly likely to cause the French much concern. While they had scant sympathy, they agreed on 26 April to a reference to future general limitation of armaments in the preamble to the disarmament clauses of the treaty. This preamble was to cause endless friction down to the mid-1930s.

The second issue, over recruitment, arose from a submission by Marshal Foch to the Council of Ten on 3 March, that the

German army should consist of 200,000 men conscripted annually. In Foch's opinion a wholly volunteer army would provide a highly trained nucleus for German military expansion. The Anglo-Americans, unlike the French wedded to the voluntary system, refuted Foch's arguments. Balfour condemned conscription as a dangerous expedient, which would provide Germany with a force of 4,000,000 men at the end of 20 years. Both Balfour and Sir Henry Wilson argued that a long service voluntary army would be more capable of preserving internal order and of policing Germany's frontiers than a conscripted one. Expense alone would encourage the German government to keep such an army to the minimum size compatible with her security, would make rapid mobilization difficult, and would so restrict the availability of reserves as to confine the German army to a defensive role.[21]

Lloyd George utilized the arguments of his political and military advisers when he opposed Foch's conscription plan before the Council of Ten on 6 March. In the end Clemenceau sided with Lloyd George and on the 10th it was formally proposed that the German army should consist of 100,000 volunteers who would sign on for 12 years. Woodrow Wilson accepted this compromise on 17 March.

Reparations[22]

Disarmament was concerned with means rather than ends, and as such did not provoke the bitter strife which occurred over reparations. On this subject there could be no Anglo-American cooperation to persuade the French to adopt a more reasonable line, since Britain was as determined as France that Germany should be made to pay as much as possible. At times the figures Britain put forward as Germany's liabilities exceeded even those demanded by her Entente partner.

The idea of exacting reparations had grown up in Britain during the later stages of the war. The alternative notion of boycotting German trade after the war had been abandoned because of official recognition of the adverse long run effects this would have on British commerce, and also because Woodrow Wilson had firmly set his face against the erection of new tariff barriers and opposed any suggestion of 'an economic war after the war'. While privately Lloyd George was irritated by American interference, he realized that Britain had depended on American aid during the war, and was likely to do so for some time thereafter, and so was not disposed to quarrel with Wilson on this issue. However, the idea of exacting compensation from Germany after the war seemed to be a much more attractive and efficacious method of punishing Germany for her transgressions. During the autumn memoranda by the Foreign Office, the Board of Trade and the Treasury suggested that Germany was capable of paying a sum of about £1,000 million, but doubted that the British Empire would be able to claim more than a small proportion.

During the election campaign, however, this issue became a major plank of the coalition platform. This was partly a result of the British electorate's desire for vengeance against Germany, a vindictiveness whipped up by the Australian Prime Minister, William Morris Hughes. One authority has recently stated that 'few men chose to quarrel with William Morris Hughes; none enjoyed doing so. Hughes was partly deaf, easily irritated and seldom afflicted by doubt. Many of his British Empire colleagues regarded him as *l'enfant terrible* to be avoided where possible and accommodated when necessary'.[23] Hughes, who turned up in Britain in the early autumn of 1918, was to represent Australia at the peace conference. Given his view that 'the Australians had, in fact, done a good deal more than the Americans towards winning the war, and had, therefore, just as good a right to a voice as President Wilson',[24] Hughes, no apostle of a soft peace, was to cause Wilson, Lloyd George and the other Empire leaders, considerable trouble at Paris.

He began to do so in fact long before the conference was opened. As early as 7 November 1918 he complained that if Germany escaped paying reparations, the British tax-payer would be faced with a staggering burden of taxation. Hughes persistently returned to this theme during the following months.

On 26 November 1918 the Imperial War Cabinet set up a Committee on Indemnity, with Hughes as chairman; Sir George Foster, the Canadian Finance Minister, Walter Long, Secretary for the Colonies, J. A. S. Hewins, an economist, Herbert Gibbs, a City of London banker and Lord Cunliffe, a former governor of the Bank of England, were the other members. With the exception of Foster, these men were all anxious to demand large sums from Germany. Lloyd George subsequently claimed that he was astonished at the magnitude of the burden the committee wanted to impose on Germany. However it is possible that he hoped Hughes and his supporters, preoccupied with these investigations, would cease their strident public demands for reparations during the election campaign.

The Prime Minister was completely mistaken if he thought that the appointment of the committee would bury the issue until the elections were over. The committee sat from 3 to 10 December and finally reported that the total cost of the war was £24,000 million and that this should be paid by Germany in annual instalments. The question of Germany's capacity to pay was not answered—indeed Hughes and his fellow committee members were not interested in this problem. As far as they were concerned Germany was to pay reparations as a penalty for causing the war. This theme was repeated avidly by coalition ministers and by the press during the long run up to polling day. Already the War Cabinet had conceived the idea of war crimes trials, and Britain and France had reached agreement on 20 December on the setting up of a commission on war crimes at the peace conference. While the cry of 'Hang the Kaiser' became a popular slogan during the elections, the demand for reparations as a collective penalty imposed on the whole German people, soon exceeded it in intensity.

Lloyd George and some of the leading ministers in the coalition had emphasized the more idealistic peace aims of the government during the early stages of the campaign, but they were soon caught up in the rising tide of anti-German feeling.

As a result, they began to concentrate on the more electorally promising theme of reparations. Lloyd George claimed that he had always insisted that regard must be paid to Germany's capacity to pay, but he came perilously close to negating this restriction when, on 11 December, he told a Bristol audience 'you may find that the capacity will go a pretty long way'.[25] As a result the more moderate voices of the Asquithian Liberals and the Labourites were drowned by the clamour, and at the 28 December elections the Coalition secured a large majority. Added to this, Lloyd George, despite the warnings of Smuts and others about the extremism of Hughes and his colleagues, allowed the Imperial Cabinet Committee on Indemnity to select the British delegates to the Peace Conference Commission on Reparation. They chose Hughes, Cunliffe and Lord Sumner, a Lord of Appeal with no knowledge of economic or financial questions. As a result the Prime Minister found himself saddled with a commitment which was to plague him for the duration of the conference and beyond.

The French, mindful of the indemnity imposed on them by Prussia-Germany in 1871 and of the colossal damage inflicted on northern France by the German armies, were equally determined to exact reparations from Germany. The French government sought compensation for the immense sacrifices her people had made during the war. It also regarded reparations as a useful weapon in its strategy of weakening, in the long term, Germany's recuperative powers.[26] It was assured of the support of Belgium, Italy, Rumania and Serbia, who all anticipated substantial compensation from the defeated powers.

Woodrow Wilson's attitude was enigmatic. Point Seven of the Fourteen Points referred to the evacuation and restoration of Belgium, Point Eight insisted that the invaded portions of France should be restored, while Point Eleven called for the restoration of the occupied territories of Rumania, Serbia and Montenegro. None of these provided a very satisfactory basis on which to claim huge sums from Germany but, on Allied insistence, Woodrow Wilson informed Germany on 5 November

1918 'that compensation will be made by Germany for all the damage done to the civilian population of the Allies and their property by the aggression of Germany by land, by sea and from the air'.[27] This note became the basis on which the Allies justified their demands, and it ensured that Britain would get a portion of whatever sums were extracted from Germany. Later Smuts secured allied agreement to the inclusion in the reparation bill of disablement allowances and pensions for war widows so that Britain would get 'a fair share and not be done in the eye'.[28]

Thus the United States had accepted that some degree of compensation to the Allies was justified. However, as the British discovered during Wilson's visit to London at the end of December 1918, the President was resolutely opposed to the vast sums demanded by the allies, which, in his view, amounted to the full cost of the war. Hankey warned Hughes early in January 1919 that 'the Prime Minister, in his conversation with President Wilson . . . found him stiffer on this subject than on anything else, and there is no doubt that the President has not yet accepted the principle of exacting indemnity . . . This is one of the battles that will have to be fought in Paris.'[29] Anxious not to disturb Anglo-American relations at the outset and thus endanger the cooperation between the two countries on which British policy at Paris was to be based, Lloyd George did not make an issue of this subject before the start of the conference.

As the conference proceeded Woodrow Wilson became even more incensed by the escalating demands of the allies. Lloyd George found himself faced with growing antagonism from the Americans while, to make matters worse, Anglo-French relations became increasingly embittered as the British struggled to secure a reasonable proportion of whatever was to be exacted from Germany. For their part the French and Belgians were determined, in view of their enormous human and material losses, that they should receive not only the lion's share of the total but priority in its apportionment. The problem for the British delegates on the reparation commission was that if

Germany's total liability was ultimately fixed at too low a figure, Britain would not get enough to satisfy the demands of her still vindictive electorate.[30] In this over-heated atmosphere, in which all these pressures tended to inflate to grotesque proportions the sums likely to be demanded of Germany, any semblance of rational discussion disappeared. The situation could only encourage hard-liners on the reparation commission like Lord Cunliffe to produce figures of what Germany ought to pay which Hankey believed were based not on any scientific investigation but 'drawn . . . rather by that peculiar instinct on which, I am told, high financial authorities in the city often work'.[31] Already by the end of February the conference was deadlocked on this issue and Edwin Montagu, the Secretary for India, who served on a reparation sub-committee, told Lloyd George that

> it would seem therefore as if the prolonged scientific investigations into bills of costs and actual claims which the Reparation Commission is considering are likely to be a work of supererogation, are likely to lead to no practical results, are likely to take much too long and are likely to lead to unnecessary international disputes.[32]

Linked to reparations, at least in the minds of the European allies, was the crucial question of the debts owed by the allies to the United States as a result of their heavy war-time borrowing. Kerr feared that the refusal of the United States, 'the only nation which has made a profit out of the war', either to cancel or reduce allied indebtedness, as well as her pressure for a modest reparation settlement, would delay Britain's post-war recovery indefinitely. If the United States would agree to the cancellation of inter-allied debts, the Allies would be able to reduce their reparations demands on Germany significantly. Woodrow Wilson would not, however, budge on this issue and on 3 May he also rejected a scheme put forward by Keynes for the provision of American financial assistance for the restoration of European credit and trade. It was rather far-fetched of the British to expect Woodrow Wilson, already faced with a hostile Congress and restive public opinion, to be prepared to grasp this particular nettle.

The British and French delegates were unable to agree during March on the total sum to be imposed on Germany, or on what the British share of this ought to be. Montagu was convinced that British public opinion would insist that 'we are not diddled by our Allies'.[33] These difficulties were compounded by the uncompromising attitude of the British reparation commissioners, Hughes, Cunliffe and Sumner, who blocked any reasonable proposals. In the Fontainebleau Memorandum Lloyd George underplayed reparations, merely pointing out that 'we cannot both cripple her [Germany] and expect her to pay', and admitting in the 'Outline of Peace Terms' that, while Germany must 'undertake to pay full reparation to the Allies', the amount 'certainly greatly exceeds what, on any calculation, Germany is capable of paying'.[34] These inconclusive comments gave no indication of how Britain was to escape from the dilemma. Hughes and his associates were adamant about any weakening of Britain's determination, while Lloyd George was well aware of the strength of Unionist feeling on the subject.

In a memorandum of 18 March 1919, the British Commissioners admitted that 'the conditions of this problem are stringent; the data scanty; the conclusions can only be a matter of forecast and opinion'. Despite these qualifications, however, they remained convinced that if Germany was made to pay too little, she would have won 'a brilliant financial victory and also palpably escaping [*sic*] the just consequences of her aggression. This would produce intense and widespread political resentment in all Allied countries'. They had no doubt that once peaceful conditions were restored, Germany would have no difficulty in meeting her obligations, since her export potential remained considerable, and she possessed abundant raw materials, machine-filled factories and a war-improved industrial base: 'Before the war she worked hard and lived well; now she has to work hard and live hard too'.[35]

The commissioners were supported by a large number of Unionists in the House of Commons who reflected the earlier punitive British attitude towards Germany. Public concern was stirred up by Lord Northcliffe's *Daily Mail,* which had irritated Lloyd George in December 1918 by pressing for penal reparations. Now the *Daily Mail* published rumours that the British delegation at Paris was weakening on the issue. This cry was taken up by other newspapers. As a result, on 8 April Lloyd George received a telegram signed by 233 Unionist M.P.s protesting against any reduction in reparations claims. The Prime Minister was forced to leave Paris to defend his conference policy before Parliament on 16 April. There he successfully outmanoeuvred his critics and won a resounding vote of confidence.

At the same time Lloyd George, as evidenced by the Fontainebleau memorandum, was becoming increasingly sceptical as to the reliability of the assessments put forward by the more intransigent of his advisers. He was also growing doubtful about the long-term desirability, from the point of view of British trading interests, of saddling Germany with huge reparations claims. Woodrow Wilson's threat to abandon the conference on 7 April unless the Allies adopted more reasonable reparations and other policies, alarmed both the French and the British. Fortified by his enhanced self-confidence after the defeat of his parliamentary critics, and the knowledge, as evidenced by the Asquithian Liberal gains at by-elections, that the tide of anti-German feeling in Britain was beginning to recede, the Prime Minister was prompted in April to adopt a more moderate line. In this he was supported by the Treasury experts in Paris, Keynes and R.H. Brand.

In contradicting Sumner, Brand and Keynes emphasized that Germany's industries were exhausted by the war, while her investments, credit and trade had collapsed. All these factors prevented any immediate and objective forecast of what she could pay. Given Wilson's opposition to excessive reparation demands and the impossibility of securing allied agreement to any moderate figure, the entire Peace Conference seemed in jeopardy. Plainly a fresh approach to the question was needed. Lloyd George perceived that the imposition of financial burdens on Germany would inhibit both Germany's industrial recovery and the revival of European trade, on which Britain's prosperity depended.

On 28 March Lloyd George accepted a proposal by the French Minister of Finance, Louis Klotz, that the final sum to be imposed on Germany should be assessed after the Peace Conference by an Inter-Allied Reparation Commission. This was at first opposed by Wilson, who feared that it would later lead to Germany being presented with unlimited allied demands. However a further refinement was added by Keynes and Smuts, who proposed that the reparation clauses should be incorporated in the draft treaty but that the space for the figures should be left blank. Lloyd George put this suggestion before the Council of Four on 29 March. He admitted that the Allies were entitled to full compensation for the losses — which he estimated at £30,000 million — they had suffered as a result of the war, but insisted that Germany could in no circumstances pay this amount. It would therefore be more reasonable to restrict allied demands to compensation from Germany both for the material losses they had suffered and for personal losses and injuries. To safeguard Britain's share, he insisted on the inclusion of disablement allowances and pensions for the civilian dependents of combatants.

Woodrow Wilson rejected these British demands because they would dangerously inflate the final figure. The British Prime Minister retorted that 'unless this were included I might as well go home as I had no authority to sign unless this were admitted'.[36] On 1 April, after reading a justification of the British case by Smuts, Wilson professed himself convinced.

The issue of fixing the final sum was by no means settled, however. Bonar Law and Walter Long warned Lloyd George from London that Unionist opinion might react very strongly against this proposal, while moderates like Lord Robert Cecil shared Wilson's fears that postponement might have a devastating effect both on international credit and on Germany's economic stability. This plan seems to me to combine the maximum of financial disturbance with the minimum of actual result'.[37]

To make matters worse, it soon transpired that French thinking was still far apart from Britain's on the subject. The French foreign minister, Stephen Pichon, told Derby that France would require Germany to acknowledge her responsibility for the damage caused by the war, although 'it might be possible [later] to say to Germany that we would arrive at some understanding which released her from such a crushing debt'. Derby summed up:

> You have Germany wanting to get money to repay her damages. You have America determined to keep the money that she made in the first few years of the War. You have us wanting to have at all events some of our great expenditure repaid and having no money to lend, and the combination of the three seems to me to make a deadlock in which I personally see no outcome.[38]

The French thus remained resolutely determined that as much as possible should be squeezed out of Germany. At the Council of Four on 5 April Klotz insisted that the Reparation Commission should base its calculations not on Germany's capacity to pay but on the total sum she owed the Allies. If this sum should prove to be greater than Germany could repay over 30 years, the Commission might allow Germany to prolong the repayments. Lloyd George countered that the Commission must at the outset determine Germany's capacity to pay. This further manifestation of French intransigence confirmed Woodrow Wilson's worst suspicions of the entire scheme, and convinced him that France had no intention of adhering to the principles he had laid down. On 7 April Wilson summoned the *George Washington* to Brest.

No doubt the President's gesture was a mixture of exasperation and bluff, but it did have the desired effect. That afternoon the French climbed down and agreed that the Reparation Commission should base its calculations on its estimates of

Germany's economic capacity. This, of course, left France with the opportunity of making further difficulties when the Commission began its investigations. However, Wilson's agreement on 10 April that the United States would participate in the work of the Commission led Lloyd George to anticipate Anglo-American cooperation on the Commission to restrain extreme French demands.

Smuts, in putting forward this scheme, reasoned that the Commission would act impartially in assessing Germany's liabilities. While Germany, under article 231 of the treaty, was to acknowledge responsibility for causing the war and was therefore technically liable to pay all allied war costs, Lloyd George hoped that the powers might agree upon a more reasonable figure when the intense passions of the war had subsided. Neither hope was, in the event, to be fulfilled. The Commission was to assess Germany's liability in accordance with her economic capacity by 21 May 1921 and, in the meantime, Germany was to pay a sizeable lump sum on account. This postponement of the imposition of a final figure on Germany merely extended the wrangling over reparations well into the 1920s. Nor were Lloyd George's immediate difficulties over reparations settled by this compromise by the Council of Four. As has been shown, Unionist opinion was angered by the failure of the conference to settle on a definite and large reparation figure. Furthermore, the opinions of the British Empire delegation at Paris had still to be ascertained, especially those of Hughes, who, predictably, was by no means reconciled to the compromise.

On 11 April the delegation assembled in Lloyd George's Paris flat to hear a statement by the Prime Minister on the progress of the draft peace treaty.[39] Andrew Bonar Law, Louis Botha, the Prime Minister of South Africa, Borden, Hughes and Wîlliam Massey, the New Zealand Prime Minister, were present, with Sumner, Cunliffe, Kerr and Hankey in attendance. Inevitably reparations proved to be the most contentious issue, with Hughes protesting vehemently that, under the compromise, Germany would escape payment of the whole costs of the war. Lloyd George retorted that if he revived this issue, the President would 'probably go home'. Botha warned the meeting that further demands would lead to a Bolshevik Germany. Lloyd George reiterated his conviction that any further pressure for greater reparations would lead to the collapse of the conference. This, in turn, would necessitate keeping 1,500,000 men under arms. In such circumstances, he asked pointedly, would the Dominions be prepared to contribute troops? Apart from Hughes, all the Dominions' representatives agreed to accept the Four's compromise as the best that could be hoped for.

At 11.00 Lloyd George had to leave the meeting and Bonar Law took the chair. Sumner and Cunliffe, now more flexible in their approach—having, no doubt, been well-primed by Lloyd George—endeavoured to persuade Hughes to adopt a more flexible line. Cunliffe admitted that, before coming to Paris, he had suggested a figure of £12,000 million as being within Germany's capacity to pay, but confessed that this was 'little more than a shot in the dark as he had been pressed to arrive at it between a Saturday and a Monday'. From his experience of the negotiations, he was convinced that the United States would not be prepared to go further than the compromise already accepted by the Council. Hughes was now in a minority of one, with even those two erstwhile hard-liners, Sumner and Cunliffe, against him. Later on the 11th he capitulated, albeit under protest.[40]

Having defeated his conservative critics, Lloyd George found himself faced, inside and outside the government, with a revolt of the more moderate elements, who considered that even the reparations compromise, intended by the Prime Minister to reduce the tension, was too harsh.

The League of Nations[41]

The concept of an international organization to prevent war had been pioneered after 1914 by academics and establishment figures like G. Lowes Dickinson and Lord Bryce. In May 1915 men of similar liberal persuasion established the League of Nations Society to propagate the League idea. It generated little enthusiasm among British politicians, officials and service advisers, who much preferred to rely on the traditional methods of guaranteeing the protection of British interests – British naval supremacy, the independence of Holland and Belgium, and the manipulation of the balance of power.

The reluctant acceptance by British officials that an international forum would have to be set up after the war was in part the result of the devotion and perseverance of Lord Robert Cecil, the Minister of Blockade from 1916 to 1918. He participated in the pre-conference planning for the League. His persistent advocacy gradually wore down the opposition of the British bureaucracy. In 1918 he received the welcome support of General Smuts, another League enthusiast. In 1917 and 1918 Lloyd George and his Coalition were more directly influenced, however, by the twin pressures of growing war weariness and increasing labour unrest. A public initiative which promised the establishment of a new international order after the war might restore morale at home and in the Entente, and undermine the will to war of the enemy populations. Left and radical elements were clamouring for a post-war settlement which would be based on a just peace, on the repudiation of selfish national aims, on disarmament, and on a league to enforce the peace. The February revolution in Russia also suggested the advantages of a more positive public approach to peace aims. Above all, there was the impact of Wilsonian idealism, with its strong appeal to British radicalism. With the entry of the United States into the war allied policy needed to keep in step with President Wilson. Lloyd George also hoped that his support for the President's principles would lead to Anglo-American collaboration after the peace conference.

In his famous war aims address of 5 January 1918, Lloyd George quoted almost word for word a Smuts-Cecil memorandum which emphasized national self-determination and the 'creation of some international organization to limit the burden of armaments and diminish the probability of war', as the goals of British post-war policy.[42] The expression of similar, although rather more definite, sentiments by Wilson in his Fourteenth Point three days later suggested that on this question Britain and the United States were ostensibly in accord.

In the same month Cecil persuaded the War Cabinet to set up a committee of experts under Sir Walter Phillimore to examine the League question. Its March report advocated an alliance of victors, whose members would agree not to go to war with each other, and to refer all disputes between them to an allied conference, which would make recommendations for peaceful settlements. A state which did not comply would be subject to economic and military sanctions by the other allies. If a non-member state refused to submit a dispute with an ally to the conference, and then proceeded to attack that ally, 'any of the Allied States may come to its [that ally's] assistance'. These proposals were hardly revolutionary in nature. The alliance was merely the concert of Europe writ large, with an ambassadorial conference which would possess a few compulsory powers with which to enforce its will. The question of the admission of neutrals and enemy states was by-passed by the committee.[43]

Despite continued pressure from Cecil, the government refused not only to allow the publication of the Phillimore Report, but also to clarify its attitude towards the constitution of the League. Lloyd George felt that he could pay only lip-service to the League ideal, since many of his ministers were opposed to a League which possessed any compulsory powers. Nor did President Wilson encourage the public ventilation of proposals, since they might stir up his Senate critics and anger idealists because they were not far-reaching enough. Lloyd George and his colleagues would have welcomed private discussions with the President on the future shape of the League, but increasing misunderstanding over other aspects of their war aims prevented any meaningful exchange of views before the end of the war.

Even in November and December 1918 the War Cabinet

gave its advisers no guide-lines as to future League policy. Matters improved, however, when Cecil was put in charge of a Foreign Ofiice League of Nations section, which studied memoranda on the subject submitted by Lord Eustace Percy and Alfred Zimmern. Both these officials adopted the cautious approach suggested by the Phillimore Report. On 14 December the section produced a 'Brief Conspectus of League of Nations Organization', which became known as the 'Cecil Plan'.[44] This envisaged annual great power summit conferences whose decisions would be unanimous. There would also be quarterly meetings of all the powers and special conferences which could be convened in an emergency. The 'Conspectus' closely followed the Phillimore recommendations about the settlement of disputes and the imposition of sanctions.

Britain's League was not to be an alternative to traditional methods of British diplomacy. The British rejected international guarantees of frontiers, favoured by Wilson. The Imperial War Cabinet was divided even over the modest degree of collective security proposed in the Cecil Plan. Lloyd George made it clear that he would not tolerate a League which possessed any independent coercive power. He maintained that decisions on all policy matters must be taken only by the member governments.

Wilson's visit to London at the end of December and his discussions with Lloyd George convinced the British Prime Minister of the primacy of the League in the President's thinking. Indeed, Wilson insisted that the League should be the first item on the conference agenda, and that its Covenant would form part of the peace treaty. As Hughes put it, Wilson

> regards the League of Nations as the great Charter of the World that is to be and sees himself through the roseate cloud of dreams officiating as the High Priest in the Temple in which the Sarcophagus or Ark containing the body or ashes of this amazing gift to Mankind is to rest in majestic seclusion for all time. Give him a League of Nations and he will give us all the rest. Good. He shall have his toy![45]

The Imperial War Cabinet agreed that the British delegation should work with Wilson to bring a moderate League to fruition. In return for British support it was felt that Wilson would be receptive to British demands elsewhere. However Britain's representatives should keep in close touch with the French, the Cabinet reasoned, so that if the United States tried to sabotage British interests, or Senate rejection of the treaty wrecked British hopes for continued Anglo-American collaboration, Britain would be able to fall back on Anglo-French cooperation.

On 25 January 1919, in accordance with Wilson's wishes, the conference set up a League of Nations Commission, consisting of two delegates from each of the five great powers, and five from the smaller powers. Cecil and Lord Eustace Percy represented Britain, and Wilson the United States. During the early weeks of the conference British and American delegates met in private to hammer out a joint proposal. This was chiefly the work of the Foreign Office legal adviser, Cecil Hurst, and an American lawyer, David Hunter Miller. It provided for an assembly on which all the powers were to be represented. On the other hand, the council, which was to determine policy, was to consist only of the great powers. At Wilson's insistence Cecil agreed to a guarantee of the territorial integrity of all member states. The sanctions provisions were modelled on those of the Phillimore Report. Finally, the dominions were to have independent membership.

The Hurst-Miller draft went forward to the Commission as the basis for its deliberations. As a result of pressure from the smaller powers, Cecil reluctantly agreed to their representation on the council. Otherwise the bulk of the Anglo-American proposals was accepted by the Commission, despite efforts by France and the smaller allies to stiffen the sanctions provisions of the Covenant. Cecil and Wilson strenuously resisted a well-orchestrated French campaign to turn the League into an instrument to police Germany and strengthen French security, by establishing an international general staff and a standing international army.

The draft Covenant was finalized on 14 February when it was presented to a plenary session of the conference. Despite this apparent success, the battle for the League was by no means won. Wilson returned to the United States in March to face a barrage of Senate criticism of the project, chiefly over its implications for United States' sovereignty. The President came back to Paris convinced that he would have to secure changes in the Covenant if the treaty was to pass the Senate. He sought a reservation about the Monroe Doctrine to prevent the League interfering in the affairs of the Americas without United States' consent. Cecil also faced critics in the British delegation (Hughes in particular) who were still uneasy about any provision for automatic sanctions. The Admiralty and the War Office opposed any clause in the Covenant concerning the limitation of armaments. British critics insisted that if there had to be a League, it should merely be a consultative body. Wilson's predicament over the Monroe Doctrine gave the British an opportunity to steer the League in a direction more in accordance with their wishes.

By the end of March, Wilson and Cecil had secured some amendments to the Covenant which met the points raised by their critics. Domestic questions were not to be discussed by the League, any member could withdraw upon two years' notice, and members could only go to war subject to the provisions of their own constitutions. Further progress was held up, however, when the project became enmeshed with the bitter disputes between the Allies about the Rhineland, reparations, and, in the case of Britain and the United States, the naval question.

Lloyd George had never been particularly keen on the League, and indeed took only minimal interest in it, except in so far as it could be used to promote an Anglo-American entente. His Fontainebleau Memorandum made only a passing reference to the organization. When the naval question erupted at the beginning of April, Lloyd George threatened to withdraw his support from it altogether if the United States refused to meet British demands for a naval agreement.[46]

Although Britain had emerged from the war with her naval primacy confirmed, the Admiralty now found that it was faced with the prospect of an American, instead of a German, naval challenge. As a result of a 1916 naval bill, by the end of 1919 the United States would have a fleet of 35 modern capital ships, superior in quality to the Royal Navy's 42 battleships, many of which were becoming obsolescent. In 1918 the American naval chiefs planned to build 16 capital ships which, when added to the 1916 ships, would eventually result in an American navy superior both in quantity and quality to that of Britain.

The motives for American determination to press ahead with her naval programme were mixed, but the Royal Navy reacted to the threat with a combination of injured pride and petulant appeals to British naval traditions. The Admiralty appreciated that if the United States decided to build a huge fleet, Britain would never be able to match it. The British government sought to reduce naval expenditure after the war, not to increase it. There were angry scenes between the naval leaders of both sides at Paris when the British demanded that the Americans abandon their construction programme. On 1 April Josephus Daniels, the US Secretary for the Navy, rejected Lloyd George's appeals for immediate cuts. The atmosphere became even more embittered when the Prime Minister asked Daniels why the United States needed a bigger navy than Britain when she possessed only a few colonies. After all, Lloyd George asserted, Britain had to protect a far-flung empire. Daniels would only hint at a reduction of the United States' programme when the League began to function effectively. This was little consolation to the Prime Minister, who was growing increasingly sceptical about the future of that organization.

Cecil now feared that Lloyd George would, in retaliation for the United States' refusal to agree to a naval compromise, oppose any concession over the Monroe Doctrine and thus torpedo the League project. The British delegate therefore reached agreement with House on 10 April whereby the United States postponed the construction of those ships of the 1916 programme not yet laid down until after the signature of the peace treaty. The United States would then consider the modification of its 1918 programme as well. In return Cecil promised that Britain would support the Monroe Doctrine amendment. In fact Lloyd George had achieved merely a face-saving compromise, since it was unlikely in the last resort that he would risk permanent American ill-will by wrecking the conference over the Monroe Doctrine.

On 11 April a new article, which incorporated the Monroe Doctrine amendment, was drawn up for inclusion in the Covenant. At the same time Wilson set aside a Japanese proposal for the inclusion of an article on racial equality, after strenuous objections by Hughes, who feared that it might be used against Australia's 'whites only' immigration policy. Nor would it have pleased Californians already upset by Japanese immigration before the war and determined to resist a new wave. The final draft of the Covenant was presented to a plenary conference on 21 April and published on the 26th. It became Part I of the treaty. Articles 10 to 13 and 15 and 16 provided for the arbitration of disputes and for combined action by League members, in case of a threat of aggression or actual aggression against a member, or of 'any war or threat of war'. The Admiralty and War Office were relieved by the paucity of references to disarmament in the Covenant. Wilson had pledged in Point Four that there would be 'adequate guarantees given and taken that national armaments will be reduced to the lowest point consistent with domestic safety'.[47] The conference left it to the League to make any necessary arrangements under Article 8 for 'the reduction of armaments to the lowest point consistent with national safety'.[48]

The Covenant evoked little enthusiasm in British official circles. Lloyd George continued to complain about the obligations which were contained in the Covenant which, since there were now to be smaller powers on the council, might involve the great powers in wars against their wishes or interests. It was not an auspicious beginning.

The German Colonies[49]

The disposal of the former German colonies became linked to the fate of the League during the early stages of the conference. The antagonism which this issue generated between Australia, New Zealand and South Africa on the one hand and Woodrow Wilson on the other provided additional fuel for the hostility of the Dominions towards the League, which the President intended should supervise the colonial administrations of the former German overseas empire. The future of Shantung was also involved in this quarrel, for Japan rejected even the face-saving formula eventually drawn up by the great powers for the management of Germany's colonies. She insisted on securing Germany's Pacific and Chinese concessions and privileges without even a formal reference to League procedures.

During the war the British Dominions had sent military and naval forces to capture Germany's African and Pacific holdings. East Africa, however, was not cleared of German troops until December 1917. Australia and New Zealand were soon in possession of the German Pacific Islands south of the Equator, while Japan conquered those to the north of that line. The main difficulty for Lloyd George and the Imperial War Cabinet was that Wilsonian idealism and Russian demands for a peace without annexations during 1917 made outright annexation an embarrassing goal. Britain therefore sought some means of satisfying domestic and foreign opinion that her intentions towards these colonies were purely altruistic, while maintaining intact the substance of imperial rule.

The latter qualification ruled out more radical suggestions put forward by E. D. Morel and Ramsay MacDonald that in future overseas colonies should be administered by an international board under the auspices of the League: even the Labour party receded from this position. In any case Australia, New Zealand, South Africa and Japan would never have agreed to this solution. Thus, when Lloyd George in his war aims speech of 5 January 1918 referred to the applicability of the principle of self-determination to the German colonies, there was consternation among the Australians, who wondered how the head-hunters of New Guinea would react to a plebiscite concerning their future. Furthermore, in February 1917, in return for the provision of additional Japanese cruisers in the south Atlantic, Britain had agreed to support Japan's retention of the German islands north of the Equator and of Germany's rights in Shantung. This was really making a virtue of necessity since nothing short of force would have induced Japan to give up her gains. Nevertheless it threatened to involve Britain in an embarrassing confrontation with President Wilson, who refused to recognize the secret treaties.

British politicians justified continued British control of Germany's colonies after the war by reference to Britain's long record of concern with the welfare of native peoples. This was compared with Germany's mistreatment of her colonial subjects before 1914. Allied propaganda was reinforced by grim forecasts of a Germany with her colonies restored raising huge black armies to attack the victors' African colonies. There was also the spectre of Germany building naval bases in her colonies, from which she could use submarines and surface vessels to challenge Britain's maritime hegemony. Thus the need to retain the colonies and yet appear to yield to Wilson's idealism suggested an approach on the lines of Smuts' proposal to the Eastern Committee in July 1918, to set up an international board to supervise the welfare of the inhabitants of all European African colonies. The altruism of this suggestion might appeal to President Wilson, who, perhaps, would also be tempted by the offer of an American protectorate over one of the conquered areas. The British could not, however, make up their minds in which area the United States would do the least harm to Britain's strategic and economic interests. Palestine and German East Africa were considered, but were eventually rejected in favour of Armenia. Smuts' development board suggestion was to lead to the adoption of the mandates scheme.

In November Smuts put forward the idea of titular League control over the liquor and arms trades, slavery and fortifications in the colonies, but with their administrations controlled by a single power. Later, in order to reduce the degree of international control even further, he refined the concept of colonies in various stages of development, graded A, B and C mandates. C mandates were to be administered as integral parts of the territories of the mandatory, which meant League surveillance over arms, slavery and fortifications but not over immigration and trade. B mandates differed little in practice, beyond League supervision to ensure open door trade practices. In both cases the mandatories had to submit annual reports to the League. A mandates suggested eventual independence and were applied to the Middle East.

Woodrow Wilson insisted at Paris that all conquered ex-enemy territories should be placed under League control. Lloyd George, who wanted the colonial issue settled before the intrusion of European questions, put the mandates proposal before the Council of Ten on 24 January 1919. Hughes, Massey and Smuts, however, tried to convince the President that the south Pacific islands, Samoa and South West Africa, were so essential to the security of the British Empire that the mandates system should not be applied to them. Japan also demanded the outright annexation of the North Equatorial Pacific Islands and her acquisition of Germany's former rights in Shantung.

On 27 January Wilson agreed to the establishment of mandates but rejected South African, Australasian and Japanese annexationist demands. Hughes led the opposition to the President. It was only after the exercise of considerable pressure by Lloyd George and Botha, who managed to convince Hughes that mandates were annexation by another name, that the system was accepted by the British Empire. Another potentially explosive issue had been defused before it could threaten the existence of the conference, although Wilson's task was made easier by Clemenceau's refusal to become involved in the dispute.

In retaliation for Hughes' opposition, Wilson deferred a decision on the assignment of mandates until early May. The United States did not assume any colonial responsibilities. German East Africa and German West Africa were awarded respectively to Britain and South Africa as B mandates. France got 60% of the Togoland and the bulk of the Cameroons, and Britain the rest, as B mandates. Belgium was grudgingly given Ruanda-Urandi, which her forces had occupied in 1914, as a B mandate. Japan secured the Pacific islands north of the Equator as C mandates, New Zealand the Samoan islands, and Australia acquired all the other islands south of the Equator (including, later, Nauru) as C mandates. France recovered the strip of the Congo lost to Germany in 1911, while Portugal gained Kionga, a coastal strip of East Africa. Italy, absent from the Council in May, was fobbed off with the Juba valley in East Africa and with minor adjustments in her favour of the Algerian border with Tripoli.

One of the motives behind Wilson's objections to the early assignment of mandates and for his earlier hopes for a greater degree of international control over Germany's former colonies, was his increasing suspicion of Japanese ambitions in the Pacific and China. The American administration feared that Japan would fortify the Pacific islands and build bases there, thus threatening American security. The Japanese also demanded the German leaseholds over Kioachow and the port of Tsingtao, and German railway, mining and commercial concessions in the Chinese province of Shantung. Japan had seized Kioachow after a short campaign between September and November 1914, and her troops had thereafter extended their occupation to key points in Shantung, including the capital Tsinan. In 1915 she presented China with a list of 21 demands which included Chinese recognition of Japan's position in Shantung and far-reaching economic concessions in China. On 25 May 1915 China agreed to Japan's Shantung demands. British support for Japan after 1917 further strengthened Japan's pressure for international recognition of her acquisitions at Paris. China countered that her declaration of war on Germany in August 1917 nullified all Germany's privileges in China, which should revert to the Chinese government. She was ignored.

Japan's claims inevitably clashed with Wilson's call for the internationalization of all foreign concessions in China, as well as increasing American uneasiness about Japan's long term aims in the Pacific. Japan's decision to despatch troops to Siberia in 1918 strengthened these American fears. Britain also opposed Wilson's internationalization schemes since she had no intention of abrogating her own economic rights in the Yangtse valley. Apart from this, Lloyd George had little sympathy for, or knowledge of, China, faced as he was with more pressing problems nearer home. The Foreign Office derided China's contribution to the war effort. Of course Lloyd George's advisers and Australia and New Zealand were as concerned as the Americans about the prospect of Japan fortifying the North Pacific islands and of excluding foreign trade. However, Lloyd George's anxieties about this could not be stressed too much, given the extent of the British Empire's claims in Africa, the Pacific and the Middle East.

When negotiations with the Japanese began in earnest on 21 April, Lloyd George insisted that Britain was bound to support Japan's claims under the 1917 treaty. Clemenceau stated that France would follow suit, so that Wilson was isolated. China rejected any formula that would allow Japan to remain in Shantung under any guise, while Japan refused to agree to the mandates system being extended to cover Kioachow. Lloyd George tried in vain to persuade the Japanese to accept a C mandate. He gave up, unwilling to risk the Anglo-Japanese alliance on an issue remote from British interests. He was followed by the President, faced with Japanese threats to abandon the conference and sign a separate treaty with Germany; he was already embroiled in a bitter dispute with Italy over Fiume and did not relish further complications. Under Article 22 of the treaty, which was drawn up on 30 April, Japan secured Germany's concessions in Shantung and the Kioachow lease. As a face-saving gesture Japan promised that ultimately the sovereignty of Kioachow would revert to China (but not the Shantung concessions) but no time limit was imposed on this transaction. As a result China refused to sign the Treaty of Versailles. Wilson had suffered a humiliating defeat but, with no support from his western partners, he had little alternative but to yield to Japan's demands.

Aftermath, June 1919

The draft treaty was presented to the German delegation on 7 May 1919 at the Trianon Palace.[50] The German Government was given 15 days (later extended to 29 May) to submit written observations. During this period Lloyd George was faced with a campaign by a number of his ministers, especially Smuts, to secure major changes in the draft treaty. The Prime Minister was not unsympathetic: he had already, in the Fontainebleau Memorandum, urged modifications on his allies and had managed to persuade the French to recede from some of their more extreme demands. When the treaty was finally read as a whole in May it appeared to many in the British delegation a harsh and uncompromising document, difficult to reconcile with the 1918 promises of Lloyd George and Wilson.

Lloyd George was therefore willing to try to meet the protests of the treaty's critics. Not only did he fear that a draconian settlement would create instability in Germany, with dire consequences for future European peace, but he now began to worry that Germany might reject the treaty outright. The victors would then have to plan forcible measures, which would not be stressed too much, given the extent of the British since the end of 1918, as Foch repeatedly argued, the Allies — particularly Britain and the United States — had substantially reduced the sizes of their armed forces in Europe. In a memorandum of 16 June 1919 Sir Henry Wilson expressed his confidence that the allied armies of 39 divisions would be able to march on Berlin. However, he somewhat weakened his argument by pointing to the large numbers of occupation troops that would be required to hold down a hostile population and protect lines of communication. Any check suffered by the advancing allied armies would have appalling consequences, and he therefore suggested that the Allies halt at the line of the Weser to see if this advance was sufficient to bring the Germans to heel. If not, the Allies should call on 'the Poles, Czechs and Italians to help and co-ordinating [*sic*] their assistance into one good sound military plan'.[51] Foch went further on 16 and 20 June when he informed an astonished Council of Four

that the forces under his command were not adequate to fight
their way to Berlin. Instead, the Allies should seize south
Germany, and then march via Prague and Posen to link up
with the Czechs and Poles to take Berlin from the east.[52]

It was a daunting prospect and partially accounted for the
British Prime Minister's receptivity to changes in the treaty.
Smuts took the lead early in May in a series of letters to Lloyd
George in which he pointed out the disastrous consequences
which would arise if the treaty was not radically revised. It
would lead to Britain, as a result of the treaty of guarantee,
being dragged into war alongside France each time there was
a Franco-German conflict over the application of the treaty.
Smuts complained specifically about the severe nature of the
disarmament clauses which, together with her other losses,
would cripple German industry for years. The Rhineland
occupation clauses 'must shock every decent conscience and
breed great perils for Europe'. Indeed, France should be
persuaded to accept the Anglo-American guarantee and the
League as adequate to protect her security.[53]

Smuts was particularly incensed by the Polish settlement. It
would leave millions of Germans and Russians under the
control of the Poles who were devoid of administrative and
governing abilities. Poland should be made to realize that
once Russia and Germany revived in strength, she would be
absolutely dependent on their goodwill. A start could be made
by excluding as many Germans from the new Poland as possible,
by reducing the size of Danzig's boundaries, placing that city
under German sovereignty (although leaving its administration
to the League) and leaving Upper Silesia to Germany.

His protests were supported by Botha and George Barnes,
a member of the War Cabinet. Botha warned the Prime Minister
that if the treaty led to a future Franco-German war in which
Britain became embroiled on the side of France, Britain could
not be certain of the automatic support of the dominions.
Barnes complained that the treaty was 'out of character with
the aims of the mass of our people'. From the War Office came
pressure of a different kind. Winston Churchill, the Secretary

of State for War, feared that if the Allies were forced to occupy Germany as a result of her rejection of the present harsh peace, it would have a catastrophic effect on Britain's dwindling military power and deprive her of her ability to defend her interests in India, the Middle East and Turkey. He too pressed for compromises which would induce Germany to sign. H. A. L. Fisher, President of the Board of Education, speaking for the Coalition Liberals, agreed, and warned Lloyd George that if war was resumed there would be 'a violent revulsion of feeling' against the Government. Lord Robert Cecil feared that if the harsher aspects of the treaty were not mitigated the United States would reject the settlement.[54]

These strictures were reinforced by Germany's observations on the treaty, which tok the form of a series of notes on specific issues, and then on 29 May, a long memorandum dealing with the whole treaty. The gist of these was that the treaty violated both Wilson's principles and the pre-armistice agreements. Germany completely rejected the war guilt clause and the onerous reparation terms associated with it, and the territorial provisions which violated the principle of self-determination. She protested about her exclusion from the League and the lack of reciprocity in the disarmament clauses. Her protests gave added weight to those who were pressuring Lloyd George to secure amendments. Bonar Law, for instance, thought the German reply 'very able' and supported concessions 'not of vital interest to the allies', to persuade the Germans to sign.[55] Lloyd George therefore summoned the British Empire delegation in Paris to discuss Britain's response to the German reply. The first meeting took place in the Hotel Majestic on Friday 30 May.[56]

The Prime Minister took the chair. Smuts and Barnes mounted a comprehensive attack on those sections of the treaty which they regarded as incompatible with the Fourteen Points. They had already rehearsed specific criticisms in their letters to Lloyd George but at the meeting they singled out reparations as being particularly vexatious. Milner supported them by urging the imposition of a moderate fixed sum. Only Hughes spoke out against reviving the issue which had been so laboriously negotiated. Lloyd George pointed out that Sumner and Cunliffe had already protested in writing against any further tampering with reparations—in Cunliffe's words, 'Germany can and will pay the whole of what is demanded'.

On the morning of Sunday 1 June the British Empire delegation reconvened. Lloyd George put two questions to each member of the delegation:

1. Was he in favour of standing on the terms proposed in the present Draft Treaty, or was he in favour of making some concessions, the nature of which could be considered at a later stage?
2. If any concessions should be made, should they be communicated in a written statement, naming a period within which the Germans must reply, or should negotiations be encouraged?

Each member said that he was in favour of making some concessions.

Lloyd George had already alluded to the possibility of securing changes in the Polish clauses, particularly over Upper Silesia and Danzig, and the delegation now unanimously supported this suggestion. None of the ministers evinced any sympathy for Poland. Lloyd George described the Poles as 'a difficult people to deal with', while Smuts described Poland as 'a historic failure'. Even Hughes thought it 'monstrous to put Germans under Polish rule'. Austen Chamberlain and Lord Birkenhead, the Lord Chancellor, supported Smuts' and Barnes' recommendation of a fixed reparation sum to be stated in the treaty, although the difficulty of settling on a figure that would be sufficient to satisfy British public opinion and ensure that Britain secured a reasonable share of the proceeds was generally admitted—even by Smuts—to be insuperable.

The delegation resumed its discussion at 5.30. Lloyd George summed up the day's deliberations as 'an earnest and sometimes passionate plea for justice for the fallen enemy'. He thought that they had 'erred on the side of consideration for the fallen enemy'. He refused to revive the question of the army of occupation and the Saar since these were both part of a package deal designed to forestall permanent French occupation of the Rhineland, although he later agreed to press for some modification of the length, cost and constitution of the occupation regime. He would certainly fight hard for a plebiscite in Upper Silesia and urge the admission of Germany to the League six months after her signature of the treaty. Turning to reparations he said that:

> He had found the subject of compensation the most baffling and perplexing of all. He did not say that the Germans could pay a particular sum or could not pay it. He did not think, for the time being, this aspect mattered much. Most experts told him that it was impossible to be quite sure that Germany could pay any particular sum. He did not think that the time had come for letting Germany off anything. There were provisions in the Treaty which enabled the Allies to reconsider the matter if they came to the conclusion that it was quite impossible for Germany to pay. She could appeal to the Commission for postponement and the Commission had power to adjudicate the request. The Commission could reduce the amount of payments. These provisions were in the Treaty, and he should have thought that the general character of the provisions would not have prevented the Germans from signing. He would have thought that this was not an appropriate moment for them to show what they could or could not pay.

Thus, despite the sustained pressure of practically the whole British Empire delegation (except Hughes and Massey), Lloyd George refused to embark on any further attempt to modify the reparation clauses, or attempt the thankless task of trying to negotiate a fixed sum. Since the delegation recognized the difficulties, they could hardly object. As a sop to the critics he agreed to propose to the Council that the Germans be invited to make a firm offer of a fixed sum three months after the treaty, but if this was unacceptable the Allies would adhere to the existing clauses. But for the Allies to forego any of their legitimate claims on Germany at this stage would create insurmountable difficulties. 'Somebody had to pay. If Germany could not pay it meant that the British taxpayer had to pay. Those who ought to pay were those who had caused the loss.' Finally the French would steadfastly refuse to abandon any of their claims. 'The hatred of the French for the Germans was something inconceivable—it was savage and he did not blame them for it.'

Then the Prime Minister listed the concessions which he was prepared to propose to his fellow allied leaders. First, the modification of Germany's eastern frontiers, leaving to her those areas where the population was unquestionably German, unless there were overwhelming reasons for transferring them to Poland. Plebiscites would be held where there were doubts as to the ethnic complexion of the population. Second, Germany should be promised early membership of the League provided that she made serious efforts to fulfil her treaty obligations. Third, the allied occupation armies in the Rhineland should be reduced both in numbers and duration of occupation. Finally there should be a concession about reparations which Lloyd George had already outlined. If the Council refused to consider these concessions, the Prime Minister would inform them that the British army would not cooperate in any attempt to enforce the treaty, such as a march on Berlin, and Britain would refuse to re-impose the blockade on Germany.

Lloyd George had secured British Empire approval to propose certain modifications to the draft treaty which, he hoped, would demonstrate Britain's firm commitment to a lasting peace based on Wilsonian principles, satisfy the clamour for a revision of the existing draft treaty and, even more important, persuade Germany to sign it. He anticipated that these concessions would be acceptable to the French, since they did not amount to a radical change in the terms so far agreed, nor did they affect French security preoccupations.

British interests were unaffected—indeed Massey had inter-jected earlier in the debate that he hoped concessions involved no alteration in the German colonial settlement, to which Lloyd George had replied with an emphatic 'No'.[57]

While Lloyd George had steered a skilful course between the positions of Smuts and Barnes on the one hand and Hughes on the other, and had formulated a set of proposals which were in line with opinion in the Imperial War Cabinet, these did not satisfy Germany's demands. Nor did they quell the protests of the bitterly disillusioned Wilsonians in Britain and the United States who felt that tinkering with individual clauses was insufficient. Indeed, the changes proposed and the manner in which they were compiled reflected the *ad hoc* approach which Britain adopted towards the entire peace settlement. To this extent continental critics were justified in their assumption that once essential British interests had been satisfied Britain possessed no coherent strategy towards the European settlement. This was partly the product of faulty organization, since, towards the end of the war, ministers possessed a huge collection of recommendations amassed by the Foreign Office, the Treasury and other Departments. Paris was also full of expert advisers. Lloyd George had neither the time nor the inclination to read much of this material. He had little use for expert advice, preferring to rely upon his debating skills, his own quick intelligence and the advice of a few intimates.

Thus British policy at Paris was inconsistent. For example, where reparations were concerned her approach seemed to depend on the vindictive and mercurial behaviour of her public opinion. To some extent this was conjured up by Hughes before the December 1918 elections and encouraged at that time by Lloyd George. The Prime Minister was seeking to extract as much as possible for Britain from reparations and yet at the same time was concerned about the likely effects of this on Germany's recovery and on Europe's economic recon-struction. This inconsistency was equally evident in General Smuts' attitude. Having devised the British demand for pensions and disablement allowances to ensure that Britain secured a large proportion of the total amount, he then made a fuss about what he considered to be the unreasonable demands on Germany. During the British Empire delegation's meeting of 30 May, in response to a suggestion by Lloyd George that the Allies put forward a demand for a figure between £5,000 and £11,000 million, Smuts expressed his fear that if this figure was too low, Britain might secure nothing. In the circumstances it was hardly surprising that Lloyd George refused to do more than try to make a few relatively minor changes to the compromise he had so laboriously negotiated with the other powers. In any case the French would have rejected any more radical proposals.

Lloyd George was mistaken if he thought the British Empire delegation meeting had satisfied the critics of the draft treaty. On 2 June Barnes offered to 'clear out' if an agreed sum was not presented to Germany in the final treaty.[58] Smuts complained that the very limited amendments put forward at the meeting did not satisfy the strong pleas put forward by practically every minister for substantial changes. He now demanded the recasting of the entire treaty so that it fulfilled the allied promises of a just peace. Germany should be allowed to enter the League immediately, while the occupation of the Rhineland ought to be abandoned. He pressed for the removal of all provisions which conflicted with President Wilson's various war-time promises and the review of all clauses dealing with the eastern boundaries of Germany. Finally he urged that reparations needed to be fixed at a reasonable yet high level.

Lloyd George was by now thoroughly exasperated. He informed Barnes that he should have objected to Britain's reparation policy when it was discussed in the War Cabinet during the general election. The Allies could neither agree on a fixed figure nor on what proportion of it each should receive. If Barnes could work out a practical alternative 'you will have solved the most baffling problem of the peace treaty'.[59] Barnes presented no threat to Lloyd George since he had no political muscle. Smuts, of course, had considerable international prestige, but his more far-reaching demands had not been supported by his colleagues. Nor had he protested against the resolutions put forward by Lloyd George during the meeting. The British prime minister informed the South African that he regarded those resolutions as binding.

Lloyd George also posed some pertinent questions for Smuts. He wanted Smuts to specify the clauses which conflicted with Wilsonian principles and to suggest more concrete modifications. Did Smuts have a specific sum for reparations in mind? If the Rhineland occupation was abandoned, how were the Allies to collect this sum if Germany proved recalcitrant? How were the Allies to be induced to accept a British figure and how was it to be distributed between them? Was Smuts prepared to forego the claim for pensions and disablement allowances so that material damages could have priority? And, most telling of all, was Smuts prepared to allow Germany to retain South West or East Africa as an inducement to her to sign the treaty? Smuts gave in: he issued one more protest, probably for the record, against Lloyd George's assumptions and concluded that 'this Treaty breathes a poisonous spirit of revenge, which may yet scorch the fair face of . . . Europe'.[60]

On 2 June 1919 Lloyd George accordingly informed the Council of Four of the unanimous decision of the British Empire delegation that unless major concessions were made to Germany, the British Empire would not assist her Allies in renewing the war or the blockade against Germany. He had gravely miscalculated if he expected this bombshell to move either Clemenceau or Woodrow Wilson. Clemenceau was not to be blackmailed by Germany's threat not to sign the treaty or by Britain's refusal to assist France if she did not. He rejected Lloyd George's proposals and warned the Prime Minister that if he pressed the issue he (Clemenceau) would be forced to resign, leaving Britain and the United States to deal with less conciliatory French statesmen. While the American commission favoured changes in the treaty, Woodrow Wilson did not. He was tired and had no wish to reopen the frenzied discussions of the last few months, as he told the American commission on 3 June. He was disgusted with the opportunism of Lloyd George and his associates who had earlier wanted to insert in the treaty the most extreme demands on Germany, and then had only been stopped by Wilson's pressure. Now in the face of threats by Germany not to sign the treaty and fears of renewed British involvement in the war, the British delegation wanted substantial amendments to conciliate Germany. Wilson was convinced that the treaty was just. All his disgust at Germany's war-time behaviour welled up during this meeting and he refused to be swayed either by the feeling in favour of changes in his own commission, appeals from Smuts or threats by the British Prime Minister.

On the afternoon of the 3rd Wilson rejected Lloyd George's demands for plebiscites in Upper Silesia and elsewhere on the German-Polish border, despite Lloyd George's reminder, to Wilson's obvious irritation, that his principles were at stake. Nor would he agree to any changes in the reparation clauses. Germany was guilty, in his opinion, of the crimes of which she had been accused and must, at least in principle, agree to full restitution. He reminded the British Prime Minister that the United States had long demanded the fixing of a definite sum but had been over-ruled by her associates. Nor was he favourable to Germany's immediate admission to the League. However, Wilson was not blind to the desirability of going some way to meet Lloyd George's wishes, especially when these were based on the President's own principles.

Wilson, followed by Clemenceau, gradually climbed down. The modifications eventually approved did not affect French interests. Nor, of course, did they entirely meet Lloyd George's earlier demands. The row continued at further meetings of the Council, in the course of which there were angry exchanges between Lloyd George and the Polish Prime Minister, Ignacy Paderewski, who was summoned to the Council when the Polish-German border was being discussed. Lloyd George managed to persuade his colleagues to agree eventually to a plebiscite in Upper Silesia to be held within 18 months, despite the vociferous protests of Paderewski. Since the British would still not agree to the fixing of a definite reparations figure and Lloyd George had, in any case, made clear his opposition to raising this issue again, the Council agreed that the clauses should remain unaltered, unless Germany made an offer of an acceptable fixed sum within four months of the signature of the treaty.

On 10 June Lloyd George persuaded the Council to agree to inform the Germans that evidence of their good behaviour would entitle them to admission to the League 'in the near future'. This was as far as Clemenceau was prepared to go. He also accepted slight changes in the Rhineland clauses—but only to the extent that the period of occupation might be reduced if the Allies considered that Germany was genuinely fulfilling her obligations under the treaty.[61] The allied military authorities were to be ordered not to interfere with the German civil administration there—a direct snub to Foch, whose generals had been fostering independence movements in the French zone.

The British Empire delegation met again on 10 June to review the modifications so far achieved. They had no alternative but to suport Lloyd George's initiatives, although Barnes protested vehemently about the failure to secure a definite reduction in the period of the Rhineland occupation.[62] The German delegation was equally dissatisfied when, on 16 June, the draft treaty, with the alterations shown in red ink, was re-presented to them. It was accompanied by a covering letter, drafted by Kerr, reminding Germany that she had not only planned and caused the war but had also carried it out in a savage and inhumane manner. She was ordered to sign the treaty within five days.

The Germans secured an extension of this time-limit to 23 June. During this period a frenzied debate was carried on in the Cabinet and the National Assembly. In the course of this Brockdorff-Rantzau, the Foreign Minister, whose bearing and tone had irritated the Allies at Versailles, resigned in protest against acceptance of the treaty. He was followed by the entire Scheidemann Government on 20 June. A new Cabinet under Bauer was hastily assembled, which decided to sign the treaty if the Allies would erase the war guilt and reparations clauses. The Council of Four rejected this on 22 June and issued an ultimatum calling either for the signature of the treaty by Germany within 24 hours or for her to face the termination of the armistice. The German army leaders advised Bauer that the Landwehr was too weak to resist an allied advance and Germany had no alternative but to sign the treaty. That historic event took place in the Hall of Mirrors at Versailles on 28 June 1919.[63]

Epilogue

A. Germany

With the departure of Woodrow Wilson from Paris on 28 June and of Lloyd George the following day, the work of the Peace Conference became the responsibility of the heads of the allied delegations in Paris. Balfour became the chief British delegate until 12 September 1919, when he was replaced by Eyre Crowe.

Remaining were a rag-bag of issues ranging from reparations to 'the German request that Allied officers of control in Germany wear civilian clothes after the entry into force of the Treaty of Versailles'. Anglo-French relations on these and other issues began to deteriorate during the second half of 1919. In December Clemenceau wanted to send a strong note to Germany threatening allied military action if she continued to place obstacles in the way of the ratification of the peace treaty. Lloyd George and the cabinet demurred, though Crowe supported the French Prime Minister. Germany appeared to be denying the authority of the reparations and disarmament commissions until American representatives were appointed, she was delaying the surrender of those the Allies considered guilty of war crimes, and she was attempting to avoid payment of compensation for the sinking of her fleet at Scapa Flow.

Lloyd George bitterly denounced Crowe for his support of Clemenceau. The British Prime Minister told Curzon that

Crowe had 'blundered very badly' in giving the Cabinet insufficient warning of the threat to use military force against Germany.[64] In fact Crowe had warned Clemenceau that he could take no action on the ultimatum until he had received the approval of his government. The action was intended to demonstrate that the Allies were fully determined to secure German compliance with their wishes. In any case the French were convinced that Germany would give way. Lloyd George sent Kerr to Paris on 7 December to confer with Clemenceau, and, as a result, a much toned down note was sent to Berlin on the 8th. Clemenceau was irritated by Lloyd George's intervention. The entire incident boded ill for future Anglo-French cooperation.

B. The Control of Foreign Policy
The muddle over the control of foreign policy, already evident in the first half of 1919, became even more pronounced after the departure of the Allied leaders from Paris. The Peace Conference could not deal expeditiously with the complex problems still unsettled—relations with Germany, the treaties with Bulgaria, Hungary and Turkey, the future of Russia—when every decision had to be referred to London, Rome and Washington for final approval, and when detailed questions were being studied simultaneously by the Paris Peace Conference and by the foreign offices of the great powers. The confusion was made worse by Woodrow Wilson's preoccupation with the congressional elections, with the Senate hearings on the Versailles treaty, and with his own deteriorating health. In London Curzon replaced Balfour as Foreign Secretary in October 1919, and insisted on being closely involved in the Near Eastern negotiations.

However, foreign office participation in the outstanding settlements was likely to be spasmodic given Lloyd George's view that 'in spite of possible delay. . . great questions should be discussed between principals meeting alternatively in London, Paris and Italy'.[65] Thus the Prime Minister's peculiar brand of peripatetic diplomacy, which he had begun during the war, continued down to his fall in October 1922. He visited Paris in October 1919 and January 1920, while Clemenceau came to London in December 1919 to discuss the Turkish treaty. Lloyd George believed that the war had shown clearly the need for personal leadership in foreign affairs. His dynamism obscured the disadvantages and dangers of the 'new diplomacy'.

C. The United States, Versailles and the League

The most serious blow to British calculations about the future was the American Senate's rejection of the Treaty of Versailles. Since, on Wilson's insistence, the Covenant of the League of Nations was incorporated in that treaty, the League had to start its life without the participation of the United States.[66] Lloyd George had always been lukewarm about the League but, as Woodrow Wilson had placed that organization at the forefront of his vision for the future, and as future British policy was to be based on Anglo-American cooperation, the Prime Minister was compelled to support the League during the conference. If American enthusiasm for the League waned during 1919, that of the British public did not, if demonstrations in its favour, such as the mass rally of the League of Nations Union at the Mansion House on 13 October 1919, were any indication. In the words of a recent historian of the League, 'with a good press and powerful backing from the churches, the League enjoyed a public support that the government could not afford to disappoint'.[67]

Nevertheless the British Government made it clear that it was not prepared to abandon any of its historic safeguards for the sake of the flimsy and dubious protection offered by the League organization. In a June 1919 White Paper the Government insisted that the best protection against aggression was 'the public opinion of the civilized world'.[68] Since this was the only sanction on which Britain was prepared to base the League system, it was obvious that she intended to maintain her future security on the traditional instruments of the balance of power, the British Empire and British naval strength.

British leaders regarded a League which included the United States as a shaky enough enterprise, likely to be held together only by continued cooperation between the two powers. A League without the United States was regarded with acute misgivings. In order to maintain close relations with Wilson and to coordinate Anglo-American policy over naval relations, Ireland and the League, the British government sent Lord Grey of Fallodon, the former foreign secretary and a president of the League of Nations Union, on a special mission to the United States in September. This mission was a complete failure. Grey never even saw the ailing President. By the end of 1919 it was clear that the American Senate would never ratify the Treaty of Versailles.

Lloyd George and his supporters could see little future in a League of Nations without the United States. On 5 November Cecil Hurst, the foreign office legal expert, lunched with Hankey, Kerr, Balfour and Drummond and reported to Hardinge that 'the view was expressed very strongly by Mr Kerr and Sir Maurice Hankey that the League of Nations could not really exist if the United States was not a member and I think Mr Balfour is inclined to agree'.[69] Lloyd George certainly agreed, but was compelled by popular opinion to support the League, at least in public. In part because of British doubts and hesitations about the League, it was to fulfil none of the hopes of its originators. And with the failure of the United States to ratify the Versailles Treaty, the main plank in Britain's post-war plans, close and cordial relations between Britain and the United States, collapsed.

In the same period American participation in the shaping of post-war Europe virtually ceased. Frank Polk remained as the American delegate to the Peace Conference after Lansing had departed in August. Polk could seldom secure coherent instructions from Washington and so Britain and France were left, with haphazard support from Italy, to resolve the remaining issues without either American interference or support. After December 1919, when the conference was dissolved, and executive powers were transferred to the conference of ambassadors in Paris, the American ambassador attended its meetings only as an observer. The lingering hopes of the defeated nations that the United States would mitigate the harsher aspects of the settlements vanished.

Conclusion

For many in Britain the aftermath of the Treaty of Versailles was one of disillusionment and despair. This was fuelled by the outspoken attacks on the treaty by Keynes and other intellectuals, who represented the settlement as a betrayal of the promises made by Woodrow Wilson during the war. Repeated German protests about the harsh nature of the treaty kept the issue alive during the 1920s and beyond. In fact, from the point of view of her national interests, Britain had not done badly out of the post-war settlement. The German fleet no longer presented any threat to Great Britain while Germany's colonies were, for the most part, controlled by Britain and her empire. She had secured at least a promise of a share in whatever reparations could be extracted from Germany. Germany had also been confined to reduced boundaries.

Lloyd George and his associates could at least congratulate themselves on having protected Germany from the more extreme demands of the French, and had even secured last minute adjustments in the treaty in Germany's favour. However the British Government also believed that Germany, by her conduct during and after 1914, justly deserved all the other impositions of the treaty. Punishment was a central motif in Britain's policy towards the defeated nations. While right-wing *enragés* like Hardinge insisted that 'the big stick is what bullies like them [the Germans] understand better than anything else',[70] a recent writer has commented that 'the punitive overtones of the moralism of the moderate left have to be taken seriously'.[71] Both Woodrow Wilson and Lloyd George shared the assumption that the aggressor must make amends for his wrong-doing, and their attitudes corresponded to that of broad cross-sections of allied public opinion.

Woodrow Wilson hoped that the harsher aspects of the treaties could be mitigated later by the League of Nations, which was presumably to engage in a continuous process of treaty revision. His faith in the future efficacy of the League must explain his almost cavalier attitude towards some of the more outrageous treaty provisions, despite Lloyd George's frequent reminders that Wilson's own principles were at stake. Lloyd George hoped that Germany would, after initial protests, settle down within her new frontiers and concentrate on economic reconstruction. When she showed no signs of doing so, he began to champion a more conciliatory approach. The French had every reason to be irritated by Britain's behaviour. At Paris Britain had led the way in insisting on a very high level of reparations. Later, however, she gave little or no support to French efforts to extract them. Britain used America's rejection of the guarantee to France as an opportunity to renounce her part of the pact. She had played a leading role in the peace settlements, but showed no inclination to assist France in upholding them.

The British argued, with some justice, that foreign policy must evolve in the light of changing circumstances. After a short term post-war boom, unemployment in Britain climbed to relatively high levels. Lloyd George began to search for a long term recovery of Britain's trade which, in turn, seemed to depend on the recovery of German (and Russian) economic life. French insistence on the extraction of large sums from Germany threatened the success of his plans, as well as keeping alive German resentment about the treaty. By 1921 post-war passions in Britain had subsided; those in France had not.

Franco-British differences widened after the ratification of the Treaty of Versailles on 10 January 1920. Woodrow Wilson's miscalculations resulted in the withdrawal of the United States from active participation in post-war European policies, while increasing Anglo-French disputes destroyed the possibility of meaningful cooperation between them. France, deprived of the Anglo-American guarantee, adopted an intransigent attitude towards every German infringement of the Versailles Treaty. Of course the lines of French post-war policy were by no means clearly defined in 1920. Nor did Britain exhibit much consistency in her approach to European questions, but the beginnings of a more conciliatory approach towards Germany and Bolshevik Russia were already becoming evident.

Both Britain and France were more or less able to thwart the other's German policies but were unable individually to impose a coherent long term unilateral solution. It was not the Treaty that was at the root of the problems of the inter-war period. It was the inability of France and Britain, the two great powers with most at stake in the settlement, either to agree to uphold the Treaty or to find some means of alleviating it.

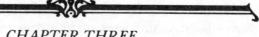

CHAPTER THREE

THE EAST EUROPEAN SETTLEMENT

Throughout the war British policy towards the Habsburg Empire swung between two alternatives: defeating the Austro-Hungarian armies and negotiating a separate peace with its rulers.[1] The continued survival of Austria-Hungary was considered primarily in the context of its contribution towards the defeat of Germany. The Tyrrell committee of Foreign Office experts recommended in 1916 that, since Austria-Hungary would always remain closely tied to Germany, European security required the break-up of the Habsburg empire and the creation of independent Poland and Yugoslavia as barriers to Germany's eastward expansion. On the other hand, during 1917, the British Government wanted to conclude a separate peace with Austria-Hungary and for this reason discouraged public speculation about the future of the nations who constituted the empire. When, in 1918, it became clear to Britain that Germany would not allow Austria-Hungary to sign a separate peace, the Government decided to promote the cause of the separate nations in order to weaken the morale of the central powers.

Since 'the political problems of eastern Europe . . . were . . . of secondary importance to the British government',[2] the war ended with no clear definition of British aims in the area, beyond Lloyd George's January 1918 promise of independence for Poland and ministerial expressions of sympathy for Bohemian and South Slav aspirations. The issue was settled for the Allies at the end of October when the Poles and the Bohemians declared their independence and the South Slavs resolved to federate with Serbia. The Habsburg empire thereupon collapsed. The armistice with Austria-Hungary

[87]

was imposed hurriedly by the allied military leaders on 3 November since they were anxious to occupy strategic positions within the empire as a prelude to an allied invasion of Germany. Germany's capitulation on 11 November put an end to the Allies' plans for a march on Berlin and their troops did not occupy any part of Austria or Hungary. Thereafter the Allies had no forces in central Europe with which to enforce their decisions. The Italian and Rumanian armies could not be relied upon to execute supreme council resolutions, especially when their own interests were at stake.

In the absence of great power supervision the emerging successor states seized as much territory as they could during November and December 1918. Inevitably they clashed with each other over border districts and fighting soon broke out across northern, central and southern Europe, prompting Lansing's comment that 'the Great War seems to have split up into a lot of little wars'.[3] On 24 January 1919 the Council of Ten attempted to forestall further violence by issuing 'a solemn warning that possession gained by force will seriously prejudice the claims of those who use such means',[4] the first of a series of similar exhortations which more often than not fell on deaf ears.

France was the only great power to have formulated a clear and consistent set of aims. She generally supported the territorial aspirations of the new states and hoped that they would become economically and strategically viable enough to resist any future German attack until France could come to their aid. She wanted them to form alliances so that collectively they could perform the role that Russia had abdicated in 1917.

Italy often opposed French designs as she did not wish to see the Habsburg empire replaced by a collection of French-dominated states and so, in the territorial committees, she objected to the claims of the successor states, particularly those of Yugoslavia. However, her policy could not be consistent as, in order to legitimize her hold on the Brenner Pass, she dared not be too antagonistic towards states who also based their claims on strategic necessity. Eager to preserve the sanctity of

[88]

the Treaty of London of 1915, she supported Rumania's territorial claims under the Treaty of Bucharest. She also shared France's hostility towards an Austro-German federation.

While the American delegation often opposed the transfer of alien peoples to the successor states as inconsistent with the principle of national self-determination, none of its members fully understood the President's interpretation of that principle. Were strategic and economic arguments to be taken into consideration? Woodrow Wilson gave them little advice and frequently contradicted himself, with the result that they had to interpret his principle as best they could. This uncertainty and the lack of a carefully prepared programme for the future of the Habsburg empire played into the hands of the well-briefed French.

The British delegation was equally confused. While a political intelligence memorandum of November 1918 insisted that 'the Germans in Bohemia and the Magyars must be treated on exactly the same principles as the Czechs and Rumanians', this proved to be difficult to implement. The British wanted to act as mediators on frontier questions, while at the same time protecting their commercial interests:

> it is needless to say that the position is one which will give an unprecedented opportunity for the legitimate extension of British influence: a good political understanding will afford the best basis for commercial and financial openings.[5]

In the last resort the British usually sided with the French, sharing as they did their suspicions of German ambitions, and their desire to punish the guilty states. The junior officials frequently sympathized with the aspirations of the new states. Although Lloyd George occasionally expressed concern about the incorporation of large numbers of Germans and Magyars in the successor states, except in the case of Poland, he seldom translated his concern into positive action on their behalf.

During the early months of the conference the attention of Britain, France and the United States was concentrated on Germany and Russia and, despite Italian protests, the problems of Central Europe were dealt with by relatively junior staff. The Allied leaders had not time to devote to the minutiae of boundary problems and, as Hardinge put it, 'most people recognize the critical situation prevailing in Central and Eastern Europe, but the problem is so huge that a quick solution is made difficult by the magnitude of the task'.[6]

British policy-makers insisted that Britain should not be saddled with any obligation to uphold the settlement in central Europe, beyond the vague terminology of the League Covenant. British interests in these areas would best be protected by the establishment of a Danubian federation, to promote economic and financial cooperation and to act as a barrier to German or Russian expansion. Britain wanted the formation of an organization of Habsburg states without the Habsburgs—a project which was directly contrary to the successor states' determination to maintain their new-found sovereignties intact.

In March Lord Curzon pressed for the despatch of an inter-allied financial and economic commission to Vienna. 'It is my opinion that when this Commission is constituted and sitting at Vienna, the various States will realize that it is in their best interests to co-operate rather than to continue their present policy of aggression and mutual mistrust.'[7] Hardinge proposed the appointment of an allied 'High Commissioner for the Habsburg Empire' to organize the supply of food and financial assistance and thus promote regional economic collaboration.[8] Lord Robert Cecil wanted to use the economic lever 'to get all the representatives of all the States in the old Austro-Hungarian Empire into a room together and tell them that they must not erect economic barriers against one another or if they do we'll starve the lot'.[9] Smuts also put forward a plan to the Council of Four, after his return from his mission to Hungary, for a sub-conference of all the former Habsburg states in Paris under allied auspices. He hoped that this would enable them to settle their financial and economic differences and, 'while teaching them the new habits of co-operation, would help to allay the old historic bitternesses which still remain'.[10] All these plans foundered on the opposition of the successor states to any cooperation with their former rulers. Hardinge thought that:

> the whole question depends upon whether the Governments decide upon a definite policy to be pursued in connection with the remains of the Habsburg Empire, or whether we continue to follow a policy of drift which is tending towards Bolshevism in German-Austria and Hungary, with the eventual union of German-Austria with Germany.[11]

In default of a Central European federation British representatives in Paris concentrated on establishing stable frontiers. This was a complex task. While the new German borders could be reconciled with allied interpretations of Wilsonian principles, the proposed frontiers in central Europe could not. The mixture of nationalities and the outdated and unreliable population censuses forced the peacemakers to examine economic, historical and strategic factors. It was impossible to hold plebiscites in all the disputed areas, especially as allied troops were not available to police them. Furthermore, France was opposed to plebiscites since they might encourage Germany and Austria to insist that they should be applied to areas they disputed. Given the French desire to reward former allies in order to enlist them on her side, the successor states were assured of staunch – and usually successful – French support for their territorial aspirations.

At the beginning of April Balfour drew attention to the inconsistencies caused by conflicts between the principle of self-determination on the one hand and strategic and economic considerations on the other. The conference had proposed that Danzig, on account of its German majority, should be granted autonomy rather than incorporated into Poland. Yet the Czechoslovak committee had advised Czech retention of

German Bohemia on grounds part economic, part geographic ('meaning, I suppose, that the semi-circle of mountains dividing Bohemia from Germany makes a nice-looking semi-circle on the map'), part historical, and part strategical. 'I would point out . . . the dangers we run if we adopt one set of principles when we leave Germans in Bohemia and another set of principles when we take Germans from Poland.' Economically, Danzig was as important for Poland's future as the Bohemian mountains were to Czechoslovakia. Balfour insisted that the Allies must demonstrate that, despite superficial appearances, there were vital distinctions between the two cases:

> What it all comes to is that we have to guard against the danger of being supposed to use our principles to further our fancies. It is perfectly true that a pedantic striving after consistency is always a blunder and sometimes a crime. But we have to deal with States which are passionately sensitive on these questions of territorial boundaries: whatever our decisions they are sure to be violently attacked; we cannot be popular, our only chance is to be just; and we shall not be thought just unless we make it clear that our different treatment of *apparently* similar cases is really capable of a justification that the plain man can be made to understand.[12]

Britain's policy towards central Europe did not have the dynamic, determined quality which characterized her initiatives in western Europe or the Middle East. Apart from a small group of Slavophils, British public opinion was largely indifferent to the fate of the central and south European peoples, while Britain's military weakness necessitated a fairly passive approach. French troops were stationed in central Europe but they were thin on the ground and relied for logistical support and supplies on the goodwill of the successor states. It proved to be difficult for the great powers to reach a consensus on their policy in central Europe, and even more difficult to enforce it. In April General Henry Wilson called for the withdrawal of the remaining four British battalions in southern Europe as they were needed in Egypt and Turkey. The Foreign Office pressed in vain for their retention since it was felt that their presence exercised some restraint on the Italians. Crowe, referring to Montenegro, lamented in March that 'we have, by the withdrawal of all our units, lost every chance of promoting a just solution of the conflicts in this important centre of international conflicts'.[13] Hardinge thought that the knowledge of Britain's military weakness encouraged 'the underhand proceedings of the Italians which are the same everywhere',[14] while Churchill warned Lloyd George that the Prime Minister could not handle his task at Paris successfully 'unless you had a great army at your back'.[15] The inconsistencies and weaknesses of allied policy in Central Europe can be partly explained by the absence of such 'a great army'.

The Council of Ten considered the claims of the central and east European states towards the end of January 1919. It soon became apparent that the Council was likely to be submerged in a flood of claims and counter-claims and that little productive would emerge from this time-consuming exercise. Accordingly, the Council set up commissions of experts from the great powers to make recommendations about frontier changes. Since, however, it gave no indication of the criteria on which these claims should be judged, beyond the injunction that their recommendations should be 'equitable',[16] they were left very much to make their own decisions. There was little political oversight and, as a result, the bulk of their recommendations were embodied in the various peace treaties without amendment.

Bulgaria

Britain did not have any direct interests in Bulgaria, beyond the broad objectives of ensuring peace and preventing the spread of Bolshevism. Britain was concerned, however, about the interests of her wartime allies in the Balkans, Serbia (which became Yugoslavia in May 1919) and—to a much greater extent—Greece, as was apparent in both the Bulgarian and Turkish settlements.[17] Britain wanted to see Greece established under Venizelos (particularly as opposed to King Constantine, whom the British and French had driven into exile in 1917) as a strong and friendly nation, which could enforce the two settlements and protect British interests in the eastern Mediterranean. Typical of Britain's attitude was Balfour's assessment that 'M. Venizelos was the only statesman in the Balkans who had sincerely tried to assist the Conference, and whose policy aimed at maintaining peace in the Balkans...'[18]

The settlement with Bulgaria, as embodied in the Treaty of Neuilly of 27 November 1919,[19] was influenced by the extremely negative view of her held by both the British and the French, a view that corresponded with that of the Greeks. That view was perhaps most succinctly and memorably stated by Venizelos when he said that 'Bulgaria represented in the Balkans the Prussia of Western Europe. She would always attempt to impose her militarism on the Balkans, just as Prussia had attempted to do in Western Europe'.[20] The Entente powers believed that since 1913 Bulgaria had acted purely out of greed and calculation. In their view she began the Second Balkan war in June 1913 in an (unsuccessful) bid to wrest territories from her allies of the First Balkan war, Greece and Serbia. The British and French maintained further that in 1915, after negotiating with both sides, Bulgaria joined the Central Powers solely because they offered the greatest spoils of war and appeared to be the side that would emerge victorious. Bulgaria then launched unprovoked attacks on Serbia and Rumania, conducting her campaigns in pitiless fashion. 'In the whole war', Balfour stated in Paris before the delegation heads of the powers in July 1919,

there had been no action more cynical and more disastrous than that undertaken by the Bulgarians. Had the Bulgarians not behaved as they had, Turkey would not have entered the war; the disastrous Gallipoli Campaign would not have taken place; the war would have ended years sooner, and needless suffering would have been saved.[21]

These hostile feelings were scarcely eased by frequent reports before the treaty was signed of Bulgaria's failure to disarm, and of unrest within the country and the possibility of resistance to the terms.. The Allies were particularly concerned because they were acutely aware of their weak military position in Bulgaria. As the British military representative made clear on 4 August, 'the Allies had no troops, and, if a national rising were provoked, it would be impossible to stop it'.[22]

In dealing with Bulgaria the British and French were largely at one, in sharp contrast with their relations over Turkey and the Middle East, even if Britain was keener on keeping the Greeks happy. Against the Entente powers supported by Japan, however, stood the Italians and Americans, who formed a dissenting minority over virtually all the major sections of the treaty. As was the case with so many other parts of the world, the British were far from happy with the performance of the Italians over Bulgaria. Rome tended to favour Sofia's claims in order to win her support with a view to thwarting the Yugoslavs and extending Italy's influence into the Balkans. In April the General Staff opined that the Italians and the Bulgarians were intriguing with one another against Yugoslavia and Greece, while Eyre Crowe blamed Rome's 'hostile and gravely menacing' attitude towards the new Slav state for the lack of a satisfactory Balkan settlement.[23] Though British officials were also annoyed with America's 'interference' on questions relating to Bulgaria, and blamed that power for various delays,[24] Balfour was insistent that the United States—which more than any other power wanted the settlement to be based upon the principle of self-determination—must be a party to all decisions concerning the Balkans, in order to bind it closely to the European powers.[25]

The drafting of the treaty with Bulgaria was entirely left by the Council of Four to the foreign ministers of the five principal allied powers, and to the appropriate committees, as was the case with the treaties with Austria and Hungary. The territorial questions proved to be the most difficult to resolve. One of the most important and controversial changes was the transfer of Western Thrace from Bulgaria (which had won most of it from the Turks in 1913, and acquired a further piece from them in 1915 as an inducement to enter the war) to Greece. The British, supported by the French and initially by the Americans, advanced four arguments in support of the change.[26] Firstly, they contended that since there was no question of returning the area to the Turks, who constituted a majority of the population, it should be handed over to the Greeks. They were the next largest ethnic group, and — according to Venizelos' evidence, which was questioned by the Americans — they were preferred by the Muslim population to the Bulgarians. Secondly, while critics had charged that the loss of the territory would cut Bulgaria off from the Aegean Sea, British policy-makers pointed out that she would still have access to the Black Sea and thence to the Aegean, since the Straits were to be internationalized and left open. Moreover, Greece promised free commercial access to Bulgaria through Thrace to a port on the Aegean. The British feared that German economic preponderance in Bulgaria would be aided if this was not done.[27] Thirdly, the British argued that since even the Americans had to admit that Eastern (hitherto Turkish) Thrace with its absolute majority of Greeks should go to Greece, it was geographically essential to give Western Thrace — the territory linking the two — to the same power. Lastly, it was maintained that if Bulgaria with its terrible wartime record did not lose Western Thrace, 'she alone of enemy powers will emerge from this war with practically no loss of territory', and her presence on the Aegean would be a menace to the Straits and, if allied with Italy, Greece.

The Italians had made known their reservations, on ethnical and economic grounds, to the planned transfer in the Greek Committee Report of 6 March.[28] It was not until July, however, that the Americans, who had agreed in the Report with the British and French position, aligned themselves on the side of the opposition, expressing the fear that Bulgaria's resentment over the loss could lead to war. British officialdom fulminated against this 'eleventh hour repudiation' and Crowe, reflecting Britain's great concern for the interests of Greece, went to see Venizelos. Their meeting led Crowe to express his fears to the Foreign Secretary that unless Western Thrace was ceded to Greece before the signature of the Bulgarian treaty, Venizelos would return home 'absolutely empty handed', with the result that 'he would almost certainly have to resign, and the dangers of a Constantinist reaction would become very real'.[29]

In the end, an apparent compromise was arrived at: Western Thrace was handed over and occupied by the allied powers themselves. Although the Bulgarians claim to have believed that this was the stepping stone to an international regime or mandate for the territory, the Allies, as was to be expected, passed it on to the Greeks at San Remo in 1920, who thus ended up with both Eastern and Western Thrace.[30]

Greece and Serbia were confirmed in their possession of the portions of Macedonia which they had won at the Turks' expense in 1913, despite the fact that in their portion the Greeks were outnumbered by the Bulgarians, and despite an American proposal for a plebiscite and another for the establishment of an independent Macedonia. The peacemakers claimed that they were refusing to touch any pre-1914 frontiers,[31] regardless of whether they were established by means fair or foul, or whether they reflected the objectives of nationality and self-determination. This was a sensible principle, since going back to before the war would have opened up a Pandora's box. It was also in the interest of the Allies, because Serbia and Greece, their friends and fellow victors in 1919, had been victors over Bulgaria in 1913. When the principle was not in the Allies' interest, they did not hesitate to violate it, as was the case with Western Thrace.

The Allies were in a particularly acute dilemma when it came to deciding the future of the Southern Dobruja, which Bulgaria had lost to Rumania in 1913. The problem was that Rumania lacked even a passing ethnical claim to the area, given that it was inhabited by 122,000 Turks, 112,000 Bulgarians,

10,000 Tartars and a minuscule 7,000 Rumanians. Because of this the Allies feared that unless the territory was turned over to Bulgaria, peace in the Balkans would be threatened. Hence the United States pressed to have part or all of the Southern Dobruja returned to Bulgaria, or at least to have a clause included in the treaty providing for bilateral talks on the subject. Although an indirect and unsuccessful attempt was made to persuade Rumanian Prime Minister Ion Bratianu to cede part of the Dobruja voluntarily, no mention of the territory appeared in the Treaty of Neuilly. Britain and France did not want to abandon the above-mentioned principle, and were insistent that they could not force a wartime ally to surrender territory to a wartime foe, however badly their erstwhile ally might be acting.[32] So the 1913 border was not changed — 'though', as Balfour candidly admitted, 'this might be neither equitable or conducive to peace in the Balkans'.[33]

Strategic considerations clashed sharply with the ethnical principle when the Allies turned to Bulgaria's frontier with Serbia. The British and French believed that the vulnerability of Serbia's pre-war eastern frontier had helped to make her a victim of Bulgarian aggression in 1915. They therefore argued that it was essential to adjust the line — particularly along the lower section of the Belgrade-Salonika railway — in order to strengthen Serbia's defensive capacities, even though this meant putting several small but overwhelmingly Bulgarian areas under Serbia. The Americans and Italians disagreed. They contended that a vanquished and disarmed Bulgaria was not a threat, but that the proposed changes would give Serbia offensive capacity and an open road to Sofia. They maintained that unless the conference adhered to the ethnical principle and followed the wishes of the people concerned, lasting resentment and ultimately war between Serbia and Bulgaria would result. Crowe's apt comment on the view that ethnical arguments must always be put ahead of strategical ones was that 'In preparing the treaties, they had to make compromises on all points. Why maintain that in this question particularly principles were sacred?'[34] In the end, though not all of Serbia's claims—to the vitally important Dragoman Pass, for example—were granted, the frontier was altered in four places, with the United States and Italy disassociating themselves from the decision and its consequences.

The guiding principle as far as reparations were concerned was, according to Balfour, that Bulgaria should pay the highest sum that her resources permitted.[35] In practice, however, this principle was weakened by several considerations. Firstly, officials such as Crowe and Nicolson believed that in order to ensure compliance with harsh territorial terms, the Allies should settle for relatively lenient reparations terms. As Crowe minuted for the Foreign Secretary on 11 July:

> Our general policy towards Bulgaria has been determined largely by the consideration that she would see her territory diminished by cession to the Allies. For this reason we have ourselves urged that in the field of Reparations and Finance, Bulgaria should be treated rather tenderly.[36]

And as Nicolson had earlier pointed out, 'we have not, ourselves and never will have, the necessary physical force to exact a large sum'.[37] The territorial exactions, by comparison, could be enforced by Bulgaria's neighbours, since they were the beneficiaries. Secondly, the fact that Bulgaria was almost exclusively an agricultural country meant not only that a blockade to starve her out would not work, but also that she had a limited capacity to pay, particularly when considered alongside her adverse balance of trade. As Lord Sumner saw it, 'the limits of her capacity to pay would be reached long before her moral responsibility was exhausted'.[38] Lastly, the British realized that from the point of view of their own commercial interests, they were wiser to try to re-establish Bulgaria's finances through an international financial commission than to impose harsh economic demands. The result of these and other considerations was that the Allies required Bulgaria to pay 2.25 milliard gold francs (about £90 million at 5% interest) over 38 years, though the Reparations

Commission was given the power to postpone or reduce the payments required.

When turning to the military clauses, it should be remembered that they were drawn up amidst recurring complaints that Bulgaria was not carrying out the disarmament terms of the armistice, and against the fear of unrest or even a rising in Bulgaria. The most important debate was over compulsory military service. The Bulgarians argued that as inhabitants of an agricultural country where most people were tied to the land, it would be impossible to raise an army without conscription. The Allies (with the exception, at first, of the Italians) demurred. Crowe successfuly contended that the Allies could not give Bulgaria the advantage of conscription, having denied it to their other wartime foes; that its abolition was a valuable step towards eventual disarmament; and that the admitted difficulties of voluntary service would deter Balkan states from pursuing a warlike policy.[39] Bulgaria was allowed to maintain an army of 20,000, as well as 13,000 other men under arms, such as gendarmes and frontier guards. While these restrictions were to prove troublesome to Bulgaria, the Allies' statement that Bulgaria undertook to observe the military clauses 'in order to render possible the initiation of a general limitation of the armaments of all nations'[40] was to cause them a great deal of difficulty and embarrassment.

The Treaty of Neuilly was drafted according to a variety of principles — ethnic, strategic, economic and moral. Bulgaria was punished for what was seen as bad behaviour during the First World War, with the peacemakers touching only on those pre-war and wartime arrangements which could be altered either to the detriment of a wartime foe, or to the benefit of a wartime ally.

As a result of Neuilly and the overall settlement in the Balkans, the Allies achieved their goal of reducing Bulgaria's importance in south-east Europe. After the gains of the First Balkan War, therefore, Bulgaria lost twice; after the Second Balkan War in 1913 and again in 1919. Though Bulgaria underwent only a relatively small reduction in area and population as a result of the peace conference, her position vis-à-vis her neighbours was greatly diminished. Rumania emerged from the conference with her pre-war area and population doubled; Serbia, metamorphozed into Yugoslavia, was tripled, while Greece at Sèvres in 1920 was enlarged by 50%. As well as this, Bulgaria was no longer on the Aegean, and was forced to disarm and pay reparations.

While opinions vary on the wisdom and justice of these terms, there is no doubt that they left a powerful legacy. On the positive side of the ledger, Bulgaria was left without major domestic nationality problems: the only large minority left, the Turks, had long been integrated.

Less happy was the legacy of Bulgarian bitterness, irredentism, and difficulty in fulfilling the terms. Bulgaria refused to reconcile itself to the loss of Western Thrace, after its demand at the Lausanne Conference for internationalization was rejected. The interwar years witnessed frequent border incidents with Greece, whose offer of free access to the Aegean was indignantly rejected. Macedonia similarly remained an international problem, and its refugees seriously disrupted domestic life in Bulgaria. Moreover, after the death of Prime Minister Stambolsky in 1923, Bulgaria's relations with her new neighbour Yugoslavia were poor. Sofia was unable to meet her reparation demands, finding relief only with moratoria and reductions, and finally with renunciation. In total she paid about a third of what was demanded of her in 1919. Lastly, as anticipated, Bulgaria had great difficulty in raising an army because of the prohibition of conscription.

As for the great powers after 1919, Britain had little involvement in Bulgaria, and the United States withdrew into isolation, leaving France and Italy to compete in attempts to extend their influence in south-east Europe.

Rumania and Hungary[41]

Most of Rumania's claims were at Hungary's expense, and were based on a treaty with the Entente signed at Bucharest on

17 August 1916. In return for joining the Entente, Rumania was promised Transylvania to the river Theiss, the Banat and the Bukovina. At Paris the Serbs, who claimed West Banat, questioned the validity of the Bucharest treaty, on the grounds that it had been abrogated when Rumania had signed a separate peace treaty with the Central Powers in 1918. Rumania countered that she had re-activated the treaty by re-entering the war on the Entente side early in November 1918. While Italy supported Rumania, the United States refused to recognise the treaty. France and Britain wanted to satisfy Serbia's more modest demands, and thought that they had conceded too much to Rumania in 1916, especially in view of Rumania's poor record during the war.

On 31 January and 1 February 1919 the Ten heard Ion Bratianu, and Nikola Pasic, the Serbian delegate. Pasic demanded a plebiscite in West Banat, a reasonable proposition when contrasted with Bratianu's insistence on all the territories which Rumania had forced the Entente to concede in 1916. The Rumanians further angered the Allies by advancing beyond the Theiss river in January. In desperation the Ten adopted a plan drawn up by Marshal Foch to stabilize the Hungarian-Rumanian frontier by establishing a neutral zone between them in Transylvania. As a result Hungary was required to pull back her troops, causing Hungarian protests, the resignation of the pro-Entente government of Count Karolyi on 21 March and the advent of a coalition of socialists and communists led by Bela Kun, who established a Bolshevik regime in Hungary.

Meanwhile the committee on Rumanian affairs recommended that Rumania should obtain the bulk of Transylvania, although not as much as she was entitled to under the 1916 treaty. Yugoslavia was granted West Banat, and on American insistence Hungary retained a small Magyar enclave around Szeged, with Rumania securing the rest of the province. The Ten were too preoccupied with the Bela Kun regime to pay close attention to this report. Neither Britain nor the United States would agree to send troops to Hungary to crush the Bolsheviks, while France refused to undertake the task without Rumanian assistance. Moreover Lloyd George sympathized with the Hungarians, telling the Council of Four that 'there are few countries which need a revolution so much'.[42] However Lansing received no support from Balfour when, on 8 May, he too protested in the Council of Foreign Ministers about the extent of Hungary's losses. The Council of Four, preoccupied with the German treaty, approved the new Hungarian frontiers without discussion on 12 May. Bratianu, however, continued to clamour for the 1916 Transylvanian line, much to Lloyd George's exasperation.[43]

When the Rumanian Prime Minister refused to order his army to retire behind the Theiss, Lloyd George and Wilson contemplated the expulsion of Rumania from the conference, but were restrained by Clemenceau. Although he had little sympathy for Bratianu, the French premier was only too well aware of the pro-Rumanian tendencies of the French president and chamber. In these circumstances there could be no question of using the Rumanian army to smash Bela Kun. On current performance a Rumanian army of occupation would have been difficult to dislodge—as subsequent events were to demonstrate. On the other hand, the British Foreign Office staff in Paris longed for the Rumanian army to be launched against Bela Kun. They justified the loss of purely Magyar districts to Rumania 'as a symbol of the new order of things and as part payment for the heavy losses inflicted by the Magyar Government on the Rumanian population through the War'.[44] Fears that Bolshevism would spread from Hungary into Austria and Czechoslovakia permeated the Foreign Office and resulted in bitter recriminations about allied passivity. Hardinge commented that

the situation everywhere is deteriorating rapidly and in favour of the Bolsheviks, owing to the Allies drifting without a policy. It is difficult to know what measures can now be taken to relieve the situation but a policy is needed in the first instance.[45]

[103]

The Council of Four sent General Smuts on a fact finding mission to Hungary early in April to bring Rumanian-Hungarian hostilities to an end. Arriving in Budapest on the 4th, Smuts promised Bela Kun that if the Hungarians would accept a favourable rectification of the demarcation line in Transylvania, the Allies might lift the blockade. When, on the following day, Bela Kun tried to secure further concessions, Smuts abruptly terminated his mission.

On his return to Paris Smuts urged the Four to lift the blockade, 'since the blockade and famine are now the principle allies of Bolshevism'.[46] This was rejected since the blockade was the only instrument available to influence the situation. His other suggestion—that all the successor states, including Austria and Hungary, should be invited to Paris to discuss economic reconstruction—was allowed to die a natural death. The new states refused to accept Austria and Hungary as co-equals.

The British delegation became increasingly frustrated by the inability of the Four to decide how to deal with Bela Kun. Crowe suggested to the Supreme War Council (the allied generals and admirals at Versailles) that an allied force be sent to occupy Budapest. While the British General Staff sympathized with this suggestion, they refused to agree to the use of British troops. Finally, the whole question was referred to Marshal Foch. On 30 May Crowe minuted:

It is most unfortunate that it seems impossible to decide on any action in Hungary. Whenever the question is raised of encouraging the Rumanians or Serbs or Czecho-Slovaks to enter Budapest, or even of finding a small detachment of French, Italian or British troops, we are told that Marshal Foch is studying the question. But no decision emerges.[47]

On 14 June the Four published the new southern boundaries of Hungary. Once more Bratianu demanded the 1916 line. While Lloyd George and Woodrow Wilson were outraged by Bratianu's behaviour, allied policy changed after the two leaders left Paris. Balfour supported Rumanian action against Bela Kun, since he felt that the failure of the Supreme Council to overthrow the Budapest regime was not only a public display of its impotence but also provided Rumania with a pretext for keeping her troops on the Theiss. Balfour accordingly adopted a more pro-Rumanian stance than had Lloyd George and, in effect, served notice on Rumania that she was free to advance to Budapest. She was supplied with the opportunity to do so when the Hungarians attacked Rumanian positions on the Theiss on 20 July. A Rumanian counter-offensive on the 29th carried them all the way to Budapest, forcing Bela Kun to flee the capital.

The peace conference was then faced with an even greater turmoil in Hungary, as the Rumanians not only refused to evacuate Budapest but also began to seize Hungary's industrial and agricultural assets. The Allies feared that these depredations would reduce Hungary's ability to pay reparations and in the long run necessitate Entente economic assistance. The conference was also anxious to see the formation of a government in Hungary which would sign the peace treaty. This could only be achieved in the absence of Rumanian interference. The United States favoured severe action against Rumania if she failed to evacuate her troops from Hungary, suggested her expulsion from the conference and, in September, pressed for the despatch of an allied naval force to the Black Sea. Neither Clemenceau nor Balfour wanted a breach with Rumania. These divisions between the great powers were shrewdly exploited by Bratianu, who continued to insist on the 1916 frontiers as a pre-condition for Rumania's withdrawal, and studiously ignored allied ultimata. There could be no peace treaty with Hungary until the Rumanians had withdrawn from Budapest.

Yugoslavia and Italy[48]

Italy based her territorial claims on the Treaty of London of 26 April 1915, whereby the Entente, in return for Italy's entry into the war, promised her the Tyrol to the Brenner frontier, Trieste, Gradisca, a large part of Istria and the off-shore islands, and part of the Dalmatian coast. Fiume was to remain part of Croatia. Italy was also promised Valona and a protectorate over Albania, although Greece, Serbia and Montenegro were to receive border areas of that country. Italian policy sought the mastery of the Adriatic and the reduction of Serbia's influence along the coast.

The United States refused to recognize the treaty, whose contents could not be reconciled with the principle of national self-determination. Apart from a few cities, the area Italy claimed was populated by Slavs. On 4 December 1918 the kingdom of the Serbs, Croats and Slovenes was proclaimed (Montenegro had already voted for union with Serbia) and Italy was faced with an adversary on the Adriatic who would vigorously contest her territorial demands.

From the outset the Italians, represented at Paris by their Prime Minister Vittorio Orlando and their Slavophobe Foreign Minister Sydney Sonnino, adopted a hostile attitude towards Yugoslavia. After the armistice with Austria-Hungary Italian troops occupied the areas promised to Italy under the Treaty of London and in mid-November seized Fiume. Italy had no intention of relinquishing it to Yugoslavia, although, if the city was included with its suburb, Susak, it was predominantly Slav. Italian troops also occupied Valona and the bulk of Albania, while Serbian forces were in possession of north Albania and Scutari.

Balfour had made it clear to Woodrow Wilson on 31 January 1918 that Britain and France considered themselves to be committed to the Treaty of London:

a treaty is a treaty and we—I mean England and France (of Russia I say nothing)—are bound to uphold the treaty in letter and in spirit. The objections to it are obvious enough: it assigns to Italy territories which are not Italian but Slav, and the arrangement is justified not on the grounds of nationality but on grounds of strategy.[49]

This commitment did not endear Italy to the British delegation at Paris, whose members privately derided her wartime exertions and condemned as greedy her territorial claims. The Italian government was variously described by British officials as 'objectionable', 'mischief-makers', 'very awkward', and 'a stumbling block and a mill stone everywhere'.[50]

Thus most of the British delegation opposed the transfer of the Tyrol to Italy, but the British government, despite the German majority in the north, adhered to the Treaty of London. The British General Staff admitted that, in the case of Italy's annexation of the Tyrol, 'the principle of nationality is at variance with the requirements of military security', and suggested that Italy should give a large measure of autonomy to the German populated districts and that the entire Tyrol should be demilitarized.[51] The American delegation at first refused to accept Italy's outright annexation of the German Tyrol, but Italy refused to agree to any half-measures. On 2 April Woodrow Wilson accepted Italy's annexation of the Tyrol on strategic grounds, perhaps in the hope that Italy would respond by evacuating Fiume.

Lloyd George had told Orlando in December 1918 that British acceptance of the Treaty of London precluded support for Italy's retention of Fiume. Italian nationalist clamour for the port mounted during the early months of 1919. While Italy and Yugoslavia engaged in heated arguments about their respective claims on the Adriatic coast, the focus of the dispute between Italy on the one hand, and Yugoslavia and the United States, supported by Britain and France on the other, eventually centred on Fiume. While the western powers believed that Fiume was vital to Yugoslavia's trade, Woodrow Wilson regarded the future of the port as a supreme test for his principles.

Yugoslavia's position at Paris was strengthened when, on 7 February 1919, Woodrow Wilson recognized the new state, although Britain and France did not follow suit until June. But Yugoslavia, with her army fighting on all her frontiers except that with Greece, was in no position to force Italy to yield Fiume: for this she depended on Wilson. She was additionally embarrassed by an earlier decision of the powers to reserve a place for Montenegro at the conference. Italy denied the legality of Montenegro's declaration of union with Serbia, claiming that it had been promoted by the bayonets of the Serbian army. In January the Italian commander in the Adriatic was restrained from sending troops to restore the King of Montenegro, Nikita, to his throne, by the commander of the British Adriatic cruiser squadron, who argued that the Montenegrins 'should be permitted to retain their inalienable right to murder each other, as and when they considered it necessary, provided that no inconvenience to the Allies is caused thereby'.[52] Italy continued to support the king, although Anglo-French distrust of the former monarch led the conference to reject his claims in November 1919.

The British delegation was pro-Yugoslav. British officials and military advisers hoped that Yugoslavia would eventually raise a strong army to guarantee peace in what had hitherto been an unstable area, and block any future German drive into the Balkans. Nicolson, Crowe and Hardinge were convinced that Yugoslavia's viability depended on her securing Fiume. An Italian Fiume would, in Crowe's words, be 'contrary to all justice. . . [and] must lead to perpetual discord'.[53]

The Four did not deal with Italy's claims until April. Faced with Orlando's declaration that 'Italy considered it within her right to demand the natural frontiers fixed for her by God and the inclusion of certain populations of other races should not be a bar',[54] it was evident that a long struggle lay ahead. Nicolson outlined British policy as seeking 'to unite French interests with American principles and join with both in imposing an adequate settlement upon Italy'.[55]

While Orlando was willing to trade Italy's claims in Dalmatia for undisputed possession of Fiume, Wilson's attitude hardened. He would not agree to Italy's receiving Fiume in any circumstances, and the utmost he would concede was that a Yugoslavian Fiume should be made a free port, with Istria partitioned between Italy and Yogoslavia and Italy receiving some of the islands, in additon to Valona. When Italy rejected this, Lloyd George tried to arrange a compromise whereby Italy would get East Istria, while Fiume and its environs would be placed under League control. This too was unacceptable to Orlando. On 21 April Lloyd George and Clemenceau met the Italian prime minister in a further effort to patch up an acceptable compromise, but without success.

Wilson then issued a public appeal to the Italian people which was published in the Italian press on the 24th. Entitled 'Regarding the Disposition of Fiume', it was widely interpreted as an interference in Italy's internal affairs. Orlando abandoned the conference in protest and was greeted as a hero on his return to Rome. Italy did not return to the conference until 6 May, after Britain and France had threatened to denounce the Treaty of London. The round of compromise efforts was resumed, with Colonel House now promoting direct Italo-Yugoslav talks, which resulted in an agreement that Fiume should be a free city. However these conversations collapsed when neither side would agree on the size of the free city.

Then the French attempted to mediate. They proposed the establishment of a demilitarized, independent state of Fiume to comprise Susak and the disputed territory of Istria. This greater Fiume was to be administered by an international commission for 15 years, when a plebiscite would be held to enable the inhabitants to determine their own future. Italy would receive Zara and Sabonica in Dalmatia, together with some islands. This plan was opposed by Wilson on ethnic grounds, while Yugoslavia insisted that she should receive Susak and the hinterland. Further progress was interrupted by Orlando's resignation on 19 June.

The new Prime Minister, Francesco Nitti, and Foreign Minister, Tommaso Tittoni, required time to study the issue before resuming negotiations. Wilson returned to the United States and the dispute was left to the heads of delegations. On 19 May Hardinge summed up the British reaction to Italy's behaviour:

The Italians have been a sore trouble during the Conference. Their incapacity and rapacity are extraordinary when one comes to think that they have never yet been able to administer or finance any colony in their possession. It really seems grotesque to add more to their undigested possession. . . As much as I sympathise with Italy in every way, they are in my opinion, the most odious colleagues and Allies to have at a Conference. . . and 'the beggars of Europe' are well known for their whining alternated by truculence![56]

Czechoslovakia[57]

Czechoslovakia, which proclaimed its independence of Austria-Hungary on 28 October 1918, was another new state whose territorial demands were supported by France, which recognized the strategic importance of her position in central Europe. The British delegation's attitude was partially shaped by the 'highly favourable opinion we have formed of the character and political principles of the leading Czecho-Slovak states-men'.[58] Czech territorial demands were referred to the committee on Czechoslovak affairs on 5 February . In the face of some Anglo-American hesitation about the number of aliens the new state would absorb if her demands were accepted, France and the Czechs argued that, unless strategic and economic factors were taken into account, Czechoslovakia could not survive. The Czechs demanded portions of Prussian Silesia and of Austrian and Hungarian territory. They also pressed for Carpatho-Ruthenia (to which they promised automony) and a land corridor to Yugoslavia. With the exception of this last, they eventually secured the bulk of these demands.

The American and British approaches to these frontiers were not, however, consistent. The British delegation supported Czechoslovakia's retention of the German-Austrian areas of Bohemia because of their valuable coal and industrial resources and the strategic importance of the mountain border with Germany. It ignored German-Bohemian protests, arguing that 'the Germans in Bohemia probably make a lot of money by their exports and will have no desire to saddle themselves with any fraction of German indebtedness'.[59] The French insisted on the strategic necessity of Czechoslovakia's retention of German-Bohemia and, while Woodrow Wilson concentrated on other aspects of the German treaty, House was more concerned to 'bring about peace quickly than. . . to haggle over details'. To this end he was aided by '[Lloyd] George seeming to know but little about it'.[60] On 4 April the Four, with House deputizing for the ailing Wilson, agreed that the 1914 frontiers between Germany and Austria should be maintained, leaving the German-Bohemians inside Czechoslovakia.

Austria[61]

As an ex-enemy state Austria was refused direct access to the conference and her later written protests were overruled. Her leaders could only envisage the survival of a shrunken and economically weak Austria in a federal association with Germany. Indeed, they could appeal to Wilson's principles in support of this solution. The Anglo-American delegations were not at first entirely opposed to this, especially as the prospects for a Danubian federation were so dismal. The inclusion of Austria in a federal Germany might reduce the influence of Prussia, in Allied mythology the source of all Germany's ills. However France and Italy were implacably opposed to such a union, while Czechoslovakia and Switzerland did not relish the prospect of being surrounded by German territory. An Austro-German union might encourage Berlin to press for the inclusion of all German peoples within the Reich, a somewhat embarrassing interpretation of the principle of national self-determination. Headlam-Morley described this prospect as:

> very dangerous . . . We do not wish to encourage the growth of these large units of Government on the Continent and we wish to use the League of Nations to maintain the existence of the smaller multi-national States such as Belgium and

Switzerland. Quite apart from questions of balance of power we have enough nationalism and we want the tide flowing in the other direction.[62]

On 15 March the Central territorial committee recommended that Austria should be independent with the same frontiers with Germany as existed at the outbreak of the war. Britain accepted this, although her delegates resisted French pressure for a clause in the treaties which would not only make the separation permanent but would bind the Allies to oppose any future union by force. Instead, a vague reference to a possible future revision of the article by the League was inserted in the treaties. The Allies hoped that once financial and economic stability had been restored to the region, Austria would prefer her independence.

In the south Austria became involved in a conflict with Yugoslavia over the future of Klagenfurt, which had been occupied by Yugoslav troops in November 1918. Austria protested that this area contained a German majority. Italy supported Austria, since she did not want that part of the Trieste-Villach-Vienna railway controlled by Yugoslavia. The Four ordered a plebiscite in Klagenfurt which took place in 1920, when a majority of the inhabitants voted in favour of remaining Austrian.

Austria also demanded that the Burgenland in West Hungary should be ceded to her on economic and ethnic grounds. While the Allies at first rejected this transfer, they changed their minds during the summer. Anxious to weaken a Bolshevik Hungary, they agreed to assign this area to Austria, and Hungary's protests were ignored.

The Austrian treaty, like the German, contained a war guilt clause and provision for the payment of reparations. There were considerable delays in finalizing the Austrian treaty, and the discussions dragged on through the summer. In August Austria protested against the accusation that, of all the nationalities of the former Habsburg Empire, the German Austrians had been alone in supporting the war. She also denounced both her territorial losses and the sizeable reparations demands of the allies.

Headlam-Morley embarked on a last minute effort to secure modifications in the treaty. He agreed with the Austrian argument that Austria was a new, rather than an ex-enemy, state and should be treated accordingly. Balfour, Crowe and the French opposed him, since acceptance would entail the re-casting of the entire treaty. He received rather more encouragement when he proposed that the Austrian reparations clauses should be abandoned, although Sumner insisted they should stay. Eventually Austria received only meagre concessions—a promise of her admission to the League as soon as possible after her signature of the treaty (she became a member in December 1920), the easing of some of the economic clauses, and her annexation of West Hungary. Clemenceau would not even allow her to style herself German-Austria. Not until 1921 did the Reparations Commission formally admit that Austria could not pay reparations. An allied note accompanying the treaty in September 1919 declared that, since the Austrian people had done nothing to resist militarism during the war, and had fully supported the Habsburg government, Austria must therefore take 'her entire share of responsibility for the crime'. Austria signed the Treaty of St Germain on 10 September 1919.

Poland

Of all the frontier disputes, those of Poland excited the most bitter animosities. Poland had been left to her own devices after the armistice and had made the most of the opportunity to seize as much territory as she could. As a result, by January 1919, she was involved in conflicts with all her neighbours.

President Wilson's resolve to establish a large and viable Poland was stiffened by the pro-Polish attitude of his delegation, and the large number of Polish-American voters in the United States. Here the Americans were in agreement with the French, who also wanted a strong Poland as a barrier to Germany, and had a long tradition of friendship with Poland. The British were more cautious. Lloyd George feared that Poland's absorption of a large number of non-Poles would have a destabilizing effect on the new state. He complained of the 'miserable ambitions' of the successor states,[63] including Poland. He pointed out to his fellow allied leaders that, since the Poles had secured their independence as a result of the war-time sacrifices of the Allies, and since many of them had fought on the side of the Central Powers, it was disgraceful that they should demand allied support for their imperialist designs. He doubted their ability to govern themselves, telling the Ten on 11 March that 'the Poles had no idea of organization: they had no capacity to direct or govern'.[64] Woodrow Wilson also became disgusted by some of their more rapacious demands and gradually moved over to Lloyd George's position.

The British approach to the Polish question was complicated by serious divisions within the British delegation. Esmé Howard, the pro-Polish head of the Polish section, thought that if the Allies did not support Poland, she would become vulnerable to Bolshevik aggression, which he believed was supported by Germany. Early in February he and Dr Robert H. Lord, the equally pro-Polish American adviser on Polish questions, agreed to support the transfer of Danzig and a corridor separating east from west Prussia, together with the bulk of Upper Silesia, to Poland. Eric Drummond was also a Polish sympathizer. He told Kerr that:

> the Germans are bent on pursuing the policy of securing compensation in the East for any losses they may suffer in the West . . . if they succeed in their plan there will be nothing to stop German expansion towards the East and ultimately throughout Russia. The Allies must help Poland to form a solid national barrier against Germany on the one side and Bolshevism on the other.[65]

The Poles were eager to adopt this suggestion.

The future of Danzig caused the most dissension within the

British delegation and later in the Council of Four. A British expert, G. W. Prothero, hotly disputed the transfer of Danzig to Poland since it was historically and ethnically a German city:

> The annexation of West Prussia and Danzig to Poland will create a sense of gross injustice in the mind of Germany which will be fatal to the peace of the world. If the League of Nations is ever to be what it is designed to be, and not merely an alliance of certain powers, a repetition of the Quadruple Alliance of 1815, Germany will have to be admitted to it; and how can Germany accept membership of a Society . . . one of whose most important clauses she is bound to repudiate . . . There comes a point when the cumulative sense of loss becomes unforgettable and intolerable, and this point would, I believe, be reached by the mutilation now proposed . . .[66]

Headlam-Morley described these arguments as 'unanswerable'. He suggested to a receptive Lloyd George that Danzig should become an autonomous city under a League commissioner.[67]

The Polish delegate, Roman Dmowski, outlined Poland's claims to the Council of Ten on 29 January. As well as the frontiers of 1772, he demanded Upper Silesia, parts of west and east Prussia and Danzig. These demands were referred to the committee on Polish affairs, which accepted most of them in March, although it suggested a plebiscite in Allenstein and Polish annexation of Marienwerder, which contained the vital Danzig-Warsaw railway. Lloyd George, in the face of Franco-American support for these recommendations, vigorously campaigned against them in the Council of Ten. He warned the Ten that either Germany would refuse to sign a treaty based on such proposals or the German government would collapse. Would Britain and the United States, he asked, be prepared to go to war in the event of future German-Polish hostilities over Danzig and Marienwerder? 'To hand over millions of people to a distasteful allegiance merely because of a railway was, he thought, a mistake'. He feared that the Council was in danger of abandoning its principles, endangering not only Poland but the peace of the world.[68]

Woodrow Wilson countered by pointing out that he had, in the Fourteen Points, promised Poland free access to the sea. He also thought that the Council must take account of Poland's strategic needs. In areas of such mixed population it was impossible to exclude alien peoples from the new states. Nonetheless, Lloyd George insisted that the report be referred back to the territorial committee. On 22 March the committee informed the Council that it would not modify its proposals. This led to a further anti-Polish outburst by Lloyd George. He agreed to accept the proposals provisionally but reserved the right to seek their revision later after he had examined the whole treaty. In view of the fuss he was later to make over Fiume, Wilson's acceptance of this procedure suggested that he was less than comfortable about the transgression of his principles involved in handing Danzig over to Poland.

Despite its differences over Danzig and the corridor, the British delegation had little sympathy for Poland's 'exaggerated ∴ . . claims' in the east. In November 1918 fighting had broken out between the Poles and the Ukrainians in Eastern Galicia, a former Austrian province. Subsequent Supreme Council efforts to secure Poland's evacuation of the province had been ignored. Paton summed up the British view in January 1919:

> The Poles are trying to use the temporary menace of Bolshevism as an excuse for annexing large areas in the east which do not belong to them. They still have to prove themselves capable of governing themselves, and there is no warrant for believing them capable of ruling other and bitterly hostile nationalities . . . If they are to be in conflict with both Powers [Germany and Russia] a new Partition will be the inevitable result. The only way of securing the future of Poland is by enabling her to develop her natural resources within her proper ethnographical limits.[69]

On 19 March Lloyd George refused to agree to Eastern Galicia being assigned to Poland, on the grounds that the White Russians contended that the province ought to be part of Russia.

However, the British reached agreement with the Americans over Danzig, and the French were forced to acquiesce. Headlam-Morley worked out a plan with Dr Charles H. Haskins of the American delegation and Tardieu for Danzig to become a free state under a League Commissioner. Lloyd George and Woodrow Wilson accepted this compromise early in April, with Clemenceau adding his grudging assent. Shortly thereafter the Four also provided for a plebiscite in Marienwerder. Despite subsequent French and Polish efforts to reopen the question, the Council of Four adhered to the compromise, although Balfour remained sceptical: 'If "the independent city" like other independent cities, quarrels with the Poles, its Allies, its High Commissioner, or its own constitution, who is going to manage it? What if it turns Bolshevik?'[70]

Elsewhere on Poland's borders conditions continued to deteriorate during April as heavy fighting was reported between the Poles and the Ukrainians and between the Poles and the Lithuanians. Disagreement continued over Eastern Galicia. The Anglo-Americans wanted it placed under League control, while the French wanted it incorporated in Poland. Balfour opposed the League solution: 'it will overload the League of Nations — and probably kill the High Commissioner'.[71]

Despite allied efforts to secure an armistice during May, the Poles launched a new offensive into Eastern Galicia. They claimed that, by expanding to the east, they were keeping Germany and Russia further apart, a notion derided by Paton as likely 'to bring Russia and Germany together in a common interest — the annexation of territory occupied by the Poles'.[72] By June the Poles had overrun most of Eastern Galicia. The committee on Polish Affairs could not reach agreement on the future of the province. While there was general agreement that the western part of Eastern Galicia should be assigned to Poland, France wanted this dividing line pushed as far to the east as possible. Each delegate had his own proposal for dealing with the rest of the province. The deadlock continued until July, when Lansing decided to support France in allowing Poland to annex the whole of Eastern Galicia. This was blocked by Lloyd George from London. In November he insisted that Poland should have a mandate to administer Eastern Galicia for 25 years. Finally, in 1923, Poland annexed the province.

The Poles were also in dispute with Czechoslovakia over the duchy of Teschen. While each country rejected the other's population statistics, there was little doubt that the majority in this important mining and industrial belt was Polish. The Poles and Czechs provisionally divided the duchy between them in November 1918 but, in the following month, the Czechs drove the Poles out of their section. Despite their irritation at Czechoslovakia's high-handedness, both the Czechoslovak and Central Territorial Committees recommended that Czechoslovakia should secure East Teschen, which included the Odenberg-Teschen-Jublunka railway and a valuable coalfield, although this meant placing a large number of Poles under Czech control. On 27 September, after further debate, the Supreme Council accepted recommendations from both the Czechoslovak and the Polish committees that plebiscites should be held in Teschen. This proved impossible owing to the disturbed state of the duchy and in 1920 it was divided between the two countries, leaving Czechoslovakia with the railway and coalfield.

The Baltic Provinces[73]

Latvia, Lithuania and Estonia had been occupied by German troops since the collapse of Russia in 1917. When Germany capitulated, the Allies decided against sending their own forces to the area and therefore, in accordance with the armistice, German troops were ordered to remain in the provinces until the Allies decided that conditions were suitable for their withdrawal. This seemed the only alternative to a Bolshevik takeover.

The British delegation was anxious that the provinces should become a British sphere of influence, partly to offset French influence in Poland, and partly in the hope that they would become centres for the revival of British trade in north-eastern Europe. Neither the British government nor the peace conference had the time to devote much attention to this area. At the end of 1918 part of Estonia was overrun by the Bolsheviks, who proceeded to occupy Latvia in January 1919. The Royal Navy did what it could to assist Lithuania and Estonia against the Red Army, but naval assistance was intermittent and could not be a substitute for land forces. These were provided by the local militias, White Russians, Swedish and Finnish volunteers and von der Goltz's German brigade, who between them ejected the Red forces from Estonia in February and from Latvia in May 1919.

The Admiralty, anxious to maintain British naval predominance in the Baltic, argued that Britain should aid the provinces, whose populations were pro-British, and whose ports were important for British trade. Furthermore, Poland could survive only if she was assured of secure northern borders. Although Paton agreed about 'the urgency of reaching some decision about the border Russian nationalities and the danger of German influence increasing unless some help is offered by the Allies',[74] the Council of Foreign Ministers refused to deal with the issue except as part of the overall question of the future of Russia. Hardinge feared that 'by drifting, we shall lose in the East what we have gained in the West'.[75]

The worst fears about German ambitions seemed to be confirmed when a group of Baltic Germans, supported by von der Goltz, overthrew the Latvian government in April. This led to the imposition of a British blockade on German shipping in the Baltic and to a meeting between Esmé Howard and Dr Samuel E. Morison of the American delegation on the 23rd to discuss the situation. They suggested that the Allies should demand the release of the Latvian ministers and the evacuation of German forces from the Baltic provinces. The Allies should then give the three governments *de facto* recognition and provide them with military equipment, food and credits. On 3 May the Council of Foreign Ministers postponed further discussion of these recommendations.

The problems of the area were further complicated by Polish designs on Lithuania. In May the Poles, having driven the Bolsheviks out of Vilna, refused to hand the city over to the Lithuanians. Balfour, after a warning from Hardinge that 'the Poles are certainly acting in an aggressive manner',[76] urged August Zaleski, the Polish delegate, to restrain the Polish command from further excesses, but this request was ignored.

In these circumstances the Foreign Office continued to press for 'some definite policy ... as soon as possible in these regions'.[77] At the end of April the Council of Three set up a Baltic Commission to make recommendations. This commission proposed to the Council of Foreign Ministers that the Germans be ordered to withdraw from the provinces and that local forces should then be organized by a British military mission. The Allies should supply credits to enable them to survive. Howard feared that 'unless we definitely make up our minds to a policy of assisting these Baltic States we must resign ourselves to seeing them become German colonies'.[78] The Council of Foreign Ministers sent an allied military mission to the provinces later in May to arrange the evacuation of all German forces. By December 1919 the German Baltic army had returned to its homeland.

The question of the future of these provinces remained. They wanted allied recognition but the Allies feared that this might prejudice their future relations with a revived Russia, whose representatives wanted them reincorporated into a non-Bolshevik state. The Supreme Council wrestled with the problem during the summer but could only take up a British suggestion that a non-Bolshevik Russia should promise to give the provinces a substantial measure of autonomy. With the defeat of Yudenich's Baltic based White Russian army by the Bolsheviks in the autumn of 1919, it was clear that the provinces had no recourse but to make peace with the Soviet Republic. E. H. Carr commented:

As the whole tendency of our policy has been to bring about this conclusion it does not seem to me that we are in a position to prevent them from doing so, or to penalize them it they do so.[79]

In early 1920 the Soviet Republic recognized the independence of Estonia, Latvia and Lithuania.

Russia[80]

The question of the future of Russia was fundamental to the peace of Europe since, without a solution of this problem, it seemed impossible to guarantee the stability of eastern Europe. Yet, beyond refusing to contribute any more troops to the struggle — a crucial decision as it turned out — the Allies could not agree a common policy. Lloyd George was in a particularly uncomfortable position. He did not oppose negotiations with the Bolsheviks but, in public, he was often forced to adopt an anti-Bolshevik stance in face of Unionist hostility to the idea of such negotiations, and of support for intervention in the War Cabinet, led by Churchill, Milner and Curzon. Churchill pressed vigorously for the despatch of a large allied army to crush the Bolsheviks but the British Prime Minister distrusted the White Russian leaders. He feared that a strong centralized state would seek the domination of eastern Europe, and preferred the establishment of a weak federation which would provide opportunities for British trade and not threaten Britain's imperial interests.

To some extent the disappearance of Russia eased the task of the allied leaders. They were freed of their embarrassing commitment to Russia's possession of Constantinople and the Straits, and were no longer faced with Czarist opposition to an independent Poland. Nor did Lloyd George really fear that Bolshevism would spread into Western Europe, although he occasionally brandished the threat to persuade a sceptical Clemenceau to adopt a less harsh line towards Germany. France was opposed to any discussion with, or implied recognition of, the Moscow regime, since it had repudiated Russia's external debts and taken her out of the war. France hoped that the Whites would defeat the Bolsheviks and then rebuild the country, so that it could resume its place as France's ally against Germany. Meanwhile, as an insurance against the failure of this design, France encouraged the formation of strong buffer states in the east capable of acting as a collective barrier between Germany and Bolshevik Russia.

Although Woodrow Wilson detested Bolshevism and resented its claim to be an alternative to his own brand of idealism, he consistently opposed further allied intervention in Russia. The collapse of Germany meant that the continued presence of allied and Czech troops in Russia had lost its *raison d'être*, but the Allies maintained forces on the peripheries of Russia to support the White Russians. As these forces successively failed to defeat the Bolsheviks, the Allies gradually lost confidence in them during 1919 and finally withdrew them. The American army in Siberia had been sent there to restrain Japan and played no active part against the Bolsheviks. Wilson refused to commit any more American soldiers to Russia. However hostile the right wing western *enragés* were towards Bolshevism, British, French and American opinion opposed the despatch of more allied troops to Russia.

Wilson sometimes joined Lloyd George in initiatives designed to secure an all-Russian settlement. In January 1919 both leaders persuaded the Council of Ten to invite all parties in Russia, including the Bolsheviks, to meet on the Princes Islands in the Sea of Marmara to discuss peace terms. Squabbles between the various factions prevented this meeting from taking place. Then, in March, Lloyd George and Colónel House promoted the mission of William C. Bullitt, a member of the American delegation, to Russia to probe Lenin's intentions. Bullitt returned with an offer from the Bolsheviks to consider an armistice, followed by a peace conference. In April House proposed an offer of allied food and financial relief to the Bolsheviks in return for an armistice. These peace efforts, which Lenin did not reject outright, foundered on French and White Russian opposition. Finally Wilson decided to concentrate on the German treaty and leave the League to deal with Russia.

Similarly proposals for an allied backed crusade against the Bolsheviks, using allied volunteers and the armies of the central and southeast European states, also came to nothing. Allied public opinion opposed such ventures, especially if there was any question of using allied troops. Many of these projects emanated from Marshal Foch. When Lloyd George returned to London in February, Churchill took his place in Paris and, on the 14th and 15th, began to lobby the Council of Ten for allied implementation of Foch's grand anti-Bolshevik strategy. He was repudiated by Lloyd George, who reminded the War Minister that the War Cabinet opposed operations in Russia likely to be costly in men and money. 'The main idea ought to be to enable Russia to save herself if she desires to do so'. Churchill's 'mad enterprise' would merely drive the Russian population into the arms of the Bolsheviks.[81] Foch's plan resurfaced briefly at the end of March in connection with his scheme to crush Bela Kun as part of an all-out allied drive against Lenin. 'Let us decide not to deal with Hungary as we have with Russia—one Russia is enough for us',[82] was Lloyd George's epitaph on this proposal.

There was a brief flurry of allied optimism in May, when the White Russian forces of Admiral Kolchak appeared to be on the brink of defeating the Bolsheviks. The Allies came close to recognising Kolchak's Omsk government on 13 June, when the Admiral agreed that he would establish a Constituent Assembly, without the Bolsheviks, when he came to power in Russia. Kolchak, like other White Russian leaders before and after him, proved to be a man of straw.

Thus throughout 1919 the British government and her allies were formally committed to a policy of non-interference in Russian affairs while, at the same time, supplying the White Russian forces with arms and supplies. The Soviet government was not slow to point out the hypocrisy implicit in this contradiction. Members of the British delegation tended to agree. E.H. Carr minuted on 28 May that 'our original intervention in Russia was alleged to be directed against Germany. Against whom is it directed now? If against the Bolsheviks, all talk about non-intervention in Russia is absurd'. Britain should either cease aiding the White Russians or declare war on the Bolsheviks. 'The present disingenuous policy which tries to reconcile these contradictory ideals can do us no good in the long run.' Hardinge agreed that 'there are many contradictions in our Russian policy, if it is a policy, and it can hardly be otherwise at present'.[83]

Above all the Council of Four feared a possible future reconciliation between Germany and Russia, whether Bolshevik or White. As Esmé Howard put it on 24 April:

A political entente between Germany and Russia is perhaps the greatest danger that threatens Europe and anything we can do to prevent it should be done now. It is quite possible to imagine a state of things wherein a Russian Government would be willing to give Germany such commercial and economic privileges in return for political and military support against Finland, the Baltic States, Poland and Roumania, to say nothing of Transcaucasia and Servia, as would enable Russia once more to become a menace to our interests in Asia while Germany would really dominate her economically and therefore ultimately politically. A combination of Germany and Russia, reconstituted and reorganized under Germany, would dominate Europe and there can be no doubt that all Germany's efforts will be in this direction.[84]

The Allies tried to prevent a future German-Russian entente by reserving Russia's rights in the peace treaty with Germany. Brest-Litovsk was formally abrogated by Germany, which had to recognize the independence of all Russian territories. Russia was offered a share in Germany's reparations payments, but the Bolsheviks repudiated the Treaty of Versailles and later made their own arrangements with Germany.

In late 1919 and early 1920 Allied confusion about Russia

continued as Kolchak, Denikin and Yudenich in turn were defeated by the Bolsheviks. Gradually the last remaining British troops were withdrawn from North Russia, and efforts by Lloyd George to secure a consensus among the Allies about Russian policy failed abjectly. Crowe summed up the negative results of allied policy towards Russia, which he described as 'a hand to mouth affair', on 15 November:

> You will probably remember that whenever the Russian problem has come before the Conference, it has always created difficulties. These in the last resort have generally been due to the absence of any well defined policy on which all the Allies are agreed and which has been thought out in all its bearings.[85]

While France now concentrated on building up the border states as a *cordon sanitaire* against Bolshevism, Britain finally withdrew all aid to the Whites. In 1920 Lloyd George began to listen more closely to overtures from the Bolsheviks, especially as they included enticing offers of a revival of Anglo-Russian trade. Britain recognized Soviet Russia in 1922.

The Hungarian Settlement

Rumania refused to withdraw her troops from Budapest during the autumn and winter, despite frequent ultimata from Paris. Bratianu insisted that Rumanian evacuation could only follow the satisfaction of her demands in Transylvania under the treaty of Bucharest. On 25 November, Sir George Clerk, who had been sent by the Supreme Council to Budapest to secure a settlement, recognized a new Hungarian coalition government. After further ultimata, culminating in an allied threat to break off relations with Rumania if she did not comply, the Rumanians gradually withdrew their forces across the Theiss river.

Early in January 1920 a Hungarian delegation led by Count Apponyi arrived in Neuilly. He addressed a fervent appeal to the three allied Prime Ministers, Lloyd George, Clemenceau and Nitti, to moderate the reparations clauses and to leave a greater area of Transylvania under Hungarian sovereignty. His appeal fell on deaf ears: the draft terms were handed to the Hungarian delegation unaltered on the 15th. On the following day Apponyi protested against the terms, which he described as being even more stringent than those imposed on the other defeated powers. He claimed that Hungary, given her parlous economic situation, could not possibly meet the reparations demands, especially as two thirds of her population was to be transferred to alien domination.

Hungary secured an extension of the time limit for her reply until 12 February. She presented 18 notes to the conference of ambassadors. These dwelt on the burdens imposed by the reparations clauses, protested about the war guilt and war crimes clauses, her non-admission to the League, and the emphasis placed on strategic and economic considerations rather than on ethnic factors when her new frontiers were determined. Her 'chief and fundamental demand' was for plebiscites in all areas of mixed nationality which, under the treaty, were to be annexed by her neighbours. Hungary also protested against the military clauses which allowed her an all-volunteer army of 35,000 men, 5,000 more than the Austrian army on the grounds of Hungary's larger population. She demanded that the number of forest guards and police allowed her under the treaty should be doubled, and that her army should be based on conscription.

These counter-claims were examined by another conference of allied Prime Ministers in Paris, meeting between 13 and 23 February. Millerand now represented France, having replaced Clemenceau as prime minister on 17 January. Despite Nitti's expressions of sympathy for Hungary's plight, and British press and parliamentary protests about the severity of the terms, the Allies would not agree to any major alterations. One Hungarian delegate thought this was because the Allies were 'frightfully bored by the whole Peace Conference. . . [it was] a labyrinth from which they cannot find a way out and . . . they have created in the peace treaties a great number of international problems which they will not know how to solve'.[86]

The powers replied on 6 May 1920. They rejected Hungary's request for a conscripted army but agreed that the Control Commission should be given discretion in interpreting the other military and naval clauses. Furthermore the Reparation Commission would be allowed to deduct from her reparation bill the losses Hungary suffered as a result of the Bela Kun regime and the Rumanian occupation. Thus, when the final peace treaty was presented to Hungary on 5 May, there were no major changes except for these modifications and allied agreement to send a frontier delimitation commission to look at the vexed frontier districts and then report its findings to the League. Although the Hungarian delegation resigned in protest, Hungary had no alternative but to sign the treaty. She did so at Trianon on 4 June 1920. Like Austria, Hungary secured the promise of an early entry to the League. On 13 November the Hungarian parliament reluctantly ratified the treaty.

In all these negotiations Britain played a minor role. As the Hungarians suggested, Lloyd George showed increasing signs of impatience with the slow progress of the Hungarian treaty, and tended to support French rejection of all but minor changes. There could be no question of unravelling the treaty at this late stage, and Britain was anxious to settle questions, such as the Near East, which were of greater importance to her. In the absence of American participation, Italy, despite some wavering support for Hungary, had no alternative but to yield to her partners. The settlement in Central Europe was very much a French affair. The formation in the early 1920's of the 'Little Entente' of Yugoslavia, Czechoslovakia and Rumania (who were vociferous in their opposition to any changes in the Hungarian treaty) was a further success for French policy.

Fiume

The withdrawal of the United States from active participation in the Paris negotiations also paved the way for an eventual settlement of the Fiume issue. Every effort by the conference to promote an Italo-Yugoslav agreement during the summer of 1919 foundered on Yugoslav objections.[87] On 12 September 1919 an Italian poet and freebooter, Gabriele d'Annunzio, led a small band of Italian irregulars who seized Fiume, with the connivance of the Italian military authorities. Despite allied protests the Italian government did nothing to dislodge d'Annunzio.

Nevertheless the British and French were beginning to move towards a compromise over Fiume despite a final protest, on 10 February 1920, by Woodrow Wilson against any concession to the Italians. During 1920 the French Prime Minister and Lloyd George pressed Italy and Yugoslavia to reach agreement on free city status for Fiume. In March and April the Yugoslavs, deprived of American support, began to yield to Anglo-French pressure, although they were not yet prepared to renounce the port publicly. The task was made easier, however, when Italy evacuated Albania in July and recognized its independence in August. Italy's abandonment of Albania was welcomed by France and Britain and made Yugoslavia's insistence on her control of Fiume even more difficult to sustain. Finally, in November 1920, Italy and Yugoslavia signed the Treaty of Rapallo, by which Istria was partitioned between the two countries and Fiume became a free city. Zara and some of the Dalmatian islands went to Italy while Yugoslavia acquired the rest of Dalmatia. In December 1920 the Italian army ejected d'Annunzio from Fiume. The free city existed until 1923, when Mussolini ordered its reoccupation by Italian troops.

Conclusion

Apart from Poland, Lloyd George had shown little interest in 1919 in the settlement of Central Europe. The bulk of the work had been left to relatively junior British officials. As a result the boundaries of the new states were largely shaped in accordance with French wishes. Britain had hoped that stability in the area could be maintained by the establishment of a

Central European federation of some kind. When this vision failed to materialize British statesmen remained cool towards the problems of the successor states and, until 1939, made it absolutely clear that Britain would play no part in guaranteeing their continued existence. Britain's military weakness, popular disillusionment with the war and the fruits of victory, and her absorption with her own economic problems, all dictated this neglect, although there was initially some official hope that she might increase her relatively small share in the markets of the Central and Southern European states.

During and after 1920 France adopted an active policy in Central Europe, without any interference, beyond disapproval, by her Entente partner. She signed an alliance with Poland in 1921 and a succession of agreements in the early 1920's with the 'Little Entente' of Rumania, Yugoslavia and Czechoslovakia. The French hoped that these states would form a bulwark against both the Soviet Republic and a reviving Germany. Britain calculated, correctly for the most part, that without massive aid from the West these states were individually too weak and collectively too divided to perform the role expected of them by Paris. Over all, British statesmen and officials regretted the passing of the Habsburg Empire, with which Britain had traditionally had good relations, and viewed the future of the Balkans and Central Europe with considerable misgivings.

CHAPTER FOUR

•

THE DISSOLUTION OF THE OTTOMAN
EMPIRE: THE MIDDLE EAST, 1919-1920

Introduction and Background, 1914-18

The 'Eastern Question', which referred to the problems created by the decline and gradual dissolution of the Ottoman Turkish Empire, had been a focal point of European and of British diplomacy since the eighteenth century. For the Arab lands within the former Empire, the settlement of 1919-20 has had a fateful legacy. Britain and France, almost entirely by themselves, although acting in the name of the Allied powers, partitioned these lands (which we can conveniently refer to as the Middle East), and created a configuration of states which closely resembles that of today. Emerging out of the ruins of the Turkish Empire were the new states of Syria, Iraq (formerly Mesopotamia), Palestine (now Israel), and subsequently the Lebanon and Trans-Jordan (now Jordan). Arabia, also freed from the Turkish yoke, was soon to be united under the house of Saud. With the sole exception of Arabia, none of these creations became truly independent after 1918, but were assigned to Britain or to France as League of Nations mandates.

The Arabs felt that they had been betrayed, since both the partition and the system of mandates, in implementation if not in theory, flew in the face of what they thought the Allies had promised them. It was this sentiment that fuelled the fires of anti-western, anti-imperialist Arab nationalism. The other legacy of the decisions of 1919-20 was the enormous increase in the conflict between the Jews and the Arabs in Palestine,[1] a conflict which after the Second World War set the Arab world against Israel in a series of wars that threatened global peace.

[131]

What interests did Britain have in this part of the world? Her main interest was strategic, to ensure the protection of the key points along the route to India, the keystone of the Empire. The most important of these points were, first of all, the Straits of Constantinople, and Cyprus. Secondly, there was the Suez Canal. British control of the Canal was secured by her occupation of Egypt in 1882, by French acceptance of her position there in 1904, and by Britain's declaration of a protectorate over the country in 1914. Thirdly, there was, on the western flank of the sub-continent, the Persian Gulf, which Britain had long considered to be within her sphere of influence. Before 1914 Britain believed she could safeguard these points by maintaining the independence and integrity of the Ottoman Empire. This would help to keep out foreign powers, and limit the possibility of conflicts between them in the Middle East. These strategic concerns had led to political interests, in particular agreements with Arab chiefs around the Gulf, and economic interests, largely at the head of the Gulf in Mesopotamia. Lastly, given the large number of Mohammedans in the Empire, Britain wanted to ensure the protection of the Holy Places, and if possible to avoid any acts which might be seen as inimical to Mohammedan interests.

These interests remained the same, though the means by which they could be accomplished were changed, after Turkey joined the Central Powers and commenced hostilities against Britain's ally Russia. This forced a reluctant British government in November 1914 to declare war against the Ottoman Empire. The need to reward Russia for her immense sacrifices in the war and to prevent her from considering a separate peace, combined with the need to win her assent to Italy's participation in the war, led Great Britain and France in 1915 to accept Russia's age old claim to Constantinople and the Straits. This promise predicated the breakup of the Turkish Empire, and led the Entente powers to consider their own desiderata in the area. This and other wartime difficulties in turn gave rise to a series of complex and controversial commitments which Britain made during the war, commitments which were the most important keys to the dilemmas which the peacemakers were to face.

In order to formulate war aims for Asiatic Turkey, Prime Minister Asquith established an interdepartmental committee under Sir Maurice de Bunsen, which reported in June 1915.[2] Its report is valuable because it provides a useful summary of Britain's pre-war interests, and reveals what a number of top policy-makers sought from a victorious war. Their hopes were conservative: they wanted to consolidate existing possessions, rather than take on new responsibilities.

The committee's predominant concern, not surprisingly, was strategic. British policy remained wedded to the retention of her position in the Eastern Mediterranean and above all in the Persian Gulf. To this end the treaties which she had entered into with Gulf Arab chiefs would have to be fulfilled, as well as the assurances given in November 1914, on the instructions of Lord Kitchener, the War Secretary, to Hussein, the Grand Sherif of Mecca, whose importance rested on the fact that he was the guardian of the Holy Places of Mecca and Medina. These assurances were to the effect that, if the Arabs aided Great Britain against the Turks, she would guarantee the rights and independence of the Sherifate.

Britain had long had strategic, political and commercial interests in Mesopotamia, which was composed of the vilayets or provinces of Basra, Baghdad and Mosul. The de Bunsen committee pointed out that Mesopotamia could become an outlet for Indian colonists and, with irrigation, a valuable producer of grain. Though interest in the past had concentrated on Basra in lower Mesopotamia, the committee believed that if Basra was acquired, the two more northerly provinces of Baghdad and Mosul should also be secured, since the security of Basra against encroachments by powers such as Russia was contingent upon the control of the other two vilayets. This interest in Mesopotamia was not only historical, but also reflected the wartime aspirations of, amongst others, the Government of India and the India Office. Lord Hardinge, the Viceroy, favoured its annexation, and hoped that with trade and development it would become a 'second Egypt'. Similarly, A.T. Wilson of the Indian Political Department urged that India be given its 'place in the sun' by the annexation of Mesopotamia, which could be peopled with 'martial races from the Punjab . . . '[3]

If Britain did extend her holdings into upper Mesopotamia, she would require a railway link to a naval base on the Mediterranean. Before the war, Haifa and Alexandretta had been recommended for this purpose. The de Bunsen committee opted for Haifa since the resultant railway would be shorter and less costly than one to Alexandretta. Moreover, if Haifa was acquired, the French could be given Alexandretta and would thereby be confined to the north, where they could act as a buffer between the British and the Russians. The committee reflected Great Britain's pre-war policy by considering the acquisition of a good Levantine port, but showing no other direct interest either in Palestine, which they believed was too vulnerable to be worthwhile, or in Syria, in accordance with Sir Edward Grey's 1912 declaration of Britain's disinterestedness in that province.[4]

The report emphasized the importance of ensuring, within the existing Ottoman Empire, the security of Britain's commercial undertakings, the maintenance of her markets, and the prevention of discrimination against her trade. The committee also pointed to the need for a solution of the Armenian problem. Lastly, it noted that Britain would have to ensure that Arabia and the Holy Places of Islam continued under independent Mohammedan rule.

The report recommended that an independent Ottoman Empire should continue to exist after the war in a decentralized form. It was thought that this solution—as opposed, for example, to partition, which is what actually happened—could best reconcile Britain's interests with her traditional policy of maintaining the Ottoman Empire intact. As it turned out, this solution was rendered impossible, first by allied territorial claims, then by the Turkish nationalists, and finally by Arab nationalists.

It was, however, wartime necessity rather than a British committee which was most responsible for forging Great Britain's Middle Eastern policy. The flagging allied war effort made the prospect of an Arab revolt against the Turks attractive. The price of the revolt was the promises which Sir Henry McMahon, High Commissioner in Egypt, made to the Sherif of Mecca (as the self-proclaimed leader of the Arabs), in their famous and controversial correspondence of 1915-16. The impetus for British support for an Arab revolt, and the source of the vision of a future Arab state and Arab (rather than Turkish) Khalifate under British auspices, came from the 'men on the spot' in Cairo.[5] Their influence was enormously buttressed in 1915 by Kitchener, significantly enough the former consul-general in Egypt, and the leading protagonist of this vision since the outbreak of war.

The Sherif's claims were staggering. He demanded the establishment of a vast, independent Arab Empire under his rule which was to encompass the entire Middle East, from the Mediterranean to the Persian Gulf and from the southern perimeter of Asia Minor to the Arabian Sea.

McMahon, with Grey's general approval, responded[6] that if the Sherif promised to revolt, equipped and financed by Britain, against the Turks, Britain would accept his demands, subject to two main conditions. The first was that the districts of Mersina and Alexandretta and parts of Syria west of the districts of Damascus, Homs, Hama and Aleppo, would be excluded since they were not purely Arab. Behind this stipulation lay the realization that these areas were claimed by the French, with whom negotiations were then in progress. The Sherif, however, refused to renounce his claims to the vilayets of Aleppo and Beirut and their sea coasts, with the result that this conflict was left unresolved. Secondly, 'special administrative arrangements' would have to be made for Basra and Baghdad, in order to ensure Great Britain's established position and economic interests there.

The Government of India and the India Office, despite this latter condition, reacted with dismay to these promises.

They were concerned about the security of the Gulf and their plans to bring Mesopotamia under their control. 'I have spoken to Sir E. Grey on the subject', minuted Austen Chamberlain, Secretary of State for India, amidst a chorus of departmental outrage, 'and the best comfort he could give me was that the whole thing was a castle in the air which would never materialize'.[7] Even Grey's own under-secretary referred to the envisaged Arab Empire as 'a fantastic dream', adding that 'I am surprised the [Sherif's] proposal has been seriously entertained'.[8] The problem with freely making promises in the hope that they would not have to be fulfilled was, as the assistant under-secretary in the India Office incisively argued, that whether or not the Arabs got what they wanted, 'we shall not get what *we* want without eating some very indigestible words'.[9]

That they might very well have to be fulfilled seemed all too possible when the Arab revolt broke out, ironically enough on 6 June 1916, the very day that Lord Kitchener went down on the *Hampshire* on the way to Russia. Though beset with problems, the revolt did make a modest contribution to the allied war effort against the Turks. It was to prove significant that the Arab effort was greater than that of the French, who were understandably preoccupied with the war on the Western Front.

If the promises that McMahon had made were not in keeping with the perceived interests of important sections of Britain's policy-making elite, it remained to be seen if they could be reconciled with the claims of France. The French had long had interests in Syria, and a vigorous and vociferous 'parti colonial'[10] to ensure that the French government protected these interests, in what colonialists referred to as 'la Syrie intégrale', generously stretching from the Taurus mountains to the Sinai peninsula, and from the Mediterranean to the desert. French interests in the Levant were a mixture of tradition, sentiment, religion and prestige, as well as of more concrete considerations. France claimed that her 'benevolent guidance' and 'disinterested protection' had been exercised in Syria since 1649.[11] She had established schools, hospitals, railways and religious orders there, and was the protector of the Christian populace, especially the Maronites. Before 1914 she led the European powers in investment, and in securing economic privileges in Syria.

Britain not only wanted to reconcile her promises to the Arabs with the claims of France but also, in the wake of the failure of the Gallipoli Expedition during 1915, to gain French assent for a British offensive from Egypt. A price would have to be paid for this assent, since the offensive was not in French interests. It would involve the diversion of troops away from the Western Front, and if successful Britain's occupation of Syria.

The negotiations were conducted for France by Georges Picot, former consul-general in Beirut, and for Britain by Sir Mark Sykes, a young MP. Significantly, Sykes had been appointed to the de Bunsen committee at the request of Kitchener, who utilized him at the War Office as his adviser on Eastern affairs. It is thus not surprising that the resultant agreement reflected both the work of the committee, and Kitchener's hopes for a British dominated Arab state.

According to the terms of this critically important agreement,[12] ratified in May 1916, Great Britain and France agreed to recognize an independent Arab state or states in area 'A', which included the major inland towns of Aleppo, Hama, Homs and Damascus, as well as oil-rich Mosul to the north-east, and in area 'B', to its south-east. Priority of right of enterprise and the exclusive right to supply advisers at the request of the Arabs went to France in area 'A' and to Britain in 'B'. Thanks to this latter stipulation, these areas, though nominally independent under the Arabs, could be controlled by the power in question. All but the most nominal restraint was removed for the 'Blue' area, which included the coastline stretching up through Alexandretta to include the south-east provinces of Asia Minor, and for the 'Red' area, composed of the vilayets of Basra and Baghdad. France in the 'Blue' area and Britain in the 'Red' were in effect allowed to establish whatever form of control, whether annexation or something less drastic, that they desired. Though Britain was to receive the ports of Haifa and Acre, the 'Brown' area, Palestine, was to be internationalized. Lastly, Britain was accorded the right to a railway from Haifa (through area 'B', or, if necessary, 'A') to Baghdad, and the right to use it to transport troops.

The task awaiting the peacemakers was further complicated by Britain's commitment to the Zionists in the Balfour Declaration, made by the Lloyd George government. The declaration was inspired by a number of considerations. First, there was the desire to entrust Palestine, strategically located between the proposed future holdings of France and the vulnerable Suez canal, to those who, it was believed, would support Great Britain and look to her for guidance. Secondly, the government was influenced by the (mistaken) notion that the Jews in Russia and in the United States were sufficiently influential to sway opinion in their countries significantly in favour of the Entente. A third influence was the knowledge that the Germans, in a war in which propaganda was proving to be of unprecedented value, were thinking of a similar declaration. Lastly, Lloyd George and his colleagues genuinely admired the Zionists and wanted to see them return to what they saw as their rightful homeland.

With these ends in mind, on 2 November 1917, Foreign Secretary A. J. Balfour wrote to Lord Rothschild, as the head of the Zionists in Britain, that

> His Majesty's Government view with favour the establishment in Palestine of a National home for the Jewish people, and will use their best endeavours to facilitate the achievement of this object, it being clearly understood that nothing shall be done which may prejudice the civil and religious rights of existing non-Jewish communities in Palestine, or the rights and political status enjoyed by Jews in any other country.[13]

Two points should be noted. Though this historic document significantly referred to a 'national home', British leaders were fully aware that the Zionists aimed at an eventual Jewish state.[14] Secondly, two top cabinet ministers objected to the declaration—Edwin Montagu, ironically the only Jew in the cabinet, and Lord Curzon. In a perceptive memorandum Curzon warned that the Palestinians 'will not be content either to be expropriated for Jewish immigrants, or to act merely as hewers of wood and drawers of water to the latter', and also cautioned that: 'It is impossible to contemplate any future in which the Mohammedans should be excluded from Jerusalem'.[15]

As a result of the Bolsheviks' publication in November 1917 of secret documents including the Constantinople and Sykes-Picot agreements, and of the Allies' desire to impress President Wilson, the Entente felt it necessary to give further assurances to the Arabs as to their future independence. This was done on a number of occasions throughout 1918, notably in the Anglo-French Declaration of 7 November. This unequivocally claimed that Great Britain and France were fighting for

> the complete and definite emancipation of the peoples so long oppressed by the Turks and the establishment of national governments and administrations deriving their authority from the initiative and free choice of the indigenous populations.[16]

Not surprisingly, this declaration was received with rejoicing by the Arabs, who assumed, understandably, that it signalled the supersession or at least qualification of Sykes-Picot. As Mesopotamia's civil commissioner A. T. Wilson prophetically telegraphed home from Baghdad, it 'bids fair to involve us in difficulties as great as Sir Henry McMahon's earlier assurances to the Sherif of Mecca'.[17] These assurances were reinforced by Woodrow Wilson's frequent enunciation of the principle of self-determination. The twelfth of his 14 Points contended that the non-Turkish portions of the Ottoman Empire 'should be assured an undoubted security of life and an absolutely unmolested opportunity to autonomous development . . .'. Given this pledge, and Lloyd George's similar promise in his speech to the Trades Union Congress in January 1918, it was clear that the Turks were destined to lose the Arab portions of their Empire. As it turned out, this was accepted not only by all the allies, but also, surprising as it may seem, by the Turkish nationalists.

How can we explain these promises, which severely limited Great Britain's diplomatic freedom of action at the end of the war and produced cries of betrayal? The promises were, quite simply, the product of wartime necessity. They were made under the pressure of an exhausting and costly war, the outcome of which until the very end was never certain. They were also made with a view to encouraging existing allies, such as Russia in 1915, or gaining new ones, such as the Arabs and the Jews. Each promise seemed to lead irrevocably to the next, particularly as it appeared increasingly likely that the Ottoman Empire as it existed in 1914 would not survive the war. Britain, moreover, did not want to be left out of the spoils, especially since her role in prosecuting the war in the East became greater and greater, while that of her European allies faded into insignificance.

It should be emphasized that wartime promises, particularly those to the Arabs, were made relatively freely, quickly and without a great deal of forethought, because there was no certainty that they either could or would have to be fulfilled. It was impossible to make definite pronouncements because it was impossible for anyone to foresee what would happen, particularly in 1915-16 with the failure of allied diplomacy in the Balkans, and the failure of the Gallipoli and Mesopotamia Expeditions, quite apart from the bleak news from other fronts. In the case of McMahon's letters, for example, there was widespread scepticism within Britain's governing circles as to the likelihood of an Arab Empire ever materializing. This scepticism was not without foundation, given traditional Arab disunity: in Hirtzel's view, the Arabs 'are no more capable of administering severally or collectively than Red Indians'.[18] As well as this, Hussein's claim to the leadership of the Arabs was challenged by a variety of other chiefs, most notably the much more impressive Ibn Saud. In Austen Chamberlain's opinion, the Sherif was 'a nonentity without power to carry out his proposals . . .'[19]

Lastly, the promises are explicable given that Britain's Middle Eastern policy emanated from innumerable centres— Delhi, Basra, Cairo, the cabinet, the Foreign Office, the India Office and the War Office—with very little coordination amongst them. In the case of McMahon's most important letter, that of 24 October 1915, Grey, without adequately consulting India or the India Office, authorized McMahon to promise more than either approved, and the High Commissioner compounded the error by going further than Grey wanted. The 'men on the spot', particularly in Egypt, wielded a disproportionate amount of power during the war, when quick decisions were often required and normal channels of communication and consultation disrupted. These same men, surrounded by Arabs, were likely to overestimate their importance. As Chamberlain wrote, 'Egypt sees only half the problem—which is not unnatural—but believes it to be the whole—which is dangerous'.[20]

An enormous amount has been written on the contradictions, real or apparent, between these pledges. The traditional and most prevalent view is that the British sold the same horse, or at least parts of the same horse, twice, once to the Arabs and once to the French. It has, however, been argued that the contradictions between the two most controversial sets of promises, those made by McMahon and those embodied in the Sykes-Picot agreement, were not all that numerous.[21]

It is at the very least clear that the *spirit* of the latter was contrary to what was said to the Arabs in 1915, and, even more so, in 1918. From the viewpoint of studying peace-making in 1919, however, the 'real' answer to the question of the contradictions involved does not matter because two crucial facts remain. First, at the time the Arabs and the French *believed* that they had rightful and binding claims to many of the same territories. Second, many of Britain's top policy-makers agreed with them, and believed that their own government had made

[141]

valid though opposing promises to both allies. For example,
Balfour succinctly minuted in March 1919 that: 'The difficulty
is that we have committed ourselves to two absolutely
contradictory declarations—the Sykes-Picot agreement and
the declaration of 1918. The French rely on one and we on the
other.'[22] The following August, with the situation further
complicated by the League of Nations Covenant and the
instructions given to the Commission of Inquiry sent to the
East, he commented forlornly that the McMahon-Hussein
correspondence, the Sykes-Picot agreement, the 1918
declaration, the League of Nations Covenant, and the
instructions given to the Commission of Inquiry

> are not consistent with each other; they represent no clear-
> cut policy; the policy which they confusedly adumbrate is
> not really the policy of the Allied and Associated Powers;
> and yet, so far as I can see, none of them have wholly lost
> their validity or can be treated in all respects as of merely
> historic interest. Each can be quoted by Frenchmen,
> Englishmen, Americans, and Arabs when it happens to
> suit their purpose. Doubtless each will be so quoted before
> we come to a final arrangement about the Middle East.[23]

These two facts are crucial because the single most important
problem which the peacemakers faced in 1919 was the dilemma
involved in reconciling the claims—which, whatever historians
may say about them, were seen at the time as valid—which the
French and the Arabs forwarded on the basis of the wartime
promises.

McMahon's letters have probably been the most frequent
target of critics. First, his correspondence with the Sherif shows
the danger of ambiguous or poorly worded agreements. There
has never been any question, then or now, but that his letters
were badly composed. Consequently, it is still being debated
whether or not Great Britain actually pledged herself to support
real Arab independence, whether Palestine was to be included
in the new kingdom, and whether the High Commissioner's

letters had any moral or jurisdictional validity. It has recently been argued, for example, that they were not binding, and were conditional on a revolt that was only partially fulfilled.[24] However, even if his letters were not to blame for any future complications, the myth grew up that they were.

Secondly, the controversy over the 1915-16 pledges shows that there are grave dangers involved in the practice of making far-reaching commitments out of a sense of expediency and for the sake of short term benefits, particularly when one does not have the means or the intention of fulfilling them, or the expectation of the need to do so. Apart from the moral problem, the difficulty is that while those making the promises might not take them seriously, those to whom the promises are given (as well as interested third parties) might take them for exactly what they purport to be. This is what happened in the present case.

Lastly, there has been a considerable controversy over the extent to which the British informed the Arabs and the French about the promises made to the other. It seems clear that at the very least the explanations forwarded by the British were not sufficiently prompt, explicit or full.

Britain's position and policies at the end of the war

Great Britain's post-war policy was conditioned not only by these commitments, but also by the circumstances under which the war in the East ended. British arms under General Allenby had been dramatically successful, taking Baghdad in March and Jerusalem in December 1917, and then sweeping through Syria, in a war which had seen few such demonstrative successes. As a result, by the end of the war, in which Britain had employed a staggering 1,400,000 men in the Eastern theatre, the entire Middle East was occupied by over a million foreign troops. Apart from an insignificant French contingent, these troops were British. 'This crucial fact alone', one author has written with forgivable hyperbole, about Anglo-French possession and control of Arab lands, 'was perhaps more important than all the commitments and pledges given during the War.'[25] Many top British policy-makers, including Lloyd George and Curzon, were eager to exploit this position of strength. Their argument that their pre-eminence earned them the right to dictate the peace terms for the Middle East was to be heard again and again during the peace negotiations. Needless to say, this ungenerous line of reasoning greatly upset the French, who replied, legitimately enough, that millions of their forces had been bled white on the Western Front, while Britain was winning relatively easy victories against the inferior Turks.

That the Arabs had visibly contributed to the eastern successes, with Faisal (one of the Sherif's seven sons), accompanied by T.E. Lawrence, occupying Damascus at the end of September 1918, is also significant. It seemed to indicate that the Arabs had fulfilled their obligation to help to defeat the Turks, and would thus be granted the independence they had been promised.

This appeared even more likely given the allied agreement of 30 September allocating zones of temporary military occupation. According to the terms of this agreement, the British would occupy and administer Palestine, referred to as Occupied Enemy Territory Administration (O.E.T.A. south); the French would be responsible for the coastal area to the north of this (O.E.T.A. west); while the Arabs, centred in Damascus, would look after the interior of Syria (O.E.T.A. east). This arrangement was to produce problems, especially for the French. They were not to occupy all the areas they had been assigned in 1916, and they lacked the troops and officials necessary to administer adequately the zone they were allocated. In their zone, the Arabs under Faisal began working towards a permanent Arab administration, in the face of French intentions to place the entire country under their own control. Lastly, supreme military and administrative power was exercised over all three zones by Allenby, who was named Commander-in-Chief. As virtual dictator he was able to prevent the French from acting as they pleased even in their own sphere. The upshot of the agreement was that Britain was still very much in effective control of virtually the entire Middle East.

Two subsequent events were to strain Anglo-French relations before the peace conference: Britain's unilateral negotiation of the armistice with Turkey, and her attempts to revise the Sykes-Picot agreement. This latter effort was not unconnected with her feeling that thanks to her wartime exertions and consequent strong position in the East, she could and should make gains which in her view were commensurate with her sacrifices. She argued that the agreement was out of keeping with changed circumstances, in particular the withdrawal of Russia from the war, and the entry of the United States with its espousal of self-determination. As was made clear in an 'absolutely uncompromising'[26] note of 18 November, the Quai d'Orsay refused to consider any such revision.

Clemenceau, however, thought differently, as was evident when he and Marshal Foch arrived in London on 1 December. According to Lloyd George's well known account:

> After we reached the [French] Embassy he asked me what it was I specially wanted from the French. I instantly replied that I wanted Mosul attached to Irak, and Palestine from Dan to Beersheba under British control. Without any hesitation he agreed.[27]

Though no record was kept of this secret arrangement, which has been a matter of some dispute, Clemenceau doubtless received assurances in return. Indications are that he received a promise that the remainder of France's claims in the Sykes-Picot agreement would be honoured, with an equal share of Mosul oil, and a guarantee of British support for France on the Rhine in the event of an unprovoked German attack.

This important bargain reflected not only the strength of Great Britain's eastern position vis-à-vis France, but also the intention of both powers effectively to exclude the Italians from the settlement. Britain, though ignoring Arab aspirations, made substantial permanent gains for herself, while France (apart from what was said about the Rhine) received little beyond what she had already been promised. As Zeine puts it:[28] 'It was like selling the same goods twice to the same customer, perhaps with the excuse that the Firm was now under a different management'. Thereafter, however, the French were to give away very little beyond these considerable concessions. This is shown by the fact that the final peace settlement reached at San Remo, though not arrived at for 16 months and then only after prolonged negotiations and numerous crises, was in outline identical with what had been agreed upon by December 1918.[29]

Britain embodied her pre-conference policy in a series of resolutions[30] of December 1918 adopted by the Eastern Committee, chaired by Curzon. For Syria, it was resolved to try to cancel the Sykes-Picot agreement through negotiation, though to support French claims to a special political position in the Lebanon and at Alexandretta. The committee further resolved to support Faisal as leader of an independent Arab state, centred at Damascus, and to follow the principle of self-determination as far as possible in the Syrian settlement. It was declared essential that Britain alone should be predominant in areas 'A' and 'B'. Lastly, the committee agreed that Italian claims should be considered in any readjustment that was effected in Syria.

These decisions virtually ensured that Britain would soon be at odds with the French. They were, it should be stressed, completely in accord with the views of the policy-making elite as a whole. In a memorandum of 9 December,[31] the General Staff argued that

it is difficult to see how any arrangement could be more objectionable from the military point of view than the Sykes-Picot Agreement of 1916, by which an enterprising and ambitious foreign power is placed on interior lines with reference to our position in the Middle East.

The memorandum concluded that, from a strategic viewpoint, Britain 'should aim at a politically detached Syria under our influence which must be accompanied by the retention of Mohammedan goodwill'. Similarly, a Foreign Office memorandum of the 19th[32] argued that Britain should support the Arab movement, rather than agree to the presence of France in Syria along the lines of the 1916 agreement. The latter policy would have two disadvantages: it would incur the hostility of the Arabs in particular and the Mohammedan world in general, and it would leave the door open to the spread of French influence throughout the Arab world and lead to Anglo-French conflict.

For Palestine, the Eastern Committee did not recommend internationalization but rather a mandate either for Britain, which should accept the offer if made, or for the United States. The choice would have to be based, in part at least, on the desires of the Arabs and Zionists in Palestine. Further resolutions called for a fair revision—in other words expansion—of Palestine's frontiers, and the fulfilment of promises made about the care of the Holy Places.

By this stage, most top policy-makers, perhaps influenced by Britain's military successes in Palestine, favoured a British mandate. It was because of this that Lloyd George asked Clemenceau for Palestine. According to the Foreign Office memorandum of 19 December,[33] it was desirable for strategic reasons, and because it was believed that its commercial development would depend upon Egypt. There was, however, a general—and far from misplaced—feeling, then and later, that there would be no benefits for Great Britain apart from strategic ones. As Robert Cecil said, more accurately than he could then have realized, 'we shall simply keep the peace between the Arabs and the Jews. We are not going to get anything out of it. Whoever goes there will have a poor time.'[34] It was further argued in the memorandum[35] that Britain should be the mandatory because

from all the evidence we have so far, the Arabs and Zionists in Palestine are united in desiring the protection of this country. If self-determination be the test, each of these two communities would, it is confidently believed, unhesitatingly vote for Great Britain.

This wording is curious in view of the key statement, made earlier in the same document and subsequently repeated, that

The problem of Palestine cannot be exclusively solved on the principles of self-determination, because there is one element in the population—the Jews—which, for historical and religious reasons, is entitled to a greater influence than would be given to it if numbers were the sole test.

In contrast to those who wanted Britain to assume the responsibility were those who, like Balfour, wanted the United States to become involved in Palestine (as well as at Constantinople and the Straits, and in Armenia). They thought that American involvement would help to limit the pretensions of France and Italy, and make it difficult for the United States to criticize European 'imperialism'.

The Eastern Committee recommended the protection of a 'great European power', by which it meant Great Britain, over Mesopotamia, whose oil had attracted the attention of Lloyd George, the Admiralty and Balfour. Though the youthful A.T. Wilson, whose enthusiasm for Empire was reminiscent of the earlier Curzon, was in favour of turning Mesopotamia into a British protectorate, officials in London spoke of self-determination, which they assumed would mean an Arab facade backed by British aid and advice, a status similar to that enjoyed by Egypt before the war.

Lastly, Britain wanted the powers to recognize her special position in Arabia. Her main difficulty there, apart from the fear of Italian encroachments on the Red Sea, was an internal one: while the Foreign Office supported the Sherif and his pretensions, the India Office backed his astute rival, Ibn Saud.

It is no coincidence that these desiderata could be admirably achieved through a system of mandates under the League of Nations, a device suggested the same month by Jan Smuts, the

South African prime minister who was, significantly, both a member of the Imperial war cabinet and of the Eastern Committee. As was agreed shortly after the peace conference opened, the former territories of the Ottoman Empire—specifically Armenia, Kurdistan, Syria, Mesopotamia, Palestine and Arabia—would be designated as A mandates, because they had

> reached a stage of development where their existence as independent nations can be provisionally recognized subject to the rendering of administrative advice and assistance by a mandatory power until such time as they are able to stand alone. The wishes of these communities must be a principal consideration in the selection of a mandatory power.[36]

Smuts, however, contended that there were great variations between these territories. Some, such as Mesopotamia, were scarcely capable of self-government, while others, such as Syria, were almost ready for complete statehood. Still others, such as Palestine, had heterogeneous populations which lacked the ability to cooperate, and hence for the foreseeable future at least would have to be administered to a considerable extent by an outside power.[37]

This analysis was in harmony with Britain's aims: it was geared to giving her effective control in both Mesopotamia and Palestine, while limiting the role of France in Syria. The mandates idea thus had a variety of advantages. First of all, by avoiding outright annexation, as described in the Sykes-Picot agreement, it provided a way out of the dilemma posed for Britain by that unfortunate document,(together with the promises to the Arabs), by clearing the way in Syria for an Arab government. Secondly, by involving the revision of the 1916 agreement, it provided Britain with ammunition to fight for its further revision or even supersession. Thirdly, by ruling out annexation, it eliminated the possibility that Britain (or other powers, for that matter) would fall prey to accusations of blatant imperialism. Lastly, it opened up the possibility of

American support and involvement. While the mandates scheme meant that France could not annex the 'Blue' zone as provided for in the Sykes-Picot agreement, there was a compensating advantage, which may explain why Clemenceau accepted the plan. France could now demand a mandate for the whole of the 'Blue' zone and area 'A' combined.

When the peace conference opened, therefore, the main lines of a settlement seemed generally accepted. Britain, at the 'request' of the populations concerned, would become the mandatory for Mesopotamia and Palestine, while France would become the mandatory for the whole of Syria, and as such would 'assist' a native Arab government. America, it was hoped, would take on the responsibility for Armenia.

There were, however, to be three main problems which resulted both in a 16-month delay in the assigning of mandates, and in a series of Anglo-French disputes. Contributing to the delay was the uncertainty as to whether or not President Wilson would gain the assent of the American Senate for the assumption of overseas responsibilities. Contributing to Anglo-French difficulties was the problem that the French and the Arabs, despite the great pressure exerted upon both by Great Britain, were unable or unwilling to come to terms over Syria. Lastly, Britain wanted to limit France's involvement in Syria. She was no longer willing to accept that France should have a position in Syria which was analogous to hers in Mesopotamia. The British thus proved unwilling to adhere to Lloyd George's assurance to Clemenceau that in return for the concessions over Palestine and Mosul, Britain would honour the remainder of the Sykes-Picot agreement.

Emir Faisal's claims at the Peace Conference

The Emir Faisal, representing his father the Sherif in particular and the Arabs in general, presented his case to the Council of Ten on 6 February 1919.[38] The Emir asked that all Arab-speaking peoples to the south of Turkey be granted independence, with a view to eventual unity. He based his demands on the racial, linguistic, economic and social unity of the Arabs, on the fact that they had contributed 100,000 men to the Allied war effort, on the principles of Woodrow Wilson, and on the promises of the Allies. Faisal, however, did say that he was willing to accept mandatories, if they were both desired and chosen by the populace in question. The latter's wishes, he suggested, might best be determined by an international inquiry. Throughout the conference, the British Delegation viewed the Emir, in sharp contrast to their view of his father, as a moderate and statesmanlike figure who could be trusted. It remained to be seen, however, whether this personal advantage would help him in the way that it helped Venizelos in 1919.

Though Britain never favoured nor considered viable a united Arab Empire, the British Delegation officially upheld the Arabs' most fundamental demand—their insistence upon independence and self-determination—albeit within the confines of a system of mandates held by the great powers.[39] What the British believed was required in order to ensure the fulfilment of her promises to the Arabs, was the further revision or even cancellation of the Sykes-Picot agreement. As it reminded the Foreign Office, the War Office hoped 'that every endeavour is being made to cancel the Sykes-Picot Agreement which they [the Army Council] regard as fraught with military danger'.[40] As well as this, the French were intensely disliked and distrusted by most of the inhabitants of Syria, who feared that they would become the victims of the sort of rule which the French exercised in North Africa. The British were afraid that the native Arab population might revolt against a French presence in Syria, and that Syrian Arab nationalists might then unite with nationalists in Mesopotamia, Egypt or Turkey. In short, anti-French feelings in Syria might release anti-western feelings throughout the East, which would react unfavourably upon Britain's position in Mesopotamia and elsewhere, thereby increasing her military commitments.[41]

The position of the French was made clear in a memorandum received by the British Delegation in early February,[42] which insisted that France had traditional interests in Syria which she had no intention of giving up. Hence the Sykes-Picot agreement 'remains the basis of our whole policy in the Levant, a policy founded on the Anglo-French understanding'. Since, however, the Allies had renounced annexations, the distinction between zone 'A' and the 'Blue' zone disappeared. Moreover, Syria was a geographical, historical and economic unit, which — as the populations concerned would themselves argue — should not be dismembered. These arguments made it possible for France to claim a mandate over the whole of Syria. The memorandum commented on a second change in the 1916 agreement, the cession of Mosul to Britain, and stated explicitly that its renunciation by France was contingent upon strict equality in the exploitation of oil resources. The document concluded by maintaining that the proposed settlement could be made compatible with the granting of autonomy to the Arab states, as was envisaged in 1916, and that, with particular reference to Damascus, 'France as a Moslem Power has every interest in maintaining a most amicable contact with the reigning family of Mecca. . . '

Despite this apparent sweet reasonableness on the part of the French, a whole variety of Anglo-French and Franco-Arab quarrels arose on the spot and in London and Paris. They grew out of the contradiction between Arab demands for independence and self-determination, and France's desire to control the whole of Syria. They also emerged from Britain's attempts to satisfy, in effect, the Arabs at the expense of the French, as well as her efforts to enhance her own position by negotiating expanded frontiers for Palestine, and railway provisions which went beyond those accorded to her in the 1916 agreement.

There was, for example, Anglo-French friction over the question of re-allocating occupation forces,[43] after it had been decided, on Wilson's initiative, to delay the assigning of mandates. A report of the allied military representatives recommended a scheme which would have allowed the British, as their public and most of their policy-makers desired, to reduce substantially their enormous forces in the East, in part by letting the French take over in Syria. The Prime Minister, however, successfully pressed to have the scheme abandoned. He realized that the presence of his own forces in Syria gave him considerable leverage vis-à-vis the French, and thus he refused to move his troops until a settlement was concluded which satisfied Britain's demands. and her promises to the Arabs. Moreover, British authorities were unanimous in believing that if French requests (which were obviously aimed at ensuring that they would receive what they saw as their rightful due) to increase their forces in Syria were accepted, the result would be fighting between the French and Arabs. Worse still, as Sir Louis Mallet minuted,[44] if Britain facilitated a French landing she would both incur part of the odium and, if disturbances occurred, have to intervene to restore order. Hence the requests were rebuffed, though the French were allowed to send in troops as replacements for Algerians and French-raised Armenian levies.[45] As a result of Britain's policy, a new agreement on forces of occupation was delayed until the autumn.

It was in this context of troubled Entente relations that Sir Arthur Hirtzel drew up one of the British Delegation's most incisive and far-seeing memoranda, dated 14 February and entitled 'The French Claims in Syria'.[46] His contention, which he termed unpopular, was that Britain needed an understanding with France, and hence London's support for Arab claims should not be pushed to the point of conflict with France. Hirtzel suggested cogent reasons in support of his thesis. After noting the strength of French (particularly Catholic) feeling for Syria, the influential assistant under-secretary at the India Office maintained that the Americans were becoming increasingly unpopular, and that neither the conference nor the League would succeed if based upon an Anglo-American front ranged against the Continent. Not only would the French continue to be Britain's global neighbour, but also 'it is quite conceivable that the USA may withdraw into their shell again, leaving us to bear the odium of disappointed hopes'. Hirtzel argued further that:

> It will not be many years before there is a great revival of
> German power, and France and we will have to bear the
> brunt of it. Again, and nearer at hand, there is the Bolshevik
> danger. To the USA that is nothing . . . But it is at our door,
> and France and we will have to face it together.

Hirtzel referred to 'the purely parochial importance of the
Arab question' as compared with 'the ecumenical importance
of the maintenance of cordial relations with France'. In any
case, since the Sykes-Picot agreement was the price Britain
had had to pay for French agreement to a British offensive
from Egypt in 1916, Great Britain must pay the price. In
practice, of course, the Arabs would pay the price for Britain,
a justifiable state of affairs given that: 'Without the British
offensive there would have been no effective Arab revolt; and
without the Sykes-Picot Agreement there would have been no
British offensive'. Hirtzel tartly dismissed the Allies' subsequent
profession of support for Arab self-determination: 'everyone
who knows anything about the east knows that, as applied
there, it can only be "make-believe".' In further support of
French claims in Syria he remarked that: 'Faisal would do
well to remember that France made her contribution to the
Arab revolt at Verdun. If the French had failed there, Faisal,
if still alive, would probably be a loyal Turkish subject now.'
The under-secretary also pointed out that French grievances,
if not always justified in fact, were understandable, and that
Britain would probably react in similar fashion if their positions
were reversed and France was in occupation of Mesopotamia.

What was the best policy for Britain to follow? Hirtzel noted
astutely that the proposed commission of inquiry to the Middle
East[47] 'will deceive nobody; it will be recognized as a defeat for
France, and the very fact that it will be so difficult for the
French to refuse it all makes its acceptance the more bitter to
them'. What he suggested, therefore, was for Great Britain to
act as 'honest broker' between the French and the Arabs, telling

Faisal that Britain could only support him up to a certain point,. and that he must come to terms with the French.

It was this idea of getting the French and Arabs to come to terms that became British policy. Lord Milner, who, like Hirtzel, was 'totally opposed to the idea of trying to diddle the French out of Syria' and who similarly believed that Britain should play the role of 'honest broker', met with Clemenceau on 11 February.[48] After assuring him that Britain had no intention of trying to drive the French out of Syria or of taking it for themselves, Milner bluntly told the French premier 'that the French should stop continually bullying and irritating Faisal and try to make up to him'. Until a Franco-Arab arrangement had been reached, the Colonial Secretary added, British troops would remain in Syria.

Milner drew up a compromise scheme for Lloyd George, which the latter presented to Clemenceau on 10 March. According to the plan, France would be given a mandate for the whole of Faisal's territory in the French sphere of influence. The mandate, however, was only to be of the mildest variety, and the Emir was to have an outlet to the sea at Tripoli. Milner opined that: 'The French would, of course, hate this, for what they have been looking for, despite their own Sykes-Picot agreement, is the virtual ownership of Syria'. The pill could be sweetened by giving them full control over Lebanon and most of the coast, including the key port of Alexandretta. Such generosity would only be possible if the French interpreted their promise to turn Palestine and Mosul over to the British in a liberal manner, so that the northern border of Palestine and the frontier between zones 'A' and 'B' were modified in Britain's favour.

This and subsequent attempts by the British to expand their prospective holdings, (and diminish what the French thought was theirs according to the 1916 agreement), were furiously opposed by the French, as was evident at the first meeting of the Council of Four on 20 March.[49] Open Anglo-French acrimony over their wartime agreements, combined with President Wilson's fear of 'a fight between friends, since he was the friend of France and the friend of Faisal' (reinforced by the warning of Allenby, who had been invited to the meeting, that: 'If the French were given a mandate in Syria, there would be serious trouble and probably war'), led Wilson to intervene. He was concerned about obtaining the consent of the governed, since America was 'indifferent to the claims both of Great Britain and France over peoples unless those people wanted them'. He thus supported the idea of sending an allied commission to Syria, and if necessary beyond, 'to elucidate the state of opinion and the soil to be worked on by a mandatory'. The French premier, obviously intent upon ensuring that the British would have to labour under the same incubus as the French, insisted that if a commission were to be sent it should not simply go to Syria, but also to other areas which would require a mandate, such as Palestine, Mesopotamia and Armenia.

The unhappy prospect of a commission, which the British and French feared might unsettle opinion throughout the East and produce negative verdicts for either of them, combined with Faisal's growing disquiet, led both powers into attempts to short-circuit any such inquiry. At an informal Anglo-French meeting of 25 March,[50] agreement was reached on a settlement which the French could present to Faisal. It was also agreed that any commission should meet and come to terms in Paris before making 'whatever local investigations might be judged necessary upon the basis of the agreement reached'. In other words, self-determination would be a charade. It was in this context that Clemenceau was at long last persuaded to meet with Faisal. Though they came to an agreement when they met in Paris on 13 April, the Emir proved unwilling to put his name to the arrangement—for a Syria with a right to independence under a French mandate—that Clemenceau insisted upon. In fact, in his draft letter to the French premier, which the latter rejected as unacceptable, the Arab prince perversely (and inaccurately) thanked him 'for having been the first to suggest the despatch of the Inter-allied Commission', sarcastically adding that he was 'sure that the people of Syria will know how to show you their gratitude'.[51] Faisal later reportedly confessed to General Clayton in Damascus 'that he had never any intention of carrying out the arrangement and that Syria was bitterly opposed to French penetration in any form whatever'.[52]

It was Anglo-French discord that prevented the despatch of an allied commission to the Middle East. The failure of Clemenceau and Faisal to come to terms was followed by the failure of two Entente representatives, Sir Henry Wilson and André Tardieu, to delimit new zones of occupation in Syria. A welter of unresolved issues came to a head at the Council of Four on 21 May, which witnessed 'a first class dog-fight' between Lloyd George and Clemenceau, and on the following morning,[53] no sooner had Lloyd George and President Wilson (who remained adamant in the face of attempts to reverse his decision to send an allied commission to the East), indicated that their commissioners would soon be on their way, than Clemenceau said he must drop out since promises made to him had been broken. France had made many concessions, yet nothing had been done about substituting French for British troops in Syria. Furthermore, he had been shown two completely unacceptable maps, drawn up by Milner and Henry Wilson respectively, showing an unsatisfactory frontier between the British and French zone and the railway which the British planned to build cutting across the French sphere of influence. After registering these complaints, and others concerning the Near East, Clemenceau announced that France would not send any commissioners until an arrangement for French to replace British troops in Syria had been made. Lloyd George also dug his heels in, flatly maintaining that unless Henry Wilson's map was agreed to, 'he would have to await the report of the Commission before withdrawing the British troops'. Both sides remained intransigent, with the French premier grumpily and ominously concluding that: 'As for himself, he would say plainly that he would no longer associate in connection with the British in this part of the world, because the harm done to his country was too great'.

The upshot of this bickering was threefold. First, Allenby remained fully in charge of military arrangements, and thus had the authority to refuse to allow further French troops into Syria.[54] Secondly, since Lloyd George said that if the French were not going to send any commissioners neither would he, the American commissioners, Charles R. Crane and H. C. King, left for the East alone. Lastly, it was at this time that both premiers first learned of the Long-Bérenger negotiations over oil in the East and around the Mediterranean.[55] Lloyd George, who believed that Britain's position in relation to that of France would be stronger if the question of frontiers was settled first, and who wanted the British government and not private interests to reap the benefits of this resource, wrote to Clemenceau to cancel all arrangements.[56]

The Zionists' Claims

The Zionists appeared before the Council of Ten at the end of February.[57] Britain was the initiator and leading sponsor of the Jewish 'national home' policy, and there were close and sympathetic relations between top figures in her government and leading Zionists such as Weizmann (who had, in fact, been employed by the Admiralty). The Zionists thus asked that Britain be entrusted with the mandate for Palestine. This was desirable, Weizmann had explained to President Wilson the previous month,[58] because Britain was powerful and she allowed peoples to develop freely under her protection, and because he personally believed that 'the English were, after the Jews, the most biblical nation in the world'. Before the Ten he expressed the sanguine belief that 'in Palestine there was room for an increase of at least four to five million people, without encroaching on the legitimate interests of the people already there'. Under questioning he stated that the Zionists

did not want an autonomous Jewish Government, but merely to establish in Palestine, under a mandatory Power, an administration, not necessarily Jewish, which would render it possible to send into Palestine 70 to 80,000 Jews annually.

Once the Jews comprised 'the large majority' of the population, he continued, they could form the government. A variety of interesting potential difficulties were raised by Professor Sylvain Levi of the Collège de France, who had been invited to speak at the session. He pointed out that since most of the Jews who would want to settle in Palestine would be from countries where they had been persecuted, they would carry with them 'highly explosive passions, conducive to very serious trouble in a country which might be likened to a concentration camp of Jewish refugees'.

Britain's position on these aspirations was in sharp contrast to her stance on Faisal's claims. In Britain's eyes, Palestine—for historical, religious, and more pragmatic reasons—was a special case, like Armenia, where the principle of self-determination should not be applied. As Balfour candidly admitted to the Prime Minister, a fellow ardent support of the Zionist cause,

> The weak point of our position of course is that in the case of Palestine we deliberately and rightly decline to accept the principle of self-determination. If the present inhabitants were consulted they would unquestionably give an anti-Jewish verdict.[59]

This explains why the Foreign Secretary objected so strenuously to a commission of inquiry going to Palestine.[60] Britain was committed not to self-determination, but rather to the letter of the Balfour Declaration, in the face of strong pressures on the one hand from the Zionists to expand the promise which had been made to them, and on the other hand from the Palestinians who wanted it revoked. The British expected to become the mandatory for Palestine, a role they wanted because of the area's strategic importance, their genuine belief in the legitimacy of Zionism, and their (totally misplaced) belief that the Zionists were a potent international force which would exercise influence against Germanization in Central Europe and the Committee of Union and Progress in Turkey.[61]

Since British policy-makers were intent upon the strict interpretation of the 1917 declaration, they exerted pressure upon the Zionists to moderate their programme, with the result that the latter modified the proposals they submitted to the conference, in order to avoid a programme which might generate distrust and thereby damage their own cause. Thus Britain warned the Zionists to refrain from speaking of a 'Jewish Commonwealth' or state, and by cautioning the Zionist leader Sokolov that Britain would not accept a mandate on the basis of extravagant proposals, persuaded them to drop some of their demands. These included their insistence that the governor of Palestine be a Jew, and that the executive and legislative councils have Jewish majorities.[62]

While the British were trying to keep the Zionists' claims in check, Faisal was making efforts to ensure good Jewish-Arab relations in Palestine. In January the Emir concluded an agreement with Weizmann, though he did so with the reservation that he would only be answerable if the Arabs were established in accordance with the proposals he had submitted to the British government. This called for the fulfilment of the Balfour Declaration, including the protection of the rights of the Palestinian Arabs, and measures to facilitate Jewish immigration 'on a large scale' into Palestine.[63] In a subsequent letter to the American Zionist, Justice Frankfurter,[64] moreover, Faisal expressed his 'deepest sympathy' with the Zionists, assuring the chief justice that 'we will wish the Jews a most hearty welcome home'. According to a letter of 9 April from Weizmann to Balfour,[65] relations with the Emir were excellent: 'Between the Arab leaders, as represented by Faisal, and ourselves', Weizmann wrote, 'there is complete understanding, and therefore, complete accord'.

Despite, however, the moderating influence of the British on the Zionists, and the apparent good relations between their leaders and Faisal, Zionist propaganda and activities gave rise to a crescendo of fear and unrest on the part of the non-Jewish population of Palestine. The latter, over whom the Emir had no real influence, feared that they would be dominated or dispossessed by Jewish immigrants, who would be accorded privileged positions. British policy makers were fully cognizant of the problems which the Zionists were causing for the Palestinians, for themselves, and, consequently, for the British government. So many reports of Zionist excesses and the fears of the Palestinians were received, that even the lackadaisical and strongly pro-Zionist Balfour was prompted to send letters urging caution on Weizmann and his supporter Sir Herbert Samuel. The Foreign Secretary told Weizmann that his adherents in Palestine were 'behaving in a way which is alienating the sympathies of the other elements of the population', and that local ill-feeling was reportedly 'increased by press pronouncements of leading Zionists in England, America and elsewhere and by the rash actions and words of the Jews in Palestine themselves'.[66]

The problems of the Zionists became also the problems of Britain, as was suggested by Weizmann's observation to Balfour that the agitation against the Jews in Palestine 'is as much anti-British as it is anti-Jewish'.[67] Herein lay the dangers of being too closely associated with the Zionists. The rapport was a two-edged sword. On the one hand, it virtually ensured that Great Britain would be asked by the Jews to become the mandatory for Palestine, while, on the other, it meant that as the Zionists became more unpopular in Palestine, Britain also became more unpopular. This identification made more difficult Britain's professed policy of holding the scales evenly in Palestine, and of being the mandatory not of the Zionists but of the peace conference and of the whole population.[68]

As with the Near East, Curzon was the most vociferous and far-seeing critic, if not an effectual one, since he often failed to transform words into action. He was 'absolutely staggered' by what he saw as extravagant Zionist proposals and pretensions, which he thought had to be checked. This was clear from his response to a telegram, on Zionist proposals, from General

Clayton in Cairo,[69] who concluded that: 'In view of the fact that quite 90% of the inhabitants of Palestine are non-Jewish, it would be highly injudicious to impose, except gradually, an alien and unpopular element which up to now has had no administrative experience'. The former Viceroy, after noting that in Palestine non-Jews outnumbered Jews by 573,000 to 66,000 minuted that

> I profoundly pity the future Trustees of the 'Jewish Commonwealth' which at the present rate will shortly become an Empire with a Hebrew Emperor at Jerusalem. Feisal must be very keen to get Palestine and the British interests there on his side in his dispute with the French, if he can swallow this programme.

He was certain that the Zionists were not simply after a 'homeland', but were aiming at a 'Jewish Commonwealth'. 'What then', he admonished his underlings at the Foreign Office, 'is the good of shutting our eyes to the fact that this is what the Zionists are after, and that the British Trusteeship is a mere screen behind which to work for this end?'[70] This state would be organized so that the Arabs were in a subordinate position, with 'the Jews in possession of the fat of the land, and directing the administration'.[71] This would not work, he wrote on another occasion (in agreement with the views of Allenby and General Money, the administrator of Palestine), since: 'A Jewish *Government* in any form would mean an Arab rising, and the nine-tenths of the population who are not Jews would make short shrift of the Hebrews'.[72] In view of all this, it is not surprising that in complete contrast to Balfour he favoured a commission of inquiry, which he hoped would extricate Great Britain from Palestine.[73]

The King-Crane Commission

The sending to the East of a commission of inquiry, albeit one composed solely of Americans, created a dilemma, since it was totally at odds with the actual state of affairs. The commission was supposed to determine the wishes of the inhabitants of the areas visited so that they could indicate their choice of a mandatory. This certainly was what was wanted and expected by Faisal and the people of the East, whose expectations could only be reinforced by Britain's publicly avowed intention of giving the fullest weight to the commission's advice.[74] What stood four-square in the way of all this, however, was the fact that, for all intents and purposes, mandatories had already been decided upon in Paris. In the case of Syria, Britain had stated categorically that it would refuse a mandate, and America, if asked, would have done similarly; France therefore remained the only serious candidate. As the Foreign Secretary wryly concluded, 'whatever the inhabitants may wish, it is France they will certainly have. They may freely choose; but it is Hobson's choice after all.'[75] Similarly, the future of Palestine was not to be decided on the basis of self-determination in accordance with the findings of King and Crane. Once again, as Balfour so candidly phrased it:

> The four Great Powers are committed to Zionism. And Zionism, be it right or wrong, good or bad, is rooted in age-long traditions, in present needs, in future hopes of far profounder import than the desires and prejudices of the 700,000 Arabs who now inhabit that ancient land.
>
> In my opinion that is right. What I have never been able to understand is how it can be harmonized with the declaration [of November 1918], the Covenant, or the instructions to the Commission of Enquiry.
>
> I do not think that Zionism will hurt the Arabs; but they will never say they want it. Whatever be the future of Palestine it is not now an 'independent nation', nor is it yet on the way to become one. Whatever deference should be paid to the views of those who live there, the Powers in their selection of a mandatory do not propose, as I understand the matter, to consult them. In short, so far as Palestine is concerned, the Powers have made no statement of fact which is not

admittedly wrong, and no declaration of policy which, at least in the letter, they have not always intended to violate.[76]

That the commission was a charade and hence a potential source of trouble explains the attempts to change its terms of reference or to cancel it. Quite apart from Woodrow Wilson's refusal to change his mind, the commission had to be sent since it had been promised and was enthusiastically awaited by the Eastern world, and since Britain's military authorities[77] believed that failure to send it off would lead to war. Fear of bloodshed was thus once again a major factor in determining policy.

The findings of the King-Crane commission[78] fulfilled the worst expectations of the British. The Syrian people indicated strong opposition to the separation of Syria and Palestine, and a preference for an American mandate, or, barring that, a British one; under no circumstances would they peacefully accept France as their mandatory. The commissioners also discovered that the programme of the Zionists was opposed by the Palestinians, and could only be implemented by force. 'A report hardly likely to improve Anglo-French relations', Forbes Adam of the British delegation minuted sombrely if accurately, to which the Foreign Secretary added, 'This will greatly add to our embarrassments'.[79] The conclusions of the report were generally known even though the Americans did not officially ciculate it in Paris, and it was not published until 1922. The whole idea of a commission was unfortunate. It raised false hopes in the East, made it all the more difficult for the French and Arabs to come together and, as a consequence, further strained Anglo-French relations.

The British withdrawal and French occupation of Syria, Armenia and Cilicia

Throughout the summer of 1919, while the Peace Conference was awaiting America's decision on mandates before proceeding to a final treaty, Anglo-French relations continued to deteriorate.

The French press and the Quai d'Orsay complained bitterly about British policy, while on the British side there were the usual grumbles from the usual people. Hardinge was convinced that the French did not 'score many points anywhere. People generally realize their insincerity', while Vansittart believed that the French knew they were not wanted in Syria 'but find it more convenient to "blame it off on the cat" — us, a dangerous and not very honest policy'.[80]

In spite of such complaints, however, top British policy-makers showed an increasing desire to come to terms with the French over Syria, lest the dispute over it threaten the entire Entente and Ango-French cooperation in Europe. The cabinet resolved to help the French as much as they could without breaking their commitments to the Arabs. This help took the form of allowing the French at long last to occupy Cilicia, Armenia and Syria as British troops withdrew.

Pressure for this reversal in policy came from a variety of sources. First of all, there were the complaints of the French themselves. As Kerr pointed out to the Prime Minister in a letter of 20 August, the French press 'keep on harping on what is really the weakest point in our case, that we have steadily refused to allow the French to occupy Syria as we have now allowed both the Greeks and Italians to occupy Asia Minor . . . '[81] Secondly, pressure was exerted by the British press and parliament, who objected to paying enormous sums for the 400,000 troops who were still — because of the delay in reaching a final settlement — in occupation in the East. Many of these soldiers were stationed in areas where Britain had no intention of remaining on a permanent basis. This seemed particularly intolerable given that Britain was short of troops to police more vital areas of the Empire, such as Ireland, India, Mesopotamia and Egypt, as well as to answer the numerous calls for a British military presence in various European trouble spots — calls that, for the most part, had to remain unanswered.

Armenia posed an especially pressing problem because of increasing turmoil there during the summer. The British did not want to remain in occupation, particularly since if they did and America refused the mandate, as seemed likely, Britain might find it difficult to evacuate without being accused of negligence. Given her desire to clear out, and, on the other hand, the need to maintain order, Britain had little choice, despite her justifiable suspicions, but to accept a French offer to send in troops. That these were to be sent through Cilicia, rather than via the Black Sea, which was the more logical route, betrayed the fact that Clemenceau was really interested in Cilicia and not at all in Armenia.[82]

This was made even clearer during discussion on the changes proposed by Lloyd George in his *aide-mémoire* of 13 September.[83] This document proposed that: the British army be evacuated from (and give up all responsibility for) Syria and Cilicia; the French occupy Cilicia and Syria (west of the Sykes-Picot line) while the Arabs took control of the remainder of the country; France be allowed to despatch troops to Armenia to protect the populace; France agree to let the Arabs grant Britain the rights to a railway and pipeline connecting Haifa with Mesopotamia. All troop changes were to be temporary and without prejudice to the final settlement.

Clemenceau agreed only to the replacement of British troops by French troops. He rejected the remainder of the proposals and bluntly stated that France had no interest in taking on the burdensome mantle of Armenia[84] (though she did occupy southern Armenia, where there had been little trouble). Hence the project of helping Armenia was abruptly dropped. The French, in short, got what they wanted — the occupation of Cilicia and at least part of Syria — without paying any price whatsoever.

From one perspective the British have been criticized[85] for satisfying their French ally at the expense of their Arab ally. But from another perspective they had little choice. The root of the problem was as always the contradictions, apparent or real, between McMahon's commitments to the Arabs and the Sykes-Picot agreement with the French. As Lloyd George pointed out, 'he was in the position of a man who had inherited two sets of engagements made by his predecessors'.[86]

Given that the French ultimately wanted control of the whole of Syria and were thus unwilling to compromise, it was not possible for Britain to satisfy both them and the Arabs. British policy-makers generally agreed that if only one ally could be satisfied, it would have to be France. First, French support and friendship, both in Europe and throughout the East, was more important to Great Britain than was that of the Arabs. Secondly, the Arabs increasingly seemed to pose threats to the stability of the East, while the position of Faisal and Hussein weakened. The Emir was losing ground to Arab nationalists, and there were indications that his forces would do badly in a war against the French.[87] His father Hussein had lost what little prestige he had and was coming out a bad second in his clashes with rival chieftain Ibn Saud. This apart, the British had never really believed that the Arabs were sufficiently competent or united to establish a largely independent state (let alone an Empire) without a large measure of European assistance and advice. Lastly, British policy-makers did not want the Arabs in the French sphere to be really independent, since the British government would have to accord an equal measure of independence to the Arabs in its own sphere of influence. After all, both governments had similar ends in mind, as Balfour frankly admitted:

> Neither of us [France or Britain] wants much less than supreme economic and political control, to be exercised no doubt (at least in our case) in friendly and unostentatious co-operation with the Arabs—but nevertheless, in the last resort, to be exercised.[88]

When Faisal was informed of the Anglo-French agreement he felt, as was to be expected, that he had been betrayed by Britain, the nation he had trusted, and with whom he had fought against the Turks. The arrangement reflected neither the King-Crane Commission's recommendations nor the promises which Britain had made to his father. Rather, it was based on the Sykes-Picot agreement which—as he stated in the presence of Lloyd George, Curzon and Allenby—'to the Arab nation was a sentence of death',[89] a prelude to the final partition of Arab lands and the permanent replacement of British by French influence in Syria.

The Emir's warnings that 'every Arab would shed his last drop of blood before he admitted the French'[90] were echoed by British authorities on the spot, including Allenby. There were reports that the prospect of a French occupation of Syria was encouraging the growth of a Pan-Islamic, anti-European (not just anti-French) movement with links to Mustapha Kemal. At the same time the Foreign Office was inundated with threats from Hussein that if Arab lands were partitioned he would abdicate, and if the Syrians fought for their independence he would cooperate with them. Despite all these prognostications and Faisal's plea for the cancellation (or at least suspension) of the troop changes, the arrangements went forward as planned.

The implementation of these changes had various consequences. Protests from Turkish Nationalists about the occupation of Cilicia by French troops led Curzon to comment that the French 'do not realize what they are in for',[91] a prophecy borne out by reports in February 1920 of hostilities between Turkish forces and those of General Gouraud. Disagreements and incidents also arose over the rights of occupation in parts of Syria, particularly the Biqa area along the coast. On the one hand it was part of France's 'Blue area'; on the other, it had been stipulated as Arab territory by McMahon in 1915 and by Lloyd George in his *aide-mémoire* of 13 September, and had been occupied by Arabs since the armistice. The French found it difficult, given their weakened military resources, to raise enough troops for their new responsibilities both in Syria and in hard-pressed Cilicia; this dilemma and their resolve to remain in Syria helps to explain their willingness to come to terms with Kemal.

As for the British, they found that the removal of their troops from Syria meant that they were no longer able to influence, or even to keep fully informed about, events in

Damascus. In fact, they increasingly washed their hands of the problems which the Arabs faced in Syria. After an attempt to arrange an Anglo-French-Arab-American meeting failed as a result of French opposition, Britain supported French insistence that Faisal should negotiate directly with them, and put great pressure on the Emir to do this. One of the motives behind Britain's *laissez-faire* attitude is evident in the Foreign Office's reply to an Arab request of 19 December for British assistance in ending a dispute over Biqa involving French troops. As George Kidston candidly explained to General Hadda Pasha, Faisal's right-hand man, he did

> not see how we can help or intervene in any way. We should very strongly resent any French protest as to our action in Mesopotamia or even in the Vilayet of Mosul or on its borders and the French position with regard to the Bekaa [Biqa] is somewhat analogous.[92]

Faisal's secret agreement with the French, and Anglo-French negotiations, December 1919

Given Britain's lack of support and the overall weakness of his position, Faisal had little alternative but to come to terms with the French. As a result of his stay in Paris in late 1919 he came to an arrangement over the contested areas in Syria, and took away an unsigned secret draft agreement,[93] support for which he hoped to gain from the Syrian people. The draft provided for a French mandate over the whole of Syria and over a separate Lebanon. Faisal was to be prince of an Arab state, governed with the aid of French advisers, which was to be based on the four interior towns but to include a part of the coast.

The agreement obviously fell far short of what Faisal had wanted. As Lord Derby telegraphed, the original French draft (which was essentially the same as the above version) 'establishes [the] whole country as a French protectorate'.[94] Part of the difficulty was, as Balfour had earlier pointed out[95], that the

Covenant did not recognize any distinction of authority within the sort of mandate (an A mandate) that Syria was destined to become. Hence the French, in what was supposed to be an Arab state within their mandated territory, would be able to exercise supreme control.

This was made clear in an accurate description of French intentions which Colonel Waters-Taylor, financial adviser to the Palestinian military administration, forwarded to the Foreign Office after interviews with General Gouraud and Robert de Caix. The Colonel had no doubt that the French viewed a mandate as an opportunity for the exploitation and occupation of Syria in its entirety, and that they considered an Arab state as an artificial creation of the British. 'I very much fear', he concluded prophetically,

> that the French will not accept Faisal, save as their creature, and that will result in his ruin with his own people, perhaps the end desired.[96]

Faisal knew this of course, but he felt that there was nothing that he could do. As he admitted to Waters-Taylor, the agreement which he had reached with the French

> was largely distasteful to him, and would be unpopular with his people but that the attitude of the British authorities gave him no choice and that he had been (handed over) tied by feet and hands to the French.[97]

Curzon and Berthelot, meanwhile, were trying to reach agreement in London on a number of outstanding issues, the most important of which were oil rights, Palestinian frontiers, and a British railway from Haifa to Baghdad. Berthelot demanded Franco-British equality in oil exploration in Mesopotamia and Kurdistan. France needed great quantities of oil, having none of her own, and expected generous treatment in view of her cession of Mosul to Britain. Despite this claim, oil did not become a matter of contention between the two governments. Berthelot quickly and quietly dropped his unrealistically high demand and tentatively agreed with Curzon to accept the just negotiated Greenwood-Bérenger agreement.[98] This was almost identical with the Long-Bérenger agreement which had been cancelled during the argument between Lloyd George and Clemenceau in May. According to the new document, France would get, as before, a 25% share of the Turkish Petroleum Company, which was placed under permanent British control. Native governments or interests would be allowed to participate in the company up to 20% of the share capital. The British managed to wrest assent from the French to the building of two separate pipelines and railways, to transport oil from Mesopotamia and Persia through the French zone to the Mediterranean.

No agreement was reached on the boundaries of Palestine with Syria, though the British pressed the Zionists' demands for generous frontiers. The Foreign Office wanted to ensure the prosperity of the existing and of future colonists of their anticipated Palestinian mandate, while the War Office was concerned about Palestine's security, although this could not be stated openly since this security was sought vis-à-vis France. While the French agreed to allow the Zionists the use of waters beyond the Sykes-Picot frontiers, they refused to give up any territory beyond those lines, arguing that Clemenceau's cession of Mosul and Palestine to Britain was cession enough.

British plans for a Haifa-Baghdad railway did not cause dissension in the December conversations. In the face of French opposition the British simply dropped the idea of running it through the French zone to Mosul. They announced that they were examining routes that would be entirely within their own sphere.

The question of frontiers was again raised at the Conference of London in February. The French agreed to what Britain saw as historic Palestine, from Dan to Beersheba, while the British accepted the boundary which the French proposed between Syria and Turkey.

The Syrian Coup

During the Conference of London a major crisis arose as a result of events in the Middle East. Faisal, not surprisingly, had been unable to gain acceptance in Syria for his draft agreement with the despised French, and came under increasing pressure from nationalists. In order to retain support, he agreed to convoke a Syrian Congress in Damascus. On 8 March this body, an elected assembly which was not recognized by Great Britain or France as a legitimate authority, proclaimed the independence of Syria, encompassing the Lebanon and Palestine, and placed Faisal on the throne. At the same time, a congress composed of Mesopotamian officers declared the independence of Iraq under Abdullah as king, its union with Syria, and the end of the British occupation of Mesopotamia.

Though Curzon did not hesitate to blame the turn of events on the French, whose unpopularity in the East, he told their ambassador in London, Paul Cambon,[99] was at the root of the trouble, the British and French did manage to concert policy, perhaps partly because not just French interests but also those of Britain — in Palestine and Mesopotamia — were threatened. The Allies insisted that all decisions had to be made by the Peace Conference, and not pre-judged by the unilateral actions of self-constituted bodies. They thus declared the resolutions made in Damascus null and void. Faisal's claims to the kingship of Syria and the independence of Syria and Palestine[100] could only be recognized if they were supported by an authorized Syrian assembly, and if he first accepted the special position of France in Syria and Lebanon, and Britain (with its obligation to the Zionists) in Palestine. The Emir was invited to Europe to consult on the decisions to be taken. He refused to go, however, until Britain recognized the independence of Arab lands, something which she refused to do. Faisal, therefore, did not attend the conference at San Remo.

The allied policy outlined above was upheld despite being questioned by Lloyd George, for reasons that are not clear, and by Field Marshal Allenby. The latter thought that Faisal should be given some assurances since he, Allenby, believed that the Syrian Congress represented the feelings of the vast majority of Syrians, and that otherwise Faisal would be forced by Arab opinion to commence hostilities against France and Britain.[101]

The Damascus 'coup' was no surprise in view of the Arabs' hatred of the French, who were now in occupation of western Syria, and of the belief that Britain had betrayed them, having in their view promised them independence and then delivered them to the French. Nor was the reaction of France or Britain a surprise. The French never had any intention of allowing either Syria or the Lebanon any real independence, while the British, having decided in September that if a choice had to be made they would opt for the French rather than for the Arabs, and having in consequence withdrawn their troops, merely continued to act in accordance with that decision.

San Remo

The bulk of the Middle East settlement was finalized in short order at San Remo in April. By this time Britain had come to believe that, as a conference of ministers on 23 January noted, Mesopotamian oil resources were 'so extensive that sufficient revenue should be forthcoming from them to pay for the whole administration of the country and that for that reason private exploitation should be prevented'.[102] Hence when Lloyd George met Clemenceau's successor, Millerand, the British premier refused to consider France's renewed demand for an equal share of the oil unless Mesopotamian expenses were similarly shared. What they eventually agreed upon was yet another bilateral document, the Cadman-Bérenger agreement,[103] which was virtually identical with the two previous agreements, both of which had been jettisoned by the British Prime Minister.

The remaining major question was that of mandates. At the Conference of London Curzon had argued that in order to ensure that the provisions of the League Covenant were

[173]

respected, the form of A mandates for the Middle East would have to be drafted either by the League or by the Peace Conference, and he had suggested that this task be assigned to the conference's Mandates Commission. 'It was not open either to France or to Great Britain to establish themselves in Syria or Mesopotamia by means of secret agreements'.[104] Subsequently, however, such niceties were dropped, and it was decided that the form of the mandates would be first decided by the British and the French, and then submitted to the League for acceptance.

Although Lloyd George maintained at the Supreme Council on 25 April that 'the council surely could not dispose of the countries now under discussion without giving the Emir Faisal a chance of stating his case',[105] dispose of them they did, in his absence, only minutes later. As anticipated, Syria including the Lebanon was assigned as a mandate to France, while Palestine and Mesopotamia went to Great Britain. Though Faisal was invited to attend a meeting which the Supreme Council planned to hold in May to present their peace treaty to the Turks, no such meeting took place, and as a result Faisal never participated in the discussions.

'The Frocks think they have done good work', Sir Henry Wilson noted in his diary on the 26th, after the final meeting of the conference,

> but we soldiers think they are all 'rotters'. . . .In fact the meeting demonstrated once more the total inability of the Frocks to take charge of events, and their cynicism throughout has been perfectly disgusting.[106]

Conclusions

The problem of the peace settlement in the Middle East was that of reconciling the promises that had been made to the Arabs in 1915 and 1918, with those that had been made by Sir Mark Sykes to the French in 1916. In the struggle to resolve this dilemma there was a continuation both of the efforts which had been made during the war to gain the support of the

Arabs, and of the traditional Anglo-French rivalry in the Middle East. This was partially obscured, but not ended, by the joint war effort, and was to continue long after San Remo. This rivalry was not, of course, confined to the Middle East, but included the whole spectrum of Anglo-French relations, in Europe and beyond.

During 1919-20, Great Britain made a variety of abortive attempts to persuade the Arabs and the French to resolve their differences. Faisal could not cope with the rising tide of nationalism and anti-French feeling in Syria, while the French government, pressed by its strong colonialist pressure groups for the control of Syria in its entirety, was similarly unwilling to compromise, particularly after its cession of Palestine and Mosul to Britain in December 1918. The British, unable to reconcile their promises, chose to fulfil their commitments to the French—necessarily at the expense of those to the Arabs—partially because Britain's aims were ultimately as imperialist as France's. Britain's choice was reflected in the arrangement which Lloyd George made with Clemenceau in September 1919, which provided for the withdrawal of British troops from Syria, Armenia and Cilicia, and their replacement by French (but not Arab) forces. Although this arrangement was technically provisional, everyone involved realized that the French occupation of Syria would be permanent, thereby spelling the end of Faisal's hopes for an independent Arab state. The unhappy events of the following summer—the French ultimatum to Faisal, Britain's refusal to intervene on his behalf, and the Emir's consequent flight—form no more than a predictable, ignominious finale.

Britain's final balance sheet showed both major successes (at least from her own point of view at the time) and major failures. Her assets included the awards of the mandates for Palestine and Mesopotamia, the terms of which she herself could decide. She was also able to safeguard her vital interests in the Persian Gulf. She was successful in ensuring that the mandate for Palestine was based upon the Balfour Declaration, and in achieving most of her territorial demands there. Great Britain's mandate for Mesopotamia included Mosul and the lion's share of its vast oil resources, together with generous railway and pipeline rights. Though Mesopotamian oil was not a major bone of contention in the negotiations—and commercial exploitation was still many years away—by 1920 the British were beginning to perceive its future importance.

Set against these successes was her failure to contain, or even fully to understand, Arab nationalism. Faisal was abandoned, anti-French feeling in Syria broadened to include the British, and in the summer of 1920 the Iraqi officers who had been with Faisal in Damascus led an anti-British revolt in Mesopotamia (where in 1921 the British set up the exiled Faisal as king). Added to this failure was the Foreign Office's folly in backing Hussein, who was finally defeated in 1924 by Ibn Saud, the founder of Saudi Arabia. In Palestine, of course, the failure to heed |the|avalanche|of|warnings—the accuracy of which was confirmed by anti-Jewish riots as early as Easter 1920—about the future of relations between the Arabs and the Jews, ensured that Britain would soon find herself in an invidious and exposed position. Her role as mandatory was to confirm the Arabs in their belief that their wartime ally had sold them out here by favouring the Zionists. Lastly, her Middle East policies failed inasmuch as they antagonized the French. Although Britain reluctantly conceded to her Entente partner its 1916 demands, she did so only after vigorously contesting many of the points involved. That she did this was partly a result of her desire to evade the impasse created by her wartime promises, and partly a result of her distrust of the French, and her desire to strengthen her own position in the Middle East at the latter's expense. Hence, while avowedly setting out to satisfy both her Arab and French allies, Great Britain—as a result of circumstances, suspicion, and her imperialist greed—ended up by satisfying neither.

The policy of the French throughout was a little less hypocritical, but no more wise. They made no attempt to hide what they wanted: the effective control of the whole of Syria. They argued that McMahon's pledges to the Arabs were British, not allied, promises, and that in any case they had not been informed of them at the time. In their view Faisal was simply a British pawn who would be used to further British interests. After Lloyd George agreed with Clemenceau in December 1918 that, in return for Mosul and Palestine, Britain would honour the remainder of the Sykes-Picot agreement, the French became embittered when the British not only baulked (and interfered in Syrian affairs despite France's non-interference in Mesopotamia, where, of course, France had no troops), but also tried to improve their position on matters such as Palestinian railways and frontiers.

France's final balance sheet was similar to Britain's. She obtained the mandate for Syria, without any strings attached, and Faisal was easily driven out. Her victory, however, was a Pyrrhic one. The struggle for Syria had worsened Anglo-French relations in the East, and, even more ominous for the future, fatally undermined her relations with the Arabs, thereby ensuring that the years of her mandate would be years of uninterrupted crisis.

The Italians played an insignificant role in these peace negotiations. This was largely because they concentrated their attention on the Adriatic and the Near East, and to some extent the result of the success of the British and the French in keeping the Middle Eastern peacemaking process exclusively in their own hands.

The involvement of the Americans was important, although they had nothing to do with the negotiations of December 1918, September or December 1919, or those at the Conferences of London and San Remo, (where, in their absence, their moralizing messages became subjects for contempt). After all, Woodrow Wilson was responsible for the despatch of the King-Crane Commission to the Middle East. It was assumed, reasonably enough, that he would ensure that its findings, based on his own principle of self-determination, would be implemented, an assumption that explains why Faisal urged his supporters to plump for an American mandate. That the Commission's report with its recommendation for such a mandate was buried lends weight to Gertrude Bell's assessment that the President's intervention was a 'criminal deception'.[107] That Faisal, amongst others, had been misled caused him a fatal loss of prestige in Syria and abroad.[108] Then, the prolonged uncertainty as to whether or not the United States government would accept any mandates helped to delay the Middle East settlement in the same way as it delayed that for the Near East.

The Middle East settlement arrived at in San Remo, like that concluded at the same time for the Near East and embodied in the Treaty of Sèvres, boiled down to old-fashioned imperialism in a new guise, that of mandates under the League of Nations, an organization that appropriately enough became dominated by Britain and France. Quite apart from the specific pledges given to the Arabs, the promises of self-determination, of following the wishes of the governed, whether expressed in representations to the Peace Conference or to the King-Crane commission, were patently not carried out. Arab lands were permanently partitioned, not on the basis of the needs of the states themselves, but according to the needs, desires and negotiations of the great powers.

Could, however, the final peace have been substantially different? Given both the circumstances and the aims of the powers, the answer must be no. France was ultimately bound to control Syria, given the terms of the Sykes-Picot agreement, the unwillingness of Britain or the United States to shoulder the burden, and France's resistance to the establishment of anything but the most nominal of Arab states based on Damascus. Similarly, Britain was destined to become the mandatory for Mesopotamia, where her traditional interests had been recognized both by Hussein in 1915 and the French in 1916. She was also assured of Palestine after the Anglo-French arrangement of December 1918 and America's rejection of a mandate.

There was probably nothing that the Arabs could have done to alter significantly the final outcome. Faisal was too weak to fight the French, and once the British—his only real source of strength—decided to support them in Syria, there was nothing he could do. Nor would it have done him much good to have come to terms with the French earlier in 1919, as the British urged him to do. It is unlikely that any agreement with the French could have been maintained in the face of the opposition of Syrian nationalists, and in any case the French had no intention of supporting real Arab independence, despite formal pronouncements in its favour at San Remo. One could argue either that the Arabs at this stage lacked the cohesion and experience necessary to run a viable state, or that they would have been better off running their own affairs than being run by the French, even if this meant being governed badly or inefficiently.

If the final peace was to a large extent 'inevitable', so too was the overall policy of Great Britain. In the final analysis, what else could she have done in 1919-20 to resolve the dilemma posed by the conflicting pledges which the Lloyd George government had inherited, than come down on the side of her most important ally, France, even when this was necessarily at the expense of a less important ally, the Arabs?

The Allies paid—and are still paying—a very high price for their policies and their imperialism in the Middle East from 1914 to 1920. That price was the development of anti-western, anti-imperialist Arab nationalism, and the continuation and deepening of the conflict between the Arabs and the Jews in the Holy Land. Because of their policies, the great powers—particularly Britain, France and the United States—are partly responsible for some of the woes that have afflicted the Middle East during the last 60 years.

CHAPTER FIVE

THE DISSOLUTION OF THE OTTOMAN
EMPIRE: TURKEY, 1919-1923

Introduction and background

It was the fate of the heartland of the Ottoman Empire, Asia Minor, along with Constantinople and the Straits, and Turkey in Europe beyond the capital, that had traditionally been at the core of the 'Eastern Question'. As with the Middle East, Britain's main interest in these areas (which, if taken alongside the remainder of the Balkans, can conveniently be referred to as the Near East) was strategic. Her policy, apart from considerations discussed above,[1] had always been to prevent the Russian Black Sea fleet from passing through the Straits at Constantinople, since it was feared that once the fleet was in the Mediterranean it would threaten Britain's eastern Empire, a contingency which became particularly worrisome after the completion of the Suez Canal in 1869.

Generally speaking, the Conservative party, with its belief in Empire and concern for Imperial security, was well-disposed towards the Turks, as were the military. Liberals, Nonconformists and Labourites, however, saw them as corrupt, inefficient, tyrannical rulers who had not only suppressed the voice of nationalism within their Empire, but had also been responsible for unspeakable persecutions of subject peoples such as the Bulgarians and Armenians. The most prominent exponent of this view was Gladstone, who attempted (without success) to put an end to the massacres and reform the Empire. His name became associated with the policy of expelling the Turks completely — 'bag and baggage' — from the European continent, including Constantinople.

[181]

Britain's post-war policy towards Turkey was greatly affected, as was her policy towards the Middle East, by her wartime commitments. In the spring of 1915 Great Britain and France reversed their traditional policy and accepted Russia's claim to Constantinople and the Straits, for reasons which have been cited above.[2] As a consequence of these negotiations, which culminated in Italy's decision to join the Allies, the Treaty of London was signed on 26 April. It stipulated that 'in the event of the total or partial partition of Turkey in Asia, she [Italy] ought to obtain a just share of the Mediterranean region adjacent to the province of Adalia . . .'[3] The Italians, however, felt aggrieved at such a nebulous offering, particularly after they learned about the Anglo-French-Russian division of spoils negotiated by Sykes and Picot. As a result, Lloyd George and French premier Ribot met Sonnino at St Jean de Maurienne in April 1917, and promised Italy—subject to Russian assent—a vast zone in south-west Anatolia. This zone included the vilayet (province) of Smyrna and the town of the same name, which was the most prosperous port on the west coast of Asia Minor.

The conclusion of this agreement appeared to leave the Greeks holding the proverbial bag, since they too coveted Smyrna with its substantial and flourishing Greek population. The twentieth-century version of the centuries old 'Great Idea' of a Greater Greece aimed at 'redeeming' areas within the Ottoman Empire inhabited by Greeks. This appeared especially pressing given that events in the Balkans in the years immediately prior to 1914 had driven the Turks to acts of reprisal against the Greeks in western Anatolia. The war witnessed the development of deep schisms in Greek politics, above all between the pro-Allied, imperialist Venizelos and King Constantine, a German supporter (albeit one who favoured Greek neutrality) who was married to the Kaiser's sister. In 1915 Grey, at Venizelos's prompting, promised Smyrna (and Cyprus) to Greece in return for joining the Allies, but the offer lapsed when it was not taken up. It was only in 1917, after the Allies had deposed Constantine and replaced him with his son Alexander, that Venizelos as Prime Minister was at long last able to bring his country into the war on the allied side, without, however, the promise of Smyrna or anything else as a reward.

Last on the list of relevant wartime commitments were those made by Lloyd George and Woodrow Wilson in 1918. In his Twelfth Point the President stated that the Turkish portions of the Empire should be guaranteed a secure sovereignty, while Lloyd George similarly promised that the Allies were not 'fighting to deprive Turkey of its capital, or the rich and renowned lands of Asia Minor and Thrace, which are predominantly Turkish in race . . .' Both stated their belief that the Straits should be permanently opened and neutralized under international guarantees.[4]

By the end of the war policy towards Turkey was conditioned not only by these wartime pledges, but also by a variety of sentiments. Most leading British statesmen, including Lloyd George, Balfour and Curzon, thought that nothing was too bad for the cruel, despicable and downright evil Turks who, in 1915-16 alone, had slaughtered over one million Armenians, and whose entry into the war, it was generally believed, had prolonged it by a full two years. To take one typical example of many, Philip Kerr concluded a memorandum of July 1919 for Balfour by stating that:

> After all the Turks are our enemies. They aided and abetted the Germans. For centuries they have proved themselves incapable of governing. They have murdered millions of their own subjects and have committed incredible atrocities on our own men.[5]

As is clear from the preceding chapter, Britain distrusted and wanted to minimize the post-war role in the East of her partner France. As for the Italians, the British viewed their wartime performance and pretensions with contempt. They were seen as a greedy lot with an insatiable appetite who had the audacity to claim large chunks of Asia Minor despite the fact that they had not fired a shot at the Turks. Typical was

Rumbold's assessment that the Italians were more fit to sell ice-cream than to fight a war.[6] In sharp contrast to the policy-makers' attitude towards these two allies was the view taken by many of them, above all Lloyd George, towards the Greeks. British Philhellenism had an ancestry dating back to Byron. At the time of the Balkan Wars important friendships and contacts had been formed between British and Greek leaders, and there had been talk of an Anglo-Greek Entente based on naval cooperation in the Eastern Mediterranean in return for territorial concessions to Greece.

While British statesmen and officials had agreed upon the main lines of a Middle Eastern settlement before the opening of the peace conference, the same was not the case for the Near East, which was considered a lesser priority. All that was clear was that, given the revolutionary nature of the Bolshevik regime in Russia and the fact that it had concluded a separate peace with Germany, no part of Armenia or of Constantinople and the Straits would be turned over to that regime. As for Armenia, it was generally held that it should be established as a separate state, under a French or, ideally, an American mandate. This would bring an end to Turkish misrule and provide a bulwark against Bolshevik incursions to the south. Britain's policy-makers were also agreed that their traditional policies towards the Straits—keeping them closed and in Turkish hands—would have to be reversed.[7] The role of Turkey in the war and in particular the Gallipoli campaign had shown the unfortunate military consequences of such policies. Since Turkey could no longer be relied upon to open the Straits to Britain (as she had before 1914, for example during the Crimean War), they would have to be international-ized. Though there was considerable support for the idea of forging them and Constantinople into a separate state which could be put under an American mandate, there was uncertain-ty as to whether the United States would accept such a charge, and important dissenting voices, above all that of Edwin Montagu, who feared an upheaval by Muslims in India if Turkish Muslims were expelled from their capital.

A plan which satisfied these desiderata for Armenia, Constantinople and the Straits, and the promises of Lloyd George and Wilson in 1918, was circulated to the cabinet by Curzon in January 1919. Under its terms the Turks would retain Anatolia, their heartland, in its entirety, but would end their rule over subject nationalities, in particular the Armenians and Arabs. Since he believed that

> for nearly five centuries the presence of the Turk in Europe has been a source of distraction, intrigue and corruption in European politics; of oppression and misrule to the subject nationalities,[8]

the Turks should be completely ejected from Europe, including Constantinople and the Straits, which should be opened and internationalized under the League. This scheme had a number of substantial assets, which were not shared by most later plans or by the peace treaty drawn up in 1920. Curzon's design was based on the principles of self-determination, independence and assent of all the peoples concerned, including the Turks: the single exception would be the latter's opposition to the loss of Constantinople and the Straits. The plan would have obviated the later rise of anti-Allied Turkish nationalism under Mustapha Kemal. At this stage—before the Turks had recovered their strength, and before the Greek landing at Smyrna in May 1919 drastically altered the entire situation for the worse—it could have been imposed and enforced. A number of authors[9] contend that if implemented it would have provided an equitable and lasting settlement, thereby sparing everyone the subsequent tragedies. It was, however, not implemented, because it flew in the face of the imperialistic designs of the Greeks, French and Italians, Lloyd George's intention to use pieces of the old Empire to compensate allies, and—above all—because the scheme was at odds with Britain's wartime promises.

Certainly the problem of achieving a positive settlement in the Near East was enormous. There was the question of the wartime agreements and the ambitions of the powers; of the difficulties posed by the clash of personalities and policies within the cabinet; of the uncertainty as to the future role of America; of the task of enforcing a peace when there were too few troops for too many tasks. Moreover, the problem of Turkey overlapped with that of Russia, another unpredictable quantity in the international balance. British policy-makers feared the spread of 'revolutionism' from Russia to Turkey, and the possibility of cooperation between the two powers. That the Russian and Turkish problems were intermingled is shown by the fact that Lloyd George wanted to end intervention in Russia partly so that the troops in question could be used to enforce a harsh peace with Turkey; while Winston Churchill wanted a moderate peace with Turkey partly so that the troops there could be sent to fight against the Bolsheviks.

The Conflicting Claims of the Greeks and the Italians

The British Delegation's first significant decisions at Paris were made at two conferences held at the Astoria Hotel at the end of January 1919. On the 30th it was agreed that Britain required free passage of the Straits in peace and war as well as a free port at Constantinople, with the entire area being put under international control. The following day the conflicting claims of the Greeks and Italians in Anatolia were considered.[10] Hardinge put forward the official Foreign Office view that the presence of the Greeks in Smyrna was preferable to that of the Italians. This was challenged by Major-General Thwaites, the War Office representative, who maintained that the Turks should retain Smyrna. He hit the nail on the head when he prophesied 'that to hand Smyrna over to the Greeks might give the people of Anatolia just cause for resentment and should not be done', though he added less fortunately, 'except as an unavoidable political expediency'. In the end it was decided that, subject to Thwaites' comments and the provision of an economic outlet for Turkey, there was no objection to giving the Greeks a zone in Smyrna.

Meanwhile, the Council of Ten was reaching provisional agreement on mandates to be administered on behalf of the League of Nations. During the initial session on the subject one of the first in a long series of indications was given that the United States might not take on the proposed obligations for Constantinople, the Straits and Armenia. President Wilson himself said that he believed that the American people 'would be most disinclined' to have their country act as a mandatory.[11]

Venizelos, marshalling all his charm and resourcefulness, presented the Greek case before the Council on 3 and 4 February.[12] His vast territorial claims were based on the juggling of statistics and a variety of principles designed to ensure Greek acquisitions in each area. He claimed both western (Bulgarian) and eastern (Turkish) Thrace not only on the basis of population figures, but also on the grounds that he had waived claims to Constantinople, 'a Greek town'. Not content in Asia Minor with the Smyrna vilayet, for which a case could be made, Venizelos also put in a claim for most of the villayet of Aidin and part of that of Bursa. He rested his claims on Wilson's Twelfth Point and the principle that only those areas which contained an absolute majority of Turks should remain within the new Turkey. He deftly switched arguments for the eastern portions where the Turks *did* have the requisite majority, maintaining that such areas were essential to the Greeks for economic reasons. The Ten agreed that an expert committee should examine the claims.

It was, however, the overlap between these demands and those of the Italians that hopelessly complicated matters. While Britain and France insisted that the St Jean agreement was invalid because it had not been ratified by Russia, the two powers (unlike the United States) did recognize the Treaty of London. The Greeks lacked similar treaty promises, but they did have the astute and likeable Venizelos. By comparison, the Italians had Orlando and Sonnino, who succeeded in alienating virtually everyone at the conference. Typical was Hardinge's comment that 'the Italians are exceedingly voracious and want all that they can get', a criticism scarcely mitigated by the additional remark that 'they are suffering from megalomania like the French'. Even the normally placid Balfour wrote to Rodd in mid-March that Italy's foreign policy 'almost suggests the idea that she thinks it better to have enemies rather than friends'. 'Their main object', he wrote in exasperation to Curzon a few days later, 'appears to be to disgust all their neighbours and all their Allies, and they are accomplishing this object with extraordinary success'.[13]

It was the Italians' demands in Asia Minor and for the port of Fiume which caused all the trouble. Their claim to the latter was — and was seen as — completely lacking in legitimacy. It had not been promised by the Treaty of London, had a purely Slav hinterland, and was the logical outlet for the new Slav state. Considering that the Italians did well out of the war, particularly since their traditional enemy, the Habsburg Empire, had disappeared from the map forever, they were foolish indeed to pursue such a hostile policy towards their new neighbour.

The solution to the problem of conflicting claims was not provided by the report of the Greek Committee,[14] whose experts, not surprisingly, divided along national lines. The British and the French largely accepted Venizelos's claims in Anatolia, while the Italians and the Americans were critical. The British believed that Greece should be given a zone in Asia Minor. Smyrna was, in Crowe's view, 'almost purely Greek, highly civilized and flourishing', and it would be politically and morally indefensible to leave it under the Italians, or even the Americans. Harold Nicolson was even more forthright. Britain would be 'morally lacking' if this 'sensitive and progressive civilization' was left under Turkish rule, while Venizelos's position would be wrecked — with disastrous results for Entente interests in the Eastern Mediterranean — if he did not return home as the liberator of Anatolia. Nicolson brushed the economic objections aside: 'economically it is defensible on the grounds that the Turks have never shown any aptitude or inclination to control their own commerce', a casualness which is interesting in view of his pro-Keynesian standpoint on the German treaty.[15] These views, along with the Delegation's decision of 31 January, testify to the fact that Lloyd George was not, as is usually assumed, acting against all his advisers when he came relentlessly to pursue a Philhellene policy.

The French support of Greek claims is ironic in view of later developments, but probably derived from the calculation that anything which weakened Italian ambitions in Turkey was desirable. Moreover, at this stage Paris regarded Venizelist Greece as a French client, as she had been before the war. The Americans opposed the claims on economic grounds, believing that acceptance would be 'to sever what remains of the Turkish Empire from its most important natural exits to the sea'[16], and they doubted Greek statistics. The United States, however, unwisely came to reverse its stance, probably because of the intervention of Wilson himself. The President may have been struck by reports of Turkish atrocities against the Greeks, and felt that a Greek presence would prevent an Italian one; he may also have been willing to side with the British on the claims in order to gain their support on the German settlement. Lastly, that the Italian representatives on the Greek Committee did not support the Greeks' desiderata in Anatolia was only to be expected in view of their belief that Italy had been promised much of the area in question during the war.

Despite this support for Greek claims, by April there was a growing uneasiness in the hearts of many British officials about their government's policies. On 8 April Robert Vansittart wearily took note of 'another long list of people who condemn the cession of Smyrna to Greece as disastrous', adding that he had 'not seen the name of a European well acquainted with the East who thinks otherwise'.[17] A few days later Llewellyn Smith of the Board of Trade forwarded notes to Hankey for the Prime Minister's attention in which he stressed the strength of feeling amongst Turks against the Greeks, and opined that the Paris peacemakers had been hypnotized by Venizelos's personality.[18] Lord Curzon, deputizing for Balfour at the Foreign Office, similarly raised his forceful voice. He was nervous about the signs of allied disunity, and, like Britain's military authorities, alarmed by her military weakness in the East. Given these difficulties, he feared that when the Turks realized that the little they would be left with in Anatolia would be controlled by some abhorred foreign power, they might 'think it worth while to strike another blow (even if it be a local and abortive blow) for Islam and the few remaining vestiges of their freedom'. As he eloquently lectured the Foreign Secretary on 25 March, in the midst of unauthorized landings by the Italians at Adalia, if the Greeks, Italians and French 'were to gallop about all over Asia Minor', he could not 'help thinking that this great pack of cards which is being reared will, almost at the first blow, tumble in fragments to the ground'.[19]

It is an unfortunate irony that at the very moment when members of the Foreign Office were moving towards a sensible solution, circumstances militated against its implementation. In mid-April Nicolson and Toynbee, determined 'to cut the Gordian Knot', suggested that the Greeks should get Constantinople and the European shore of the Straits, but not Smyrna. Anatolia in its entirety was wisely to be left to the Turks. While Hardinge and Crowe reacted enthusiastically, Balfour tartly enquired where the French and Italians came in. When Crowe said that the latter could go to the Caucasus, the Foreign Secretary replied that Italy, understandably, would not accept that in place of what she was entitled to by the Treaty of London.[20] Indeed, it was the problem of the Italians that provoked a crisis at the conference; on 24 April they walked out because of their failure to gain satisfaction over their Adriatic claims. Though Italian opinion supported their intransigent stand, the withdrawal from Paris was an extremely ill-considered move. It not only incensed the Big Three, but left Venizelos with the floor to himself.

The Decision to land Greek troops at Smyrna, May 1919

The fateful decision to land Greek troops at Smyrna must be seen in this context. In the absence of the Italians, the hostility of the Three to them multiplied at a geometric rate. They were fed with reports of landings along the portions of the Turkish coast which the Italians thought were rightfully theirs, and with tales — some of them supplied by Venizelos — of sundry Italian misdeeds. On 2 May President Wilson, responding to a report that the Italians were despatching ships to Fiume and Smyrna, and convinced that Italy 'is a menace to the peace', suggested that he could send America's biggest cruiser, the *George Washington,* to either port.[21] Lloyd George was not going to let the opportunity pass. On the 5th, after airing his suspicions that the Italians were on the brink of a major expedition to Asia Minor and that it would be difficult to remove them once they were in occupation, he proposed a redistribution of occupation forces. The Greeks would be permitted to occupy Smyrna, 'since their compatriots were actually being massacred at the present time and there was no one to help them'. He added, significantly, that he would like to arrange this 'before the Italians returned to Paris this afternoon, if possible'.[22] The actual decision was taken the next day, just in time to avoid the presence of the Italians, who had decided to return on the 7th. While Lloyd George's initiative was merely agreed to by Clemenceau, it was enthusiastically greeted by Wilson, who chipped in that the Greek Committee was now unanimous that Smyrna should go to Greece. He proposed that since the forces would not remain in good shape on board ship, they should be landed at once.[23]

The Big Three were at their most secretive and deceitful when they met with Orlando on 12 May and told him about their plan. Clemenceau explained that 'the Greeks had asked us to agree to a disembarkation at Smyrna, which we conceded'. He stressed that this did not presage a re-distribution of territory affecting Smyrna. He, Wilson and Lloyd George all maintained that the motive was to protect the Greeks from massacre. These statements included three misrepresentations. First of all, as Wilson himself said by way of correction, the original proposal had not emanated from the Greeks but from the Council of Three.[24] Secondly, it was clear that the latter *did* see the landing as the precursor of the cession of Smyrna to Greece. That this was generally understood is evident by Nicolson's comment in his diary that the decision 'means at least that the Smyrna question is settled. A personal triumph for Venizelos'.[25] Thirdly, the main motive was certainly not to prevent massacre; in fact, it was subsequently discovered that far from disorder existing prior to the landing, it was the landing itself that caused it! Orlando accepted the decision, agreeing that while British, French and Italian detachments would take the Turkish forts at Smyrna and re-embark, the Greeks would remain in occupation.

What were the motives behind the operation? If it is too much to say that Lloyd George engineered the whole scenario, he certainly leapt at the opportunity which presented itself in the wake of the Italian walk-out and landings. Through his initiative, he was able at one fell swoop to accomplish two interwoven objectives: keeping the Italians out of Smyrna and helping to create a Greater Greece. In the circumstances, this could be achieved with the full cooperation of the United States. That such cooperation was welcome indeed is shown by Lloyd George's statement of 3 May that: 'If there must be a break, a break with Italy would be bad enough, but not a disaster; a break with the United States would be a disaster'.[26]

The objective of keeping the Italians out must be put into perspective. The anti-Italian sentiment of early May, fully exploited and even whipped up by the Prime Minister, provided the occasion for the decision, which—as he told Venizelos—had been provoked by Italian machinations.[27] Lloyd George was only intent upon keeping the Italians out of Smyrna because he wanted it to go to the Greeks. After all, he had shown little hesitation in promising it to Sonnino at St Jean in 1917. He was certainly not against giving the Italians a zone in Asia Minor. This not only seemed essential given the Treaty of London, which Lloyd George stood by, but also might succeed in directing Rome's attention away from Fiume, her claim to which was causing friction not only between Britain and Italy, but also between Britain and the United States.

Such thinking was in line with the Prime Minister's general attitude towards Asia Minor. To him, unlike Curzon, the area was a very bad second in importance to Europe. He thus had no overall final Near Eastern settlement in mind. Far from agreeing with the former Viceroy's objections to partition, he saw it as a means by which recalcitrant allies such as the Italians could be compensated. This approach meant, however, that decisions were made on a day to day basis with little regard for consistency or for the consequences. For example, it was only a matter of days after Lloyd George had vented his wrath on the Italians and put forward his Smyrna proposal that he was suggesting that they be given a mandate for southern Anatolia. After all, he insisted, they 'were an extremely gifted race', who—curiously enough—had during the war 'developed some of the qualities for which Romans had been famous'.[28]

Lloyd George's second objective—to help Venizelos to achieve his 'Ionian Vision'—was of far longer standing and greater strength than his desire to forestall the Italians. Quite apart from the fact that favouring Greece was the logical concomitant of despising the Turks, which was *de rigueur* for all good radicals, the two prime ministers had been friends since 1912, and Lloyd George, like everyone else at the conference, was beguiled by the charming Cretan. The self-made Welshman from humble origins, the outsider who made it to the top, admired and could identify with the similarly self-made outsider from Crete. And of course Greece, like Wales, was a small and valiant nation with an impressive history, a nation which could be admired for its classical past and its liberation as a Christian power from the unspeakable Turks. More concretely, Lloyd George believed that Venizelos's unswerving devotion to the allied cause throughout the war should not go un-rewarded. There is little question as to his sincerity when he wrote to Venizelos that:

We shall never forget your tried loyalty during the great period when militarism threatened to overwhelm our liberties and when, practically alone, among the leaders of the smaller nations of Europe you never wavered in your support of the Allied cause.[29]

Above all, since Britain's strategic interests in the Eastern Mediterranean could no longer be maintained by preserving and supporting the Ottoman Empire—it had become an enemy power and was now in ruins—Lloyd George looked to a strong Greece, backed morally and diplomatically by Britain, to protect those interests. By supporting Greece he was able to fuse perfectly his belief in justice with his recognition of the need for imperial security.[30] As he enthused to his fellow premier, Greece 'has *great possibilities* in the Near East and you must be as powerful as possible in the military sense in order to take advantage of them'.[31] Hence at no military cost to Britain—which lacked the troops to enforce peace terms upon Turkey—the army and navy of Greece, experienced and still mobilized, could at one and the same time enforce its allied-endorsed claims against Turkey and help guarantee Britain's eastern interests. For their part, of course, the Greeks would retain the friendship and support of a great power and gain a golden opportunity to make good their claims. Hence it is no surprise that, in the words of the best recent authority on the Greek viewpoint, Venizelos was the 'instigator and willing accomplice' of the Three and their scheme for Smyrna.[32]

The motives of Wilson and Clemenceau were straightforward. The president had been in a moral fury over the Italians' Adriatic claims, so their departure from Paris and unauthorized landings were simply the icing on the cake. 'President Wilson would have put the devil into Smyrna', concluded Michael Llewellyn Smith, 'if that would have kept the Italians out'.[33] Wilson believed that the Greeks had to be sent in to protect their co-nationals from being slaughtered by the Turks, and in any case believed that Greek claims were justified on the basis of self-determination. Clemenceau played a much lesser role. France had few direct interests, apart from financial, in Asia Minor, so her Prime Minister felt it prudent to agree to any Anglo-American proposals. He hoped that his cooperation would help France to win concessions where she was vitally concerned: Germany and Syria. Moreover, Clemenceau was not likely to object to an action designed to dish his Latin rival and aid the Greeks, who were helping to fight the Bolsheviks in south Russia. Lastly, all three leaders were doubtlessly influenced in their decision by the fact that it would not involve any of them using their own troops.

The Smyrna decision was probably the single most important one taken in the almost five years from the armistice to the final peace treaty. It completely reversed the post-war situation in the Near East. It brought about war between the Greeks and the Turks, sealed the fate of Armenia, and ended all hope of allied cooperation in the Near East. It ultimately helped to bring about the downfall of Lloyd George. All authorities agree that it, more than anything else, explains the rise and success of Mustapha Kemal and Turkish nationalism. The decision was thus at least indirectly responsible for the birth of the Turkish Republic which has lasted to this day.

Widely criticized at the time and subsequently, this diplomatic decision was perhaps one of the least defensible of the twentieth century. As Churchill phrased it, 'the whole attitude of the Peace Conference towards Turkey was so harsh that Right had now changed sides'.[34] As discussed above, the decision was misrepresented, and was made in great secrecy without proper consultation with advisers. While Lloyd George was not acting against all advice, he certainly initiated the Smyrna scheme in the face of numerous warnings. Hankey—admittedly at the eleventh hour—summarized his misgivings for the Prime Minister, pointing out that the planned action might precipitate a further crisis with the Italians.[35] This view was reinforced by the grim accounts emanating from Rome, where Rodd reported that 'Feeling of anti-Ententism is unanimous', and that unless a satisfactory settlement was reached 'we shall permanently estrange the friendship of Italy which has subsisted for 50 years and more'.[36] The CIGS, Sir Henry Wilson, directly confronted Lloyd George, asking him on the 6th if he realized that the landing would start another war, a possibility that the latter brushed aside.[37] Curzon, Churchill, Montagu and Hardinge were critical of the decision when they learned of it.

The plan to send in Venizelos's troops completely ignored the long-standing antipathy between the Greeks and the Turks. The Three failed to realize that while the Turks might have sulkily acquiesced to the presence of certain foreign troops on their soil, they would never submit to the despised Greeks. Their occupation of Smyrna seemed to herald the division of Anatolia—the Turkish heartland of the old Empire—by the Greeks, Italians and French. Nationalism in Turkey was as little anticipated or understood as it was elsewhere.

The Three's Smyrna decision was partially the product of sentiment rather than rationality. Philhellenism and admiration for Venizelos were combined with animus towards the Italians, a feeling which was scarcely likely to aid in solving the difficulties posed by the wartime ally. The ill-feeling which helped to give rise to the decision was also largely misdirected. The most important and well-founded grievances against the Italians were over their Adriatic claims rather than their claims in Asia Minor, which were, after all, based on one if not two treaties. As one authority, Helmreich, has recently concluded: 'On balance, it would seem that in order to prevent one outcome, the powers sanctioned another that was equally unjustified'.[38]

Two caveats must be made. First of all, however foolish the decision to land the Greeks at Smyrna, it need not have been as fateful as it was. It was the failure after the landing to ensure that they acted responsibly that explains much of the ensuing tragedy. Secondly, since the Italians precipitated the whole crisis, they must share the blame. Their post-war claims, taken as a whole, and their conduct at Paris, were clearly unreasonable. They were quite simply trying to grab too much, largely because their politicians had worked up public opinion and then found they were unable to control it. It has recently been argued[39] that given the extent of Rome's appetite, Lloyd George's fears about a major Italian descent upon Turkey were not unreasonable. As Nicolson noted in his diary, Orlando and his delegation had sacrificed the sympathy of the conference 'by incessant ill-temper, untruthfulness, and cheating', while Balfour came to feel that he would not only be unable ever to visit Germany or Austria, but also Italy.[40]

The implementation of the Smyrna decision was as bad as the decision itself. A single shot fired from an unidentified source shortly after the landing on 15 May was all it took for pandemonium to break loose. According to a neutral observer, those Turks who were taken prisoner 'were made to go through no end of humiliation and received a good deal of knocking about'.[41] They suffered losses of 300 to 400 the first day thanks to Greek indiscipline and, as Llewellyn Smith indicates, to allied hypocrisy. If they had really sent the Greeks in to prevent massacres, they should not have given them a free hand. The British and American authorities on the spot blamed the Greeks for the chaos, and accurately forecast that if they were allowed to settle in the Turks would revolt and peace would be impossible.

Important developments were meanwhile taking place in Paris. On 17 May representations were made before the Four on behalf of Mohammedan opinion by the Secretary of State for India, Sir Edwin Montagu, and an Indian delegation, headed by the Aga Khan. They wanted the retention of an independent Turkey which would include all of Anatolia, Thrace and Constantinople, where the Sultan would remain as Caliph. They based their case on the principle of nationality, the Fourteen Points, and Lloyd George's wartime promises, and pointed to the substantial role that India had played in defeating Turkey. The delegates warned that the existing unrest amongst the 70,000,000 Indian Mohammedans was partly the result of fears that the only Mohammedan great power was going to be partitioned. The unrest would increase if Turkey was dealt with more harshly than the other wartime enemies. Why, it was asked, should there be talk of depriving the Turks of their capital when the Germans, the war's greatest offenders, were to retain Berlin?[42]

Montagu was to play a prominent role in the Turkish settlement. He was concerned about Turkey because the

Government of India repeatedly reported to him that anxiety about its future was the primary cause of Mohammedan unrest. By vigorously supporting a pro-Turk peace, which could be done at no cost to India, Montagu hoped to reduce the discontent and smooth the way for the reforms he wanted to implement. While the Secretary for India was correct in believing that Mohammedans were genuinely concerned about Turkey's fate, he went beyond merely representing the Government of India's views, and overestimated Mohammedans' real devotion to the Caliphate.[43] When Kemal's nationalist movement abolished the Caliphate in 1924, there was little protest from the subcontinent.

A provisional allocation of mandates had emerged by mid-May: the Americans would get Constantinople and Armenia, the Greeks Smyrna, and Anatolia would be divided in two, with France in all likelihood in the north and Italy in the south. No sooner, however, had the Indian delegation withdrawn than Lloyd George announced that he was 'much impressed' and favoured the retention of the Caliphate in Constantinople. He was now to reverse himself completely and oppose the partition of any of Anatolia apart from Smyrna. He does seem to have been genuinely moved by warnings of further trouble in the East, so that:'The more he thought the matter over, the less was he, as head of the Power which had done nine-tenths of the fighting against Turkey, willing to agree to the partition of Asia Minor'.[44] He also seems to have been influenced by a 'powerful' memorandum by Balfour, protesting the mandates schemes on the grounds that the Anatolian Turks had the right to remain united as a single people under one sovereign.[45] This view was reinforced when a majority of the cabinet at a meeting in Paris in the wake of the Smyrna landing argued against any further diminution of the area to be left under Turkish control. Hence the Prime Minister was merely reflecting the current of British opinion when he came to argue that 'the Allies had no more right to split up Turkey than Germany, in former days, had had to split up Poland'.[46] Lastly, the ever-troublesome Italians provided a reason for opposing the dismemberment of Anatolia by landing more troops on the coast.

The last substantial schemes were presented in late May. Nothing definite was decided upon, though the President came to agree with Lloyd George that partition was undesirable. A month later, just before Wilson and the British premier were to return home, the latter suggested they try 'to agree on some Peace Terms which would put Turkey out of her misery'.[47] However, the single decision reached was to delay the final settlement until the United States government could say if it would accept any mandates. Thus by the end of June a treaty with Turkey was little closer to fruition than it had been in January, while the problems to be surmounted were more numerous and intractable.

The Problem of the Greeks and Italians in Anatolia, June-December 1919

The primary concern of Britain's policy-makers between June and December 1919, when high level allied conversations on the future of Turkey were resumed, was to control the Greek and Italian forces in Asia Minor. Curzon and the Foreign Office—with the exception of the staunchly pro-Greek Crowe —fully appreciated the mess that the Allies were getting themselves into. The Greeks had advanced beyond the limit which the Four had set for them, and were encountering fierce resistance from the Turks. The Italians were also carrying out unauthorized advances in Anatolia. The men on the spot could not have been clearer to London about the unfortunate consequences of the presence of these forces, especially the Greek. Graeco-Turkish friction 'has now become most serious', wrote Admiral Webb from Constantinople, 'and of course it all dates back to the time of the occupation of Smyrna by the Greek troops'. Similarly, Admiral de Robeck claimed that 'the Greek occupation of Smyrna has stimulated a Turkish patriotism probably more real than any which the war was able to evoke'.[48] In despatch after despatch these men urged the rapid conclusion of a peace treaty and the limitation of, and then total withdrawal of, all Greek and Italian forces.

The Supreme Council feared that the advancing Greek and Italian troops would meet and clash. That possibility was lessened when Venizelos and Tittoni, the Italian Foreign Minister since 19 June, came to two agreements in July, one on respective zones of influence in Anatolia and the other involving support for each other's aspirations.[49] Further progress was made in early October, when the Supreme Council considered a report[50] prepared by General Milne, the allied Commander-in-Chief in Asiatic Turkey. The report certainly highlighted the problems the Greeks were creating, with the result that they were told to remain where they were, a requirement which left them, particularly in the vulnerable Aidin area, 'on a maddeningly tight leash'.[51]

While Milne's censure of the Greeks was not explicit, that of the allied commissioners, whose report came before the Supreme Council in November, most emphatically was. This document firmly maintained that the landing was totally unjustified in the first place:

> The internal situation in the Vilayet did not call for the landing of Allied troops at Smyrna. On the contrary, since the Greek landing, the situation is troubled because of the state of war existing between the Greek troops and the Turkish irregulars.

The Greeks were blamed for misdeeds at Smyrna and in the interior; indeed: 'Their occupation, far from presenting itself as the carrying out of a civilizing mission, at once took the form of a conquest and crusade'. The occupation had turned into an annexation, despite the fact that apart from the cities of Smyrna and Aivali the Turks were incontestably in a majority. The latter would never accept annexation except under duress, and the Greeks by themselves lacked the resources to enforce it. The commissioners thus proposed to replace the Greek troops by a much smaller number of allied troops.[52]

Reactions to this cogent document were illuminating. Crowe went so far as to state that: 'He felt that the Greeks had done their best and that on the whole they had succeeded rather well'.[53] His attitude is particularly remarkable given that Polk, the American representative, was impressed by the report, as was Clemenceau; the French, in fact, came to the conclusion that the allied support of the Greeks was a mistake. Even Venizelos, although claiming in reply to a pointed question from Clemenceau that: 'He felt assured that if the Conference should charge Greece with the task of defeating Turkey she would be able to do so',[54] realized the precariousness of the Greek foothold in Asia Minor. This is evident from an extraordinary conversation which he had in late October with Henry Wilson. 'I told him straight out,' records Wilson,

> that he had ruined his country and himself by going to Smyrna; and the poor man agreed, but said the reason was because Paris had not finished off the Turk and had made peace with him . . . He realizes that he is in a hopeless position, and is now trying to sell his 12 divisions. He begged me to tell Lloyd George that both he and Greece were *done*. I said I would. The old boy is *done*.[55]

However, since Venizelos's position at home required success in Turkey and a Greater Greece — with Greece as a significant Mediterranean power — there was no question of turning back.

The upshot of the commissioners' report was that, on Clemenceau's initiative, Venizelos was sent a letter supporting the report's indictment, and reminding him that the occupation was provisional.[56] In a biting reply Venizelos laid bare the hypocrisy and naïvety of the latter stipulation. He pointed out that the Allies could not but know how the Greeks would and did interpret the decision to land their troops at Smyrna. Their claims had been officially presented at the Peace Conference and approved by the Greek Committee, and so it was hardly surprising that they felt that they were at least morally, if not yet legally, entitled to Smyrna.[57] Sending a scolding letter to Venizelos was not going to change anything. In view of the report's criticisms and recommendations, the Allies may well have missed the one chance since 15 May to get the Greeks out without losing too much face. The opportunity was lost and the report was not even published.

In the final analysis, therefore, Britain, despite all the indications that other powers were questioning Venizelos's mission, resolutely stood by Greece. Britain had managed to become everyone's whipping boy. The Turks blamed her because they saw her, quite correctly, as the main protagonist of Greece, the Italians blamed her for not supporting what they viewed as their just claims to Turkey, and even the Greeks blamed her for not allowing them a free hand to finish off the Turks.

The rise of Mustapha Kemal

Meanwhile, the Sultan's government at Constantinople was rapidly losing control of the country to the Nationalists in the interior of Asia Minor. Their growing strength resulted from the Turks' conviction that the armistice terms had been violated by the Allies and exploited against them, and by fears that Anatolia was going to be dismembered and put under foreign control, with Armenia as a separate state. The Turks, moreover, were angry at the Allies' March demand for the handing over of 'war criminals', and the subsequent arrests, some of them questionable, and imprisonments on Malta. Above all, of course, the nationalist movement arose because of the Smyrna decision. As a result of that, Bernard Lewis writes, 'The Turks were ready to rise against the invader—only the leader was awaited'.[58] That leader was Mustapha Kemal, the 'Cromwell of the Near East', to whom the occupation of Smyrna was a piece of unexpected good fortune.

Kemal has been lauded by one of the most prominent authorities on modern Turkey as 'the brilliant and inspired leader who snatched the Sick Man of Europe from his deathbed and infused him with a new life and vitality', and by another as the man who 'transported his country from the Middle Ages to the threshold of the modern era and a stage beyond'.[59] In 1919 he was a 38-year-old general with 14 years hard experience in the field behind him. He was the hero of Gallipoli and the most successful Turkish commander of the war, with the added advantage that he had quarrelled with the wartime ruling faction, the Committee of Union and Progress, and thus was not associated with its mistakes. Kemal was a realistic, strong-willed, ambitious patriot who possessed great military and political skills. It is unlikely that any of his contemporaries could have matched his accomplishment.

It is one of the ironies of modern history that it was this man that the Grand Vizier chose to send to Samsun on the Black Sea to put an end to Nationalist activity. Kemal landed there a mere four days after the first Greeks disembarked at Smyrna, and immediately began to organize a resistance movement. He was dismissed by the Constantinople government in July, and at congresses at Erzerum and Sivas laid the basis for a cohesive Nationalist movement in Anatolia which maintained uneasy and, after a break in September, unofficial relations with the Sultan. The movement's unalterable minimum demands were enshrined in a 'National Pact'. What the Nationalists sought was a completely sovereign and independent nation-state based on those areas 'which are inhabited by an Ottoman Muslim majority, united in religion, in race, and in aim . . .'[60] This was a realistic goal which did not go beyond Lloyd George's promises of January 1918 or the Fourteen Points. Kemal realized the dangers of Pan-Islamic and Pan-Turanian movements, and, unlike most dictators, wisely refused to expand his limited programme when it met with success.

Nationalist foreign policy was shrewd and successful. Kemal exploited the divisions between the wartime Allies. He took advantage of Russia's isolation and the west's fear of her to achieve some measure of Turkish-Russian cooperation, though he was fully aware of the dangers of too great a reliance upon Moscow or anyone else.

The Allies were aware of Kemal's programme from the beginning, largely because he himself fully publicized it. Given the formidable obstacles which he had to surmount, it is not surprising that his movement was at first underestimated. It was also misinterpreted. Curzon and Montagu failed to understand the western, secular orientation of Turkish nationalism, which meant that their assumption that it was akin to Indian Muslim sentiment was incorrect. The British and French High Commissioners in Constantinople—not to mention Venizelos—inaccurately associated it with the Committee of Union and Progress. Despite these misjudgements, from the summer of 1919 onwards London and Paris were fully warned of the danger posed by the Nationalists. However, they did little more than verbally support the increasingly feeble Constantinople government, which by the autumn had lost effective control of Anatolia. There was really very little the Allies could do to curb Mustapha Kemal's activities, short of withdrawing all foreign troops from Anatolia, since allowing the Sultan to send a force against him would probably have resulted in its joining him or in full-scale civil war.

The French and Italians proved willing to come to terms with Kemal. France's desire to gain the Nationalists' favour was a by-product of the close relationship between Britain and the Constantinople government. It was also a result of their vulnerability in Cilicia, which they occupied in November after the British evacuation.[61] The Kemalists were on good terms with the Italians, although they realized that the latter's sympathy for their movement was a product of anger at their wartime allies, failure to achieve their aims in Turkey and desire for economic concessions in Anatolia.

Anglo-French conversations on the future of Turkey, December 1919

'We have all been running on the assumption', Philip Kerr wrote to Lloyd George on 15 November, 'that the great powers, including America, were going to stand together and more or less run world affairs'.[62] By this date it was clear that this assumption was mistaken. President Wilson had been incapacitated in October by a near fatal stroke and the Senate was on the point of rejecting the Treaty of Versailles and withdrawing the United States into isolation. The French thus proposed, and the British accepted, that as the only two serious remaining parties they should commence conversations on the Eastern settlement.

In the conversations of December it was decided, on Clemenceau's initiative, that the system of mandates for Anatolia should be abandoned.[63] The Turks would have nominal sovereignty over the whole of Asia Minor, while the Greeks would be placated by virtual autonomy in Smyrna and generous compensation in Thrace, the Italians by economic concessions, and the French by rights in Cilicia.

The other main question considered, now that an American mandate appeared out of the question, was the fate of Constantinople.[64] The Prime Minister and Curzon achieved one of their major aims by gaining Clemenceau's assent to the expulsion of the Turk from Europe and the internationalization of Constantinople and the Straits. The French had wanted the Sultan to remain in Constantinople but acquiesced in his removal because they needed British support against Germany, particularly since the Treaty of Guarantee had collapsed with America's withdrawal.

The Constantinople issue pitted two formidable though often myopic ministers, Montagu and Curzon, against one another. Montagu warned the cabinet that if the Turks were expelled from Constantinople, they would join with the Bolsheviks and initiate a 'Turkey irredenta' movement, which could only be subdued by hundreds of thousands of troops, none of which could be Indian. Given these views, it is not surprising that he termed the Anglo-French agreement 'disastrous and incredible'[65] and threatened to resign. For Curzon, on the other hand, it was a commonplace that the Turk had long 'been a blight and a curse to the countries

which he has misgoverned, and I know of no single good
thing that the Turk has done to a single nation or community
or interest in Europe'. There was now the opportunity presented
by the defeat of the power

> whose entrance into the war prolonged it for at least two
> years and cost us millions of treasure and tens of thousands
> of lives, to settle once and for all a question which more than
> any single cause has corrupted the political life of Europe
> for nearly 500 years.

Ignoring the antagonism between the Sultan and Kemal, Curzon
further maintained that the retention of the Turks and their
Sultan in the capital would give the Nationalists prestige and
impetus. Lastly, he feared that unless put under international
supervision, Constantinople would again become 'the prey of
rival ambitions and the cockpit of future struggles', with the
possibility of France 'assuming the role of champion of the
new Islam . . .'[66]

When the combatants faced one another at a special meeting
of ministers on 5 January 1920, Britain and France agreed
upon a plan similar to the one which Curzon had urged upon
the cabinet a year earlier.[67] Despite this agreement and the
fact that the Foreign Secretary was supported both by his
predecessor Balfour and the Prime Minister on the expulsion
of the Turks from Europe, it was Montagu, powerfully aided
by Churchill and Henry Wilson, who carried the day. British
policy was thus dramatically—and permanently—reversed.
Montagu and his supporters asserted that secret information
revealed that expulsion would produce a movement in India,
similar to Sinn Fein, favouring total separation from England.
The French would exploit the fact that the stigma for such a
decision would fall to Britain, and set themselves up as the
protector of Mohammedan interests. They also argued that
the proposed step would increase the danger of cooperation
between the Bolsheviks and the Nationalists, a particularly
bleak prospect since Britain had no forces with which to oppose

the great strides the former were making throughout the East; in fact, 'our troops were at their lowest ebb and we shortly should not have a single friend from Constantinople to China'. The Sultan could most easily be controlled if he was left where he was.

A sizeable majority of the cabinet was thus persuaded that the Turks should remain in Constantinople, with the Straits controlled by an international force. As was accurately prophesied: 'We had destroyed Austria which would cause endless trouble, and it was disastrous to destroy Turkey also'.[68] Although Constantinople was soon to lose its status as the capital, and the Sultanate and Caliphate were abolished, it was unlikely by this stage that there could have been a peaceful settlement if the Turks had lost this predominantly Turkish city which had been their capital for almost five centuries.

During these months, Britain's policy-makers could agree on very little. Lloyd George and Curzon saw eye to eye on Turkey in Europe but diverged sharply on Smyrna; Montagu took the opposite approach to Turkey in Europe, but shared Curzon's doubts about support for the Greeks in Anatolia. The importance of these divisions is shown by the reversal over Constantinople, which was primarily the work of the man who was supposed to be determining Indian, not Turkish, policy.

The Treaty of Sèvres, 10 August 1920

The Treaty of Sèvres[69] was largely drafted at the Conference of London, held from 12 February to 10 April 1920. It was dominated by Lloyd George who, along with his forceful personality and great debating skills, was aided by his position as chairman and the inexperience of the French and Italian premiers, Millerand and Nitti. The subsequent conference at San Remo finalized what had been agreed upon in London.

The terms were severe indeed. Strict limitations were placed on the armed services of Turkey, which was allowed a force of 50,000, including the gendarmerie. Although the Turks would be left Constantinople, an international commission would have complete control of the zone of the Straits, which were to remain open to all ships in peacetime and wartime. The provisions ensured that the Straits were controlled by the Allies, or rather by Britain, since she was the greatest maritime power.[70]

There were many sharp Anglo-French clashes over the financial clauses, since the British feared that international financial control would allow France to run Turkey's affairs. Finally the Allies agreed that a three-power Financial Commission should exercise tight control over Turkey's revenues and expenditures. Although there were to be no reparations as such, the French, pressured by their bondholders, ensured that funds were available for the Ottoman Debt, while the British made certain that Turkey would pay all occupation costs. Although it was intended eventually to abandon the capitulations, the long-standing system of economic and judicial privileges for foreigners that Kemal had sworn to abolish, they were continued for the moment.

The question of spheres of influence also proved difficult, given the problem of reconciling French and Italian demands with the need to avoid the appearance of partition, which would upset America and run counter to the League Covenant. Curzon found the solution. Indirect control could be exercised through a 'self-denying ordinance', whereby the Allies agreed to mutual support and non-interference in one another's spheres. In the resultant Tripartite Pact[71] France was given priority in Cilicia, and Italy in Adalia. The British, who already had more than enough responsibilities, did not want and were not given a zone.

Lloyd George's unwavering support for Venizelos ensured very favourable settlements for Greece in Smyrna and Thrace. The Welshman argued that it would be valuable in case of trouble to have 'a bridge-head at Smyrna in the hands of a Power which had the same interests as the *Entente* Powers', a view which ignored the possibility that the bridge-head itself might be the cause of trouble[72]. He successfully overcame all opposition and secured an agreement which was beyond what either the British or French Foreign Offices had envisaged in December. The Greeks would garrison and administer Smyrna, which could eventually apply to the League for incorporation into Greece. Turkish sovereignty was a farce: the Turks had the right merely to fly a flag over a single fort. Greece was generously given the whole of Eastern and Western Thrace to the Chatalja line, thanks to Lloyd George's astute bargaining and the fact that American objections were no longer considered important.

Given the Turks' talent for massacring minorities, provisions had to be drawn up in an attempt to prevent future atrocities. The Armenians were in a particularly difficult position. They were widely dispersed and a minority in most areas, so that even before the wartime massacres a state on the basis of self-determination was impossible, and they were separated by national frontiers and particularism.[73] The Republic which they had established in 1918 was soon threatened both by Nationalist and by Bolshevik forces. Both on the popular and official levels allied, and in particular, American, professions of support for Armenia had been endless. Colonel House had even made the extraordinary suggestion that Herbert Hoover would make a suitable governor of Armenia. The Supreme Council, while formally supporting Armenia's independence, was unwilling to provide the requisite financial and military aid. Advised by Marshal Foch, it concluded that while the Allies might arm the Armenians, they were in no position to send troops to defend the fledgling state.[74] In the end they turned to America, which, while refusing to take on any financial or military responsibilities—let alone a mandate—agreed in the person of Wilson to determine the Republic's frontiers. Although the Allies were undoubtedly realistic in their belief that they could not defend Armenia, Lloyd George's claim that 'There was no question of the Allies shirking their burden'[75] rings hollow, given the glaring gap between promises and performance.

These terms were arrived at in the face of innumerable

warnings of their consequences, warnings which turned out to be all too accurate. Perhaps the most incisive critique of the envisaged peace was written by de Robeck in a letter of 9 March to Curzon, who circulated it to the cabinet. The proposed terms, he maintained,

> are such that no Turk, Committee of Union and Progress or pro-*Entente* can very well accept. The Supreme Council, thus, are prepared for a resumption of general warfare; they are prepared to do violence to their own declared and cherished principles [of self-determination]; they are prepared to perpetuate bloodshed indefinitely in the Near East; and for what? To maintain M. Veniselos in power in Greece for what cannot in the nature of things be more than a few years at the outside. I cannot help wondering if the game is worth the candle.[76]

Curzon did not need convincing. As he gloomily informed the Prime Minister's secretary, he doubted if Lloyd George was

> aware of the tremendous part in the impending chaos that is going to be played by leaving the Greeks in Smyrna as well as Thrace. Venizelos thinks his men will sweep the Turks into the mountains. I doubt if it will be so.
> I believe that we shall be at war in Asia Minor in a few weeks or months time, almost entirely because of our Smyrna decision. My views are assuredly not prejudiced (because I am a strong anti-Turk).[77]

The War Office also warned the cabinet that the peace would have dire consequences. The General Staff agreed with the report of the Foch Committee that a minimum of 27 divisions would be required to enforce the peace. Since this figure was well beyond the available allied forces, and since the General Staff believed that a satisfactory settlement could only be reached if Greek ambitions were curbed, they proposed (as de Robeck had done) a complete reconsideration of the peace terms.[78] Despite this array of bleak forecasts and Curzon's direct warning to Lloyd George that: 'We must be on very strong and sure ground if we are to override all this',[79] the prime minister persisted in his policy. Encouraged by Venizelos's confident assurances, he maintained that the Allies' problems were not as insurmountable as Foch indicated, and that Turkey could be strangled if the Allies seized her strategic centres.[80]

A step in this direction had already been taken with the Allied occupation of Constantinople. In late February the Supreme Council became greatly agitated over reports that the local populace in Cilicia, aided by the Nationalists, were successfully revolting against the French and massacring Armenians. As well as this, the Allies were becoming increasingly aggrieved with the Turks' continued failure to disarm, and their election of a Nationalist dominated national assembly in Constantinople which approved the National Pact.

Urged on by Lloyd George, the Supreme Council thus decided, in his words, that: 'The time had now arrived to take strong action and to do something dramatic'.[81] That something was the occupation of Constantinople, upon which the Prime Minister became so intent that he repeatedly emphasized that, if necessary, Britain would act alone. The aim of this action was to assert allied prestige and power, prevent future massacres, punish the Turks, and show them that they could not continue to flout the Allies with impunity. It would also give the powers a lever to force Turkey to accept severe peace terms, since it was clear that these would have to be imposed by force. The seizure of key government locations, the dismissal of the assembly, and the arrest of suspected Nationalists was initiated on 16 March, and was reported to be successful.

The occupation was ill-considered. It was taken in preference to a much more sensible policy suggested by de Robeck[82] and the allied high commissioners in Constantinople. De Robeck believed that Britain could gain the support of the Sultan and other anti-Nationalists for the peace terms if these terms were more lenient—and, in particular, if the Turks were allowed to remain in Smyrna, Eastern Thrace and much of Asia Minor. This was ruled out, however, since it was completely contrary to the peace envisaged by the Supreme Council.

The occupation was the upshot of the Allies' misplaced belief, despite all the warnings, that they could readily mobilize enough men to defeat the Turks if it came to a showdown. Using Venizelos' inflated estimates of Greek troops in Asia Minor, Lloyd George calculated that the Allies could field 160,000 men against an estimated 80,000 Turks, and he commented acidly that

> if two soldiers—French, British, Italian or Greek—could not defeat one Turk, the Allies ought to start their conference anew and ask the Turk upon what terms he would condescend to make peace.[83]

He subsequently claimed that: 'No one believed that Mustafa Kemal would be able to drive the Greeks out of Asia Minor'.[84] Both this easy confidence and the cavalier fashion in which Lloyd George seemed to contemplate hostilities can be and was criticized.

The occupation was predicated on the assumption that the Constantinople government had control over Kemal and Anatolia, so that action taken in the capital would affect events in the interior. However, as Cambon, Berthelot, Nitti and Churchill warned, Kemal acted completely independently. Far from the occupation resulting in a strengthening of the Sultan, as had naïvely been hoped, it weakened his already shaky authority. There was a complete break between Constantinople and Kemal, who had been made all the more defiant by the occupation, and whose ranks were swollen by further defections from the Sultan's forces.

The treaty was completed by the end of April, although the Turks managed to delay signing it until August. Whatever illusions the Supreme Council had about its enforceability, they had no illusions about its stringency. Lloyd George himself said—approvingly—that the terms were 'very severe, and certainly not of a character to placate the enemy'. What little would be left to the Turks would be placed 'under control and practically in fetters'.[85]

The existence of so many sceptics and critics in the British camp does not alter the fact that the treaty was a triumph for Britain, 'a tribute to their negotiating ability if not their foresight'.[86] The British fully achieved their major desiderata: the opening of the Straits, a handsome settlement for their ally Greece, and the containment of French and Italian ambitions in the Near East.[87]

The treaty can only be understood in the light of the miscalculations discussed above. That the settlement bears the unmistakable imprint of Lloyd George's support for the Greeks and his hatred of the Turks can be explained by his domination of both his allies and his colleagues, and his contempt for and dismissal of 'expert' advice and warnings, whether from the Foreign Office or the military. Venizelos was as always a potent influence upon him,[88] and seems to have been at his side supplying information and reinforcing his biases whenever important decisions were to be made. Sèvres also reflected the ambitions of the Greeks, French and Italians. The French, not without misgivings, fell into line with this largely British package because it gave them a sphere of influence and the possibility of further control over Turkey's affairs, and because they needed Britain's support on the Rhine. The Italians were even more discontented with the treaty: they got less than they thought they deserved and had doubts about its durability. Their views, however, counted for little in the eyes of the British and French, who had long since decided that they alone should decide the main lines of the settlement. As for the Americans, they had cut themselves off and were alternately ignored and abused by the Supreme Council.

The Treaty of Sèvres was an attempt to resolve the Eastern Question along what were in effect nineteenth-century imperialist lines. It aimed at gratifying the victors and fulfilling their demands. It was negotiated on the basis of power politics and completely ignored the Allies' professed principle of self-determination. When allied interests were not directly involved, as in the case of Armenia, promises meant nothing, lending weight to charges of Allied hypocrisy. That the French and Italians had doubts about Sèvres and later came to terms with Kemal does not remove the fact that in Turkish eyes they were as imperialist as the British and Greeks.

Sèvres was bound to fail. The peacemakers did not come to terms with the rapidly changing circumstances of 1919-1920 — perhaps a forlorn task — or with the forces of nationalism. The treaty could not last because it was contingent upon too many elusive variables: future allied cooperation, the dominance of Lloyd George and Venizelos and the continuation of their successful collaboration, and the military strength of Greece, basically a poor country with limited resources.

Some critics of the Treaty of Versailles maintain that it would probably have been a better treaty had it been completed less hastily, and not so soon after the end of hostilities when the passions of war were still so immediate. A study of the Treaty of Sèvres leaves this thesis open to question. The Turkish settlement was arrived at over many months and not signed until almost two years after the armistice, yet it was no less vindictive than Versailles and was probably more out of tune with reality than if it had been completed earlier. The statesmen's insistence upon a pound of flesh changed much less rapidly than did circumstances. As T.E.Lawrence remarked,

> the document is not the constitution of a new Asia, but a confession, almost an advertisement, of the greeds of the conquerors. No single clause of it will stand the test of three years' practice and it will be happier than the German Treaty only in that it will not be revised — it will be forgotten.[89]

The Greek advance and the fall of Venizelos, June-December 1920

In mid-June 1920 the Nationalists, unwilling to accept either the presence of foreign troops on Turkish soil or the peace terms, attacked British troops in the Ismid peninsula, thereby threatening the Straits. When Milne requested reinforcements, Henry Wilson asked the cabinet to send Greek troops, since they were the only ones available, although he believed 'that all this means war with Turkey and Russia, and will end in our being kicked out of Constantinople'.[90] At the cabinet's behest Venizelos agreed to send a division to serve under Milne, on the understanding that he could carry out a limited advance from Smyrna. This turn of events of course pleased both Lloyd George, who gained the assent of Millerand and a reluctant Sforza to the operations, and Venizelos, who seemed (as in May 1919) to be presented by the Allies with a golden opportunity. Venizelos wanted war. He correctly realized that the only way to make the Sèvres terms a reality, and to make still further gains at Turkey's expense, was to crush the Nationalists. It appeared that this aim might now be accomplished under ideal circumstances, with Greece acting as 'mandatory' for the allies.[91]

Greek operations were so successful that Lloyd George announced triumphantly on 21 July that 'Turkey is no more', praising the Greeks—ironically in view of later events—for their ability to estimate accurately their strength and resources.[92] The problem was that the Turks were not crushed. Moreover, the operations had confirmed Lloyd George's dangerous faith in Venizelos and his disdain for his military advisers, who had not anticipated the Greeks' success.

In the autumn of 1920 the situation changed dramatically as a result of the re-emergence of the ever-divisive problem of the Greek monarchy. In October King Alexander died of a pet monkey's bite and did not leave an heir. Venizelos then foolishly decided to base the forthcoming elections on the issue of the return of the exiled Constantine. To the surprise of virtually all observers, the Prime Minister was overwhelmingly defeated.

This event broke the tenuous bonds holding the Allies together. The French hated Constantine and felt that if he returned to the Greek throne they would no longer owe anything to Greece, and could use the opportunity to pursue a pro-Nationalist policy. Such a policy would involve revising Sèvres. The Italians felt similarly liberated. While many British policy-makers agreed that revision was now essential, Lloyd George and Curzon insisted that the treaty so laboriously drawn up must still be enforced. The Prime Minister continued to see Kemal as a 'mutinous General' and argued that Greece was of vital importance to Britain and could not be betrayed simply because His Majesty's Government disapproved of the electors' choice.[93] Even Lloyd George and Curzon, however, agreed to declarations by the Allies that should the 'disloyal' Constantine be restored, they reserved complete liberty to deal with the new and unfavourable situation, and would withdraw all financial support from Greece.[94]

Constantine returned to Athens in triumph on 19 December after a referendum had decisively confirmed the desire for his restoration. The legacy of the crisis was, as one Foreign Office clerk minuted, that 'It is undeniable that Allied solidarity in the East no longer exists'.[95] Moreover, the new Greek govern-ment, which was unwisely very strongly in favour of a forward policy in Asia Minor, was now to be denied the moral and financial support from the Allies essential to make such a policy—and the still official allied policy of enforcing Sèvres—successful.

The London Conference and its failure, February-March 1921.

By early 1921 the forces favouring revision seemed too great to be denied. The Allies had not even recognized the new Greek monarch and the Sultan had managed to avoid ratifying Sèvres. Kemal alone, the *de facto* ruler of the Turks in Anatolia, appeared to be making progress. His movement had grown further thanks to the draconian treaty, and he was heartened by the fall of Venizelos and the ever-increasing signs of allied disunity. His forces were successful against the Armenians in December and repelled a Greek attack towards Eski Shehir in January. Particularly worrisome to the western powers was his continuing courtship of the Bolsheviks, which was soon to bear fruit with a treaty of alliance.[96]

By February virtually all British policy-makers, forcing a reluctant Prime Minister and an uncompromising Balfour into line, were in agreement with the French and Italians that concessions to the Turks were essential.[97] With the transfer of Churchill to the Colonial Office, that department joined the War Office, India Office and Foreign Office in urging a new settlement. 'I have yet to meet a British official personage', Churchill assured Lloyd George on 22 February, 'who does not think that Eastern and Middle Eastern affairs would be enormously eased and helped by arriving at a peace with Turkey', adding that he was grieved 'at finding myself so utterly without power to influence your mind even in regard to matters with which my duties are specially concerned'.[98] The War Office, as always, was keen

to make gracious concessions to the Turks, and so wean them from their alliance with the Russian Bolsheviks, by this means recreating Turkey as a buffer State between the Entente Powers and Russia, and removing some of the principal underlying causes of unrest throughout the British dominions in Egypt, Mesopotamia and India.[99]

Consequently, a conference which included representatives of the Greeks, the Sultan and the Nationalists, was held in London in February and March. More telling than the details of the various schemes put forward, most of which centred around an autonomous Smyrna under Turkish sovereignty and the modification of certain other parts of the treaty in Turkey's favour, were the overall reasons for their failure. First of all, British policy was too pro-Greek, and French and Italian policy too pro-Turk, for the Allies to unite either to conciliate the Turks or to support the Greeks. In any event none of the three was willing to employ sufficient of his own resources to enforce decisions of the conference. Secondly, the Nationalists, encouraged by their recent progress, and

successful during the conference in reaching separate agreements with France and Italy over Asia Minor, were unwilling
to accept the proposals offered since they were far short of
their demands. The Greeks proved even more intransigent.
They wanted to keep virtually all that Sèvres had promised
them and believed that they could enforce the treaty if they
had Britain's diplomatic and, it was hoped, financial support.
They argued that unless the Allies could raise 100,000
men — clearly an impossible figure — they alone could guard
the Straits and vanquish the Kemalists, who, they insisted,
were 'a rabble worthy of little or no consideration',[100] an
assessment shared by Lloyd George but disputed by the French.

The possibility of treaty revision was further diminished by
the fact that Lloyd George certainly did nothing to discourage
Greek ambitions. Though he did not explicitly tell the Greeks
that he supported their desire to resolve matters on the
battlefield — since he did not want to be held responsible for
hostilities — he definitely left them with the impression that
he favoured their planned offensive. The startling revelations
of an intercepted telegram to Athens of 1 March typify his
stance throughout the conference. Referring to a proposal for
an ethnological enquiry for Smyrna and Thrace, Philip Kerr
told a Greek delegation in confidence that

> the Prime Minister thinks that 'The consent of Greece to the
> decision of the Conference was tantamount to signing a
> blank cheque, but before she signed such a cheque she ought
> to know for what sum she was signing.' Kerr added that
> while we ought not to hesitate to refuse, it would be desirable
> if the Turks should be the first to decline to submit to the
> decision of the Conference.[101]

Kerr said he was convinced that the proposed Greek military
operations would be a success, and led the delegation to conclude
that 'These operations appeared to be gladly accepted', as was
the Greeks' desire to safeguard the Straits. Moreover, Lloyd
George took pains to emphasize that the powers could not

take the responsibility for preventing the Greeks from taking whatever military actions they saw fit. At the end of the conference he authorized the delegation to contact the Treasury, assuring them 'that Great Britain has consecrated a warm corner in her heart for Greece and proposes to assist her to return to her pristine glory'.[102]

Only in the most legalistic sense could all of this be construed as anything but encouragement to attack the Turks. In Churchill's words, the Greeks believed that though 'nothing definite has been said and no agreement has been made, the great man is with us, and in his own way and in his own time and by his own wizardry he will bring us the vital aid we need'. 'Now this', Churchill continued,

> was the worst of all possible situations. The Greeks deserved at the least either to be backed up through thick and thin with the moral, diplomatic and financial support of a united British Government, or to be chilled to the bone with repeated douches of cold water.[103]

The continuation of the war

The Greeks initiated their second offensive of 1921 on 23 March, a mere five days after the conference had ended, amid the widespread belief inside and outside Britain that it was Lloyd George's support that prompted them to act. The CIGS confided to his diary that the attack was 'entirely uncalled for and wholly unprovoked. And Lloyd George knew this. The whole thing is a ramp, and a disgusting ramp'.[104] At the second battle of Inönü the Greeks suffered their first major setback in Asia Minor. Their position deteriorated further in April when the Allies proclaimed a policy of neutrality,[105] which hurt them much more than the Kemalists, who continued to receive arms from the French and Italians.

On 31 May Harington warned the Cabinet that the Greeks might collapse and thereby expose the weak allied forces at Constantinople to the Nationalists.[106] Consequently, he and

Henry Wilson advocated the withdrawal of the Allies, to be followed by a policy of 'making love' to Kemal.[107] A cabinet committee decided against this 'humiliating' policy, but did agree to offer both belligerents a modified version of terms which Britain had presented at the London Conference. However the Greeks, still convinced of ultimate victory, refused, though interestingly enough Venizelos, aware of how little Greece could count on support from the powers, urged acceptance.

With the arrival of King Constantine at Smyrna in June, the first Christian monarch to touch the soil of Asia Minor since the Crusades, the Greeks were about to embark upon their greatest campaign since antiquity. Prime Minister Gounaris, revealing the inflexibility and foolishness of his government, insisted after the March offensive that:

We cannot change policy, we are obliged to continue the war until the end, even if we risk catastrophe. Otherwise the English will cease to regard us as a serious Nation, if we do not fulfil what we promise, and will abandon us and support Turkey. We must prove that we are a Nation on which a Great Power can depend.[108]

Lloyd George's spirits soared after the Greek capture of Eski Shehir on 19 July. He sent a blistering and sarcastic epistle to his hapless War Secretary, complaining that the General Staff's information (as always in his view) 'turned out to be hopelessly wrong when the facts were investigated at the instance of the despised politicians'. 'Have you no Department', he enquired caustically,

which is known as the 'Intelligence Department' in your Office? You might find out what it is doing. It appears in the Estimates at quite a substantial figure, but when it comes to information it is not visible. Please look into this yourself.[109]

The time for mediation, the Prime Minister announced confidently in the Commons, had not yet arrived.[110]

Kemal ordered the unpopular policy of a general retreat, thereby drawing the Greeks still further away from their bases. He then dug his troops in in good defensive positions beyond the Sakarya River, a mere 50 miles from Angora. The clash which began on 23 August raged for 22 days and nights, which Kemal claimed made it the longest pitched battle in history. Though both sides exhausted themselves, the Kemalists staged a counter-offensive on 8 September and the Greeks, who had sustained 18,000 casualties, were forced to retire.

This was the turning point of the entire war in Asia Minor. The Greeks, unable to crush the Nationalists' army or take their capital, had lost any chance of imposing a settlement by force of arms. As Churchill phrased it, 'the Greeks had involved themselves in a politico-strategic situation where anything short of decisive victory was defeat: and the Turks were in a position where anything short of overwhelming defeat was victory'.[111] Although Lloyd George was reported to be still 'hotheaded for the Greeks, in victory or defeat',[112] he now had little choice but to follow Curzon's advice and place their interests in allied hands

Anglo-French acrimony and the postponement of allied mediation, October 1921-January 1922

The prospects of successful allied mediation, however, were diminished, and allied conversations long delayed, by the deterioration of Anglo-French relations, which were damaged in the autumn of 1921 by French dealings with Kemal. Angora had rejected the Briand-Bekir Sami agreement reached at the London Conference, because it was contrary to the National Pact. Hence the French, desperate to extricate their 80,000 men from Cilicia, who were costing 500 million francs a year, authorized Franklin-Bouillon, a Turkophil French politician whom the British dubbed 'Boiling Frankie', to negotiate a new settlement. The consequent Angora agreement of 20 October[113] brought an end to the state of war between the two signatories, allowed the French to withdraw unmolested from Cilicia, and provided for economic concessions to France. The accord, although mutually advantageous, was above all a triumph for the Nationalists. They had in effect concluded a separate peace with one of the Allies, who recognized their National Assembly as the government of Turkey. They were now able to increase the forces they could deploy against the Greeks and, furthermore, siezed military supplies which the French had left behind. The agreement heightened the Greeks' diplomatic isolation and made the disunity of the allied camp glaringly apparent.

The outrage of the British when the full scope of the agreement became known knew no bounds. Curzon was livid. The accord made a mockery of previous French promises that they would not conclude a separate settlement. 'The atmosphere is getting decidedly heated', he scribbled, bristling with indignation, to Hardinge,

> tho' certainly owing to no fault or action of ours. We seem to be reverting to the old traditional divergence—amounting almost to antipathy—between France and ourselves, fomented by every device that an unscrupulous Govt and a lying Press can suggest.

After remarking that the French had exploded 'this dirty rocket' simply to score points for themselves, he concluded—with rumblings of retribution alongside his usual sense of injured innocence—that 'I will not say that two can play at this sort of game but there are a good many ways in which I can make our loyalty to them hitherto unqualified a little less uniform in the future'.[114] In the end, however, his realization that the Entente, however imperfect, had to be preserved, ensured that protests would be restricted to words.

The allied mediation that Curzon had tried to effect since June 1921 was further delayed when the generally well-liked Briand fell from power on 15 January 1922 and was replaced by the inflexible and punctilious Poincaré, the French politician the British most loved to hate.[115] The new premier told the British Foreign Secretary during their first encounter that he insisted upon clearing the ground through (an undoubtedly time-consuming) exchange of notes before attending any conference. Obviously thinking of Lloyd George's penchant for conferences, at which the Welshman excelled and where he seemed to get the better of his French colleagues, Poincaré declared that 'Public opinion in France was at present strongly opposed to conferences'. He also blankly stated that Curzon's peace proposals were unlikely to be accepted by the Turks, whom the French would refuse to coerce, and that: 'There was no sympathy anywhere in France for Greece'.[116] Hardinge, who was in attendance, was sufficiently struck by their mutual antagonism that he looked forward to their next encounter with perverse relish. 'It will be interesting', he confided to Gertrude Bell in Baghdad, 'to see how two men of somewhat disagreeable natures such as Curzon and Poincaré get on together in their negotiations'.[117]

The desperate position of the Greeks, and the final attempt at allied mediation

Greek fortunes had plummetted by early 1922. In January Lloyd George and Curzon told Gounaris bluntly at Cannes that Greek forces would have to be withdrawn from Smyrna and the frontier in Thrace altered in Turkey's favour. The Prime Minister added that Britain had made the conclusion of a treaty of guarantee to France, then under consideration, conditional upon a resolution of the Eastern Question and that 'there was nothing better in sight for Greece unless she were prepared to continue the war to a successful decision'.[118] This newly found British firmness, really not more than a facing of facts, was far from being the Greeks' only worry. Their financial position and army morale had grown progressively worse thanks to the endless delays in revising Sèvres.

Gounaris revealed the extent of Greece's difficulties in a letter of 15 February to Curzon, in which he outlined the problems of the troops in Anatolia and the 'complete financial *impasse'* in which Athens found herself. Although the British government had agreed in December to allow the Greeks to raise a loan on the London market, they had been unable to do so. Gounaris concluded that since the army would be exposed to grave dangers unless it received money and supplies, Greece would have to order an immediate and complete withdrawal.[119]

Curzon replied that he hoped the situation was not as critical as Gounaris indicated, 'and that the remarkable patriotism and discipline of the Hellenic Armies. . . will not fail them in any emergency that may conceivably arise'. The wisest course was to come to a diplomatic settlement as expeditiously as possible. The Greek government, having placed itself in allied hands, should listen to whatever counsels the powers offered.[120] The Foreign Secretary thus held out no promise of assistance but expressed his faith in the Greeks' ability to remain until a diplomatic solution could be achieved.

The question of withdrawal was ultimately a question that the Greeks had to decide for themselves, and hence they must bear the responsibility for their decision to remain. Nevertheless it appeared that Curzon missed a heaven-sent opportunity to encourage the Greeks to clear out, thereby sparing everyone the subsequent tragedies. He did in fact express the view that he was 'not quite certain that it would not be better to get Greece out of Asia Minor before she is beaten and before she gets a loan (if she does), than for us to incur the odium of the loan and her the ignominy of defeat'.[121] However, when he suggested this to his minister in Athens, Lindley, the latter replied that he was 'inclined to regard Greek talk about immediate evacuation as something of a bluff'.[122] In any case, a precipitate withdrawal was not in Britain's interest. It would give the Nationalists a victory in Anatolia and make them intransigent in Thrace and elsewhere, it would endanger the native Greeks in Asia Minor, and would expose Constantinople, the Straits and Mesopotamia to the Kemalists. What Curzon thus hoped for, as he explained very confidentially to Lindley, was 'to arrange for immediate evacuation of Anatolia by arrangement with Angora', adding that 'M. Gounaris will doubtless so interpret my note. . . '.[123]

The British, French and Italian Foreign Ministers finally met in Paris on 22 March for what proved to be the last concerted attempt at allied mediation. They eventually hammered out a scheme, which was drafted by Curzon[124] and communicated to the belligerents. It called for an armistice to be followed by various Greek concessions to the Turks, above all the evacuation by the Greeks of Asia Minor, which would be restored to Turkish sovereignty. The Greeks, concerned about the protection of the Greek minority after their troops had withdrawn, accepted the armistice, but were unwilling to accept the other proposals until the Turks had similarly agreed to one. The Nationalists, however, noting that Constantine had responded to the London Conference by ordering an offensive, and to the peace initiative of June 1921 by landing at Smyrna, would only accept a cessation of hostilities if it coincided with evacuation, since they feared that otherwise their adversaries would take advantage of an armistice to resume war. The Allies' refusal to accept this condition, plus the continuation of their disunity, explains the failure of this last attempt, and the ensuing deadlock through the summer of 1922.

Montagu's resignation, March 1922

Meanwhile, a crisis arose within the British government as a result of the activities of Montagu, who had not ceased stressing to his fellow ministers that it was in the Empire's interest to restore friendly relations with Turkey. In a cabinet memorandum of December 1921, the Secretary for India went so far as to claim that because of 'the admitted blunders of our pre-war diplomacy, the Turks were compelled to fight against us', a statement that must have made Lloyd George apoplectic. Similarly, he could hardly have ingratiated himself with Curzon by telling him the following February that he found Poincaré's views on the Near East much closer to his own than Curzon's.[125]

On 4 March Montagu, without consulting the cabinet, granted the Viceroy permission to publish a telegram[126] outlining India's views on the revision of Sèvres. He saw nothing wrong with this procedure because India's dissatisfaction with the treaty was well known. This prompted a stinging letter from ex-Viceroy Curzon[127] deprecating India's interference in matters outside its jurisdiction, a letter that Montagu was tactlessly later to reveal to his Cambridge constituents and characterize as 'one of those plaintive, hectoring, bullying complaining letters which are so familiar to his friends and colleagues'.[128] On the 9th Lloyd George forced Montagu to resign, thereby relieving the Foreign Secretary of what the former referred to as 'Montagu's folly' and 'unwarranted intervention'.[129]

Montagu, whose brilliant career had become bound up with his obsession with Indian Muslim concern about Turkey, believed that he was sacked to appease the coalition's die-hards who disliked his Liberalism. He never recovered from the shock of being forced to resign. He lost his seat in 1922 and died in 1924 at the age of 45. He was of course wrong to publish the telegram and to concern himself to the extent he did with the Turkish question. He was, after all, not the Foreign Secretary. He had had a considerable if resented influence on policy, particularly in May 1919 and January 1920, but he overestimated the importance of Turkey to India, and even fanned the Kilafat movement by paying such an inordinate amount of attention to it.[130]

Lloyd George and the Greeks, January-August 1922

What of the mercurial Welshman during these months? Not only was he surprisingly tough with the Greeks at Cannes, but he also told the Patriarch of Constantinople on 2 February that while 'personally I am a friend of Greece', because of the restoration of the monarchy 'all my colleagues are against me. And I cannot be of any use to you. It is impossible, impossible.' Moreover, when Gounaris wrote to the prime minister on the 27th, reminding him of the appeal he had addressed to Curzon, and asking for an interview, the request was refused.[131]

It soon became clear, however, that Lloyd George was far from renouncing his 'Ionian Vision' and from persuading the Greeks that they must realistically renounce theirs. In fact, he urged Venizelos on 30 May that

> Greece must stick to her policy. He would never shake hands with a Greek again who went back upon his country's aims in Smyrna . . . he felt most strongly that this was the testing time of the Greek nation, and that if they persevered now their future was assured. Great Britain would go back to her original ideas about Asia Minor in due course . . . Greece must go through the wilderness, she must live on manna picked up from the stones, she must struggle through the stern trial of the present time. If she did so, she would win the Promised Land . . . the tide was turning, and the Greeks must keep their hearts up until Constantine disappeared from the scene and opinion throughout the west came round to them as it certainly would do . . . A quick settlement would be a bad settlement for Greece. They must be patient and stick it out.[132]

They were to stick it out, however, without any material assistance from Britain. Apart from the fact that Lloyd George could not have persuaded his government to give aid, his basic policy was to encourage the aspirations of the Greeks without openly committing himself, and thereby running the risk of being held responsible either for continued hostilities or a Greek defeat.

Similar thinking lay behind the premier's famous Commons speech of 4 August.[133] This was a response to Lindley's warnings that the Greeks would collapse unless they received aid,[134] and to the failure of the Greeks' desperate bid, following the transfer of two of their divisions from Anatolia to Thrace, to occupy Constantinople. The Allies warned Athens that they would employ force to oppose any such attempt. It was in this context that Lloyd George delivered an indictment of recent Turkish history and a eulogy of the Greeks. Echoing the Greeks' claims, he complained to Parliament that Britain was being unfair to Greece by protecting Turkey's capital and refusing her normal belligerent rights, such as the right to search ships for arms destined for the Kemalists. Although the latter, who were solely responsible for the failure to reach a settlement, would not accept peace, the Allies were preventing the Greeks from using their full strength to wage the war. This situation, he asserted ominously, could not be allowed to continue indefinitely.

Lindley was probably correct in his belief that the speech was a substitute for assistance, while Curzon dubbed it 'partisan and unwise'.[135] Athens received the speech with rejoicing, erroneously seeing it as the prelude to British permission to occupy Constantinople. In Angora, however, Lloyd George's words and the transfer of the two divisions (not to mention the encouragement of the French and Russian representatives) convinced the Kemalists that they could now hasten the attack they had been planning.

The Chanak crisis, September-October 1922

It was with the words 'Soldiers, your goal is the Mediterranean'[136] that Mustapha Kemal inspired his troops for their offensive of 26 August, which led to a major Greek defeat at Afium Karahissar. The forces that survived the initial surprise and subsequent onslaught fled in terror and disarray to Smyrna and the Sea of Marmara. As the Metropolitan of Smyrna wrote to Venizelos, 'Hellenism in Asia Minor, the Greek state and the entire Greek Nation are descending now to a Hell from which no power will be able to raise them up and save them'.[137] Excesses and atrocities were committed by the Greeks during their retreat, and by the Turks following their entry into Smyrna on 9 September. The razing of all but the Turkish quarter of the city, blithely referred to by Kemal as a 'disagreeable incident',[138] was probably the work of Nationalists while busying themselves massacring Armenians. Rumbold felt that 'there is little to choose between the two races . . . the

Greek retreat, followed by the scenes at Smyrna, form a sickening record of bestiality and barbarity'.[139]

As Winston Churchill has written,

> The catastrophe which Greek recklessness and Allied procrastination, division and intrigue had long prepared now broke upon Europe. The signatories of the Treaty of Sèvres had only been preserved in their world of illusion by the shield of Greece. That shield was now shattered.[140]

The crisis which followed the Greek expulsion from Asia Minor arose because of British fears that the advancing victorious Turks would threaten the Straits and try to cross into Europe to seize Constantinople and Thrace, and fight the Greek forces that had fled there. The cabinet and, in particular, a militant band led by Lloyd George, Churchill and Birkenhead, was concerned about the security of the Straits. The premier referred to the Gallipoli Peninsula as 'the most strategic position in the world', and claimed that 'the closing of the Straits had prolonged the war by two years'.[141] Churchill, who had still not been forgiven for his management of the ill-fated Dardanelles Expedition of 1915, believed seven years later that if the Turks took Constantinople and Gallipoli 'we shall have lost the whole fruits of our victory, and another Balkan war would be inevitable'.[142] It was taken for granted that the return of the Turks to Europe would mean the return of oppression, corruption and massacre. What was certainly legitimate was the argument that since Great Britain had, along with France and Italy, prevented the Greeks from descending upon Constantinople and the neutral zone, Britain was bound to react in the same way when a similar threat was posed by a regime with which she was at war.

Apart from these considerations, the cabinet became obsessed with the notion that any withdrawal from the positions which Britain had taken up in the face of Kemal's troops would involve an irreparable loss of prestige, particularly since the Turks were 'Orientals'. On 20 September the cabinet went so far as to conclude that 'apart from its military importance, Chanak had now become a point of great moral significance to the prestige of the Empire'.[143] Behind the determination that there would be no backing down in the face of threats was the belief, pressed as before by Curzon, that revisions to Sèvres could only be made through diplomacy, and ultimately through a conference of all the treaty's signatories.

On 7 September the cabinet decided that they would liquidate their position in Anatolia, but stand firm and fight, if necessary alone, should the Turks attempt to advance into Europe. Authorization was given to the Commander-in-Chief to withdraw British troops from Chanak and Ismid, which were both in the neutral zone on the Asiatic side of the Straits. Harington, however, on his own initiative had already persuaded the French and Italian High Commissioners at Constantinople to send contingents to help to defend these two positions, possession of which he and Rumbold saw as essential to the security of Constantinople and the Straits. Hence, when they learned of London's policy, they urged that, in view of the apparently united allied stand and the fact that they had informed the Nationalists of this, a withdrawal 'would have a deplorable effect on prestige of Allied powers'. Rumbold believed that the Nationalists might move against the Allies and warned the Foreign Secretary that he did 'not think that in his present temper it would be safe to try to bluff Kemal'.[144] Harington's telegrams convinced Curzon that it would be a pity to withdraw from Chanak or Ismid, since they might prove useful pawns in negotiations, and since the Allies seemed to be working in unison. In short, it was Harington who initiated the policy, different from that decided upon by the cabinet, of making a stand at Ismid and Chanak, and hence he is responsible for the form the consequent crisis took.[145]

On the 15th the cabinet decided not only to transport reinforcements to the scene, but also to seek the cooperation of France, the Dominions and the Serbians and Rumanians.[146] This ambitious and unrealistic programme, which ended in embarrassment and failure, was capped the following day by a communiqué,[147] drawn up by Lloyd George and Churchill, outlining British policy and referring to the request to the Dominions for military assistance. As well as being seen by many as bellicose in tone, it was published in the press before three of the Dominion premiers had received any such request. The latter were understandably indignant, and only New Zealand offered immediate support in the form of a battalion.

The communiqué also prompted the French and Italian decisions to withdraw their forces from the Asiatic side of the Straits. On 19 September Hardinge had a heated interview with Poincaré,[148] in which this question was discussed. The French premier accepted the suggestion that Kemal should be invited to a conference but insisted that it would first be necessary to assure Angora that her territorial demands would be granted. The following day Curzon arrived in Paris to confer with Poincaré and Sforza, the Italian foreign secretary. Poincaré explained the withdrawal by pointing out that Paris had overruled the 'dangerous' offer of their High Commissioner to help to defend the Asiatic side of the Straits. Curzon was so upset that he declared that he 'could only explain to his Government that so far as Asia was concerned, the *Entente* had ceased to exist', and that it thus 'must be understood that England would be free to take a similar line of independent action in Europe—for instance, at Gallipoli'.[149]

This was a mere trifle in comparison with what was said and done at a meeting on the 22nd.[150] Hardinge claims that he made Curzon promise beforehand that for the sake of making progress he would not mention the Chanak withdrawal again. However, Curzon *did* mention just that—in terms of France's 'abandonment' and 'desertion' of Great Britain—which caused the already high temperatures of the protagonists to rise to unmanageable proportions. Poincaré insisted that Curzon withdraw what he had said; Curzon refused, and a series of accusations were exchanged. Various colourful descriptions of the encounter have been preserved. Curzon cabled afterwards that 'Poincaré lost all command of his temper, and for a quarter of an hour shouted and raved at the top of his voice . . . behaving like a demented schoolmaster screaming at a guilty schoolboy'.[151] Curzon said that he finally could stand it no longer and broke up the meeting and left the room, not returning until the French premier had apologized. Harold Nicolson's version is even more dramatic. Curzon, he writes, 'collapsed upon a scarlet settee. He grasped Lord Hardinge by the arm. "Charley", he panted, "I can't bear that horrid little man. I can't bear him". He wept'.[152] According to Hardinge's account in his memoir, *Old Diplomacy*, his chief's comments

> provoked the wrath of Poincaré and he suddenly lost his temper and shouted and screamed at Curzon, really in the most insulting manner, pouring out torrents of abuse and making the wildest statements with a flow of language like Niagara, which completely bowled over Curzon, who collapsed entirely. Curzon kept on saying to me, 'What am I to do, hadn't I better go home to London, I cannot go on, something must be done'.[153]

Poincaré, albeit reluctantly, agreed to apologize, after Hardinge told him that Curzon withdrew his statement. The plenipotentiaries reassembled, and the immediate crisis was over.

The meeting, although one of the lowest points in Anglo-French relations since the turn of the century, did lead to an invitation to Angora, reflecting French insistence that concessions be made to the Turks, to attend a meeting at Venice to negotiate a new treaty. The Allies said they viewed favourably Turkish claims to Thrace (to the Maritza River, basically the pre-1914 frontier) including Adrianople, reaffirmed their intention of eventually restoring Constantinople to the Turks, and pledged that they would use their influence to effect a Greek withdrawal, for which purpose a meeting could be arranged at Mudania or Ismid. The Nationalists, however, would have to agree to keep out of the zones which the Allies designated as neutral, and promise not to cross the Straits.[154]

On the 23rd, the day on which the invitation was despatched, over 1,000 Turks entered the neutral zone south of Chanak. It was immediately clear, however, that the Nationalist troops had been given orders not to open fire, since they were content to make faces through the barbed wire at the British. In the subsequent confrontation, the Turks had good reason to stay their hand, since they had in effect been promised Eastern Thrace. Nonetheless, it was by no means a foregone conclusion that Kemal, facing much the same dilemma as the more level-headed of Britain's policy-makers, would or could restrain his more bellicose followers. Moreover the Turks, like the British, were concerned about the loss of prestige which withdrawal would entail. The 'shadow-boxing' at Chanak was brinkmanship on the part of both powers, since a minor incident or accident could easily have produced an explosion.

War, therefore, was a real possibility. This was particularly so after London received Kemal's 'thoroughly unsatisfactory'[155] response to a personal telegram from Harington demanding the withdrawal of Turkish troops. Kemal denied any knowledge of a 'neutral zone' and said that his army was merely pursuing the Greeks. Furthermore, when news of the abdication of the hated Constantine reached Lloyd George, he responded by conjuring up the vision of the Empire supporting the Greeks under Venizelos to keep the Turks out of Europe. Hankey, who dined on the 27th with Lloyd George and Churchill, recorded that 'All talk was of war'.[156]

The telegrams from the men on the spot stressed the alarming nature of the situation at Chanak. On 29 September the conference of ministers, determined not to make concessions while Kemal was defiantly occupying the neutral zone, rejected compromises suggested by Harington, Rumbold and the French High Commissioner. The ministers accepted the service chiefs' advice that, in view of intelligence reports that Kemal was going to attack the next day, and the consequent need to protect British forces, an ultimatum was necessary. Harington was told to notify the Turkish commander at Chanak that, unless his troops were withdrawn, 'all the forces at our disposal, naval, military and air will open fire on the Turks'. The G.O.C. was instructed that the 'Time limit given should be short'.[157]

The response of the men on the spot was determined by their strong desire for peace, and their belief that the crisis could be satisfactorily resolved through diplomacy. They had pressed for concessions over Thrace, and for a meeting with Kemal, which by the 30th seemed a possibility. Harington wired London that the foothold at Chanak could withstand all but a very serious offensive and that the overall situation 'was never dangerous'.[158] The cabinet was furious when it learned that the G.O.C. and Rumbold favoured delay and that the former had not delivered the ultimatum. As Hankey confided to his diary: 'I think everyone felt a little that after his telegrams about the seriousness of the situation [which had brought about the ultimatum in the first place] we had been "spoofed".'[159] Rumbold and Harington clearly did not appreciate, the cabinet concluded with annoyance, 'the danger to peace' which their attitude 'seemed to involve'.[160]

The hysterical mood of the cabinet was vividly portrayed by Curzon in a letter of 1 October to Hardinge. The Prime Minister, Churchill, Chamberlain and others 'have been wild for ultimatums, advances, gunfire and war'. As for himself, however: 'I mean at all costs if I can to avoid war and above all war with Greece on our side', though it would be difficult since 'the struggle is not yet over for some of my colleagues literally smell of gunpowder'.[161] Hardinge had suspected as much. 'I have felt all along', he replied,

> that there has been a violent section in the Cabinet who were simply longing for war and of course I knew that Churchill would be amongst that crowd, for he always advocates expeditions and military operations which end in failure. Antwerp and Gallipoli are classical examples.[162]

Despite the sabre-rattling, the Chanak crisis was effectively over on the same day. Since the Nationalists indicated that they were willing to begin negotiations at Mudania and that they had ordered the cessation of all movement of their troops, the cabinet no longer insisted upon the delivery of the ultimatum. The subsequent negotiations resulted in an armistice on the 11th. By the **Mudania Convention the Greeks** would withdraw from Eastern Thrace, which would be controlled by the Allies for 30 days before it was turned over to the Turks, who agreed to respect the neutral zones until a peace treaty was signed.

Although it is of course true that, in retrospect, many crises appear totally unnecessary, the Chanak crisis seems even more unnecessary than most. It would not have arisen in the form it did, (if at all), had not Harington decided to make a stand on the Asiatic side of the Straits. In the end, after days of tension and the threat of war, an armistice was signed which gave the Turks virtually all they had wanted without a shot being fired. British policy, as exemplified by the communiqué and the ultimatum, was mismanaged, inflexible and irresponsible. It was folly to try to defend a position as vulnerable as Chanak, and self-defeating to act so brazenly in the face of public opinion, France, Italy and the Dominions. London overreacted to each development and preferred confrontation to compromise. War was treated cavalierly and was evidently anticipated with enthusiasm by Lloyd George and Churchill. As one observer graphically wrote:

> The fighting 'bloods' at home, have been straining at the leash. Winston longing to drop the paint brush for his sword and L.G. murmuring at every meal, We will fight *to the end!*[163]

The concern over the freedom of the Straits was not in keeping with international realities in 1922. There was a failure to make the mental leap from the concern of the early war years, when Britain vainly attempted to open the Straits for her ally, Russia, to the post-1917 years when Russia became an uncertain quantity in the international balance. Lloyd George, Winston Churchill and Birkenhead thought largely in terms of the past, rather than the present.

Moreover, one cannot but think that the obsession with Imperial prestige was manifestly out of joint with the times by 1922. By continually asserting its importance the British government succeeded in backing itself into a corner which proved difficult to get out of without either a loss of face or war. If Chanak became 'a point of great moral significance to the prestige of the Empire', it did so solely because the cabinet saw it as such. The irony is that Britain had already lost prestige through her ineffectual support for the Greeks, while her stand at Chanak was to lose her more, since it was followed by an armistice which was effectively a victory for the Turks. Finally, the débâcle contributed to the fall of Lloyd George.

The Conference of Lausanne, 20 November-July 1923

The international conference which began at Lausanne on 20 November was the last, the longest and by far the most successful of the peace conferences held after the First World War. It was convened by the British, French and Italians to negotiate a treaty with Turkey to replace the still unratified document that had been signed at Sèvres in 1920 under totally different circumstances.

The changed circumstances were entirely in Turkey's favour and she held the strongest diplomatic cards. She had victory on the field behind her and an army in being, and the attendant prestige, psychological benefits and leverage. As Allenby in Cairo reminded Curzon on 3 November: 'The defeat of the Greeks is, as you know, widely advertised as a victory of the Turks over the English; and many people look on the Turks as the final victors in the War'.[164] The latter, moreover (unlike the Allies, with the possible exception of Greece) were willing to resume hostilities if their basic demands were not met. Secondly, at Lausanne the Turks could at last speak with one voice, that of the Nationalists. That voice was infinitely stronger, surer, more determined and representative than the Sultan's could ever have been. In response to the allied invitation to both governments to attend the conference, the Grand National Assembly abolished the Sultanate. The Sultan mercifully put an end to the problem posed by his continued presence in Constantinople by fleeing to Malta aboard a British warship three days before the conference met. Henceforth Constantinople was no longer the seat of a government which could be pressured by the resident allied High Commissioners backed by their forces of occupation. Thirdly, the Turks had been treated to innumerable examples of allied disunity and thus had good reason to hope that the French and Italians could be won over, as well as the Soviets and the Americans. The Turks' greatest advantage over their former position (and that of all the defeated powers in 1919-20), was that they went to Lausanne to negotiate terms as an equal rather than to receive a dictated treaty as a supplicant.

The key figures at the conference were Lord Curzon, head of the British delegation during its first phase, and Ismet Pasha, who headed the Turkish delegation throughout. Curzon had what appeared to be unbeatable advantages as a negotiator. He was unrivalled in his knowledge of the East, debating skill and eloquence, and he had great prestige and a daunting air of authority. He saw as essential the need to maintain the apparent allied unity established in meetings between himself, Poincaré and Mussolini immediately before the conference. He anticipated, however, that his allies would let him down. Commenting on the 'bigoted refusal' of the French to take action against Turkey, Curzon suggested that Britain might trying to maintain allied unity, to restore British prestige in even an opportune Senegalese— in order to get them to budge from this attitude of craven weakness...'[165] His aim was, while trying to maintain Allied unity, to restore British prestige in the East and in particular to ensure the freedom of the Straits, win Mosul for Iraq and drive a wedge between Angora and Moscow.[166]

Ismet, by comparison, was a soldier with virtually no

diplomatic experience, who had accepted the job reluctantly at the urging of Kemal. His knowledge of many of the questions under consideration was imperfect, as was his command of French, the language he used; he was a poor speaker, unable to extemporize, and he was deaf. He had rigid instructions, the essence of which was to base his stance upon the National Pact and to defend at all cost Turkish independence and sovereignty.

At the outset of the conference[167] Curzon forcefully and effectively took advantage of his authority and experience. Over the protests of Ismet, he secured for himself the presidency of the whole conference and of its most important commission (on territorial and military questions), with the chairs of the other two commissions going to France and Italy as convening powers. The result was that Curzon was able to control the time-table of the conference.

The first question dealt with, the future of Thrace, was resolved with comparative ease. Ismet demanded the pre-1914 frontier for Eastern Thrace and a plebiscite in Western Thrace. The first was agreed upon, as were demilitarized zones on both sides. The second, however, was rejected, quite simply because the Allies and the Balkan nations were unanimous in their desire to limit the Turkish presence in Europe. In any case, the fate of Western Thrace had already been decided by the Treaty of Neuilly.

The Straits settlement was equally palatable to Britain since it effectively ensured the continuation of her naval domination of the Eastern Mediterranean. Curzon presented proposals on behalf of the Allies which stipulated that in peacetime the Straits were to be open to all ships, though a limitation was placed on the number of warships allowed into the Black Sea. In wartime, there was to be complete freedom of passage when Turkey was neutral, but freedom for neutral ships only when she was a belligerent. Specified zones along the Straits were to be demilitarized, with an international commission under Turkish presidency, responsible for supervision and inspection. Ismet generally accepted the allied proposals. He realized the importance of the Straits to Britain and the risks involved in being intransigent, and felt that Turkey's bargaining position would be strengthened if she was conciliatory over this question. Once again, moreover, he was faced with a united front on the part of the Allies and the Balkan powers. That Turkey accepted, while Russia rejected, the proposals, in Curzon's view, 'marked a definite break away by Turks from Russian thraldom'.[168] Curzon had skilfully divided the erstwhile comrades-in-arms by warning Ismet against the dangers of becoming overly influenced by Russia's viewpoint, and by making it explicit that the two nations' views were not as similar as Chicherin, the chief Soviet delegate, pretended. Ismet and the Allies, but not Russia, signed a draft Straits Convention on 1 February.

The negotiations over minorities, which aroused great passions, had mixed results from Britain's point of view. On the debit side of the ledger Curzon admitted that the minority section of the treaty was weak but realized, in his own inimitable phraseology, that 'it is probably [the] most that could have been extracted from an enemy swollen with pride and in a position to dictate rather than to accept conditions'.[169] The Turks were determined at whatever cost to assert their sovereign rights and leave the Allies no openings to interfere in their domestic affairs under the guise of protecting minorities. 'Turkey was acutely sensitive on this matter [of sovereignty]', Ismet maintained,

> and her fears were unfortunately well-founded, for up to the present day, Turkish sovereignty had always been infringed on the plea of humanitarian considerations. The integrity of Turkey had frequently been guaranteed by means of promises from the highest authorities and also by solemn treaties, and yet Turkish sovereignty had repeatedly been violated and Turkey had been dismembered again and again. How could Turkey help having misgivings?[170]

Nothing, as could have been anticipated, was to be done for Armenia, which became part of the USSR in December 1922.

Curzon also regretted that the Turks and the Greeks agreed upon a wholesale, compulsory exchange of population, based not upon language or race but upon religion. He feared, quite rightly, that this would produce great suffering, although he did realize that it would remove a deep rooted cause of dispute between them. As implemented frcm 1923 to 1925, over 188,000 Christians were transferred to Greece while 355,000 Muslims were moved from there to Turkey.[171]

On the positive side was the Turks' unexpected pledge to join the League of Nations upon the conclusion of peace. This meant that they would be subject to its minority guarantees. The decision marked a further widening of the breach that Curzon had helped to create between Turkey and the Soviets, who viewed the League and its members with contempt. Curzon attributed this success to his threat to leave Lausanne over the minority question. He isolated Ismet by forcefully playing the Allies' single card, international opinion, warning that if the conference broke down over minorities, 'not a voice would be raised anywhere in her defence'.[172]

Other problems proved to be even more difficult, such as the question of whether oil-rich Mosul should become part of Turkey or of the newly created kingdom of Iraq, of which Britain was mandatory under the League. The problem was a complicated one, and, since both sides were intransigent, no agreement was initially reached. Ismet's case was based on the National Pact, on historical, geographic and ethnical grounds, and on Turkey's need, as a poor country, for the oil. Curzon, who was particularly concerned about Mosul's strategic importance to Iraq and the entire East, rejected all but the last of these arguments. He maintained that Mosul, by right of conquest, administration as part of the mandate and the wishes of the inhabitants (of whom 7/12 were Kurds, 1/4 Arabs and 1/12 Turks) was an integral and necessary part of Faisal's kingdom.

Economic and financial questions, and the problem of the capitulations proved insoluble during the first phase of the conference. Beneath the welter of complicated negotiations two quite simple positions were coming into collision. On the one side the Allies believed that Turkey could not survive without foreign help. According to Rumbold, the 'Kemalist Turk' was 'inspired by blind chauvinism, hates all foreigners and thinks that he can run his country himself without any foreign intervention'.[173] The Allies, particularly the French and Italians, wanted to expand their economic activities in Turkey, while they all wanted the continuation of the privileges and protection which the capitulations provided. On the other side the Turks, while desiring help, were bent upon ensuring that it did not involve any infringements on their independence and sovereignty, and were steadfast about the need to end the capitulations, which they saw as the symbol of such infringements.

When Curzon decided in mid-December to draw up a draft treaty, many issues seemed hopelessly deadlocked. He increasingly felt that he was fighting a solitary battle against Turkish obstinacy while the French and Italian delegates were 'overflowing with unctuous civility to the Turks and showing an inclination to bolt at every corner from the course'.[174] Ismet argued every point *ad nauseam* and appeared impervious to reason, so that Curzon despairingly commented that: 'One might just as well argue with the Pyramid of Cheops' and concluded that 'Ismet like all other Turks is doubtless at bottom a true-born son of the bazaars'.[175] As for the Turks' obsession with sovereignty, Curzon compared their mentality with that of King William, who talked so often about leading the charge of the Guards at Waterloo that he eventually convinced himself that he had in fact done it, even though he was really a hundred miles distant.[176]

The New Year brought further problems for the British delegation as a by-product of the Anglo-French rift over reparations and Poincaré's occupation of the Ruhr. Curzon's desire to be as firm as was consistent with arriving within a reasonable time at a settlement was not shared by his Prime Minister. Bonar Law, as head of the Conservatives, a party that was traditionally pro-French and pro-Turk, made it clear that he wanted peace concluded rapidly and at virtually any price. As the Foreign Secretary gloomily reported on 1 January 1923 after meeting the premier in Paris,

> I found Bonar longing to clear out of Mosul, the Straits, and Constantinople, willing to give up anything and everything rather than have a row; astonished at the responsibility I have assumed at Lausanne and prepared for me.to back down everywhere. . . [177]

The Prime Minister had two 'vital' concerns. First; in order to prevent any further deterioration in Anglo-French relations and to avoid the risk of acting in isolation, he categorically insisted that 'if the French, as we know to be the case, will not join us, we shall not by ourselves fight the Turks to enforce what is left of the Treaty of Sèvres'. Second, to save money and to avoid appearing as an oil-hungry imperialist, he wanted if possible to get out of Mesopotamia and under no circumstances to go to war over Mosul.[178]

The Ruhr crisis led to pressure on the British delegation to pursue a policy of concession not only from Bonar Law but also from the French. This was clear to Curzon on 21 January when he saw the proposals that Bompard, who was to replace Barrère[179] as the chief French plenipotentiary, had brought back from Paris. To Curzon the proposals constituted a 'policy of abject surrender', and, in the wake of Chanak, a 'culminating effort at desertion'. Insult was added to injury by the fact that between the Turks and Britain's Allies

> there is abundant hob-nobbing over champagne. . . the spectacle may be witnessed nightly of the French and Italian delegates joking and clinking glasses with the men by whom the Allies were openly affronted in the conference chamber only an hour or two before. '

Since the 'Italians wobble from one side to the other with an invariable preference for retreat' the British were in a constant minority, 'for the two other allies and the Turks may be said to constitute a working alliance'.[180]

Curzon responded to these pressures and problems with a combination of skill and impatience. In the face of his Prime Minister's warning he achieved a great coup over Mosul. As a result of an oratorical *pièce de résistance* on 23 January he won agreement for his proposal to have the question settled by the League of Nations, a proposal vindicated by the latter's decision in 1925 to award the vilayet to Iraq.

In order to expedite proceedings he announced his intention to leave Lausanne by 4 February, and he obtained his allies' agreement to place the draft treaty before the Turks on 31 January for ratification. The latter, undoubtedly encouraged by the French government's statement that they considered the draft as no more than a basis for discussion, refused to sign. As planned, the British delegation steamed off on the Orient Express on the evening of the 4th, thereby indefinitely suspending the negotiations. To Curzon,

> Perhaps the most characteristic sequel was that within the next hour Ismet Pasha twice telephoned to find out whether I had really gone. Like a true Turk he thought that he could still catch me before I turned the corner of the street in order to have a final transaction over the price of the carpet.[181]

In retrospect, even the rupture of the conference had positive results, since it is virtually certain that if the Allies had dragooned the Turks into signing the draft treaty on 31 January it would not have lasted.

The conference resumed at Lausanne over 2½ months later, after the Turks had put forward counter proposals which the Allies deemed reasonable.[182] The final negotiations were primarily over complex economic questions and the capitulations. Both Ismet and Rumbold, who had taken over as head of the British delegation, were determined to bring the negotiations to a successful conclusion. Rumbold was aware of the pressure that was being exerted upon Ismet by his own government. The High Commissioner pursued a conciliatory policy and often acted to effect a compromise between the Turks on the one hand and the French, Italians or Greeks on the other. The prospect of another breakdown, or of renewed war between Turkey and Greece, which loomed large as a result of the bellicose attitude of the latter over reparations, was successfully averted.

In the end Ismet, who in the final meeting was reportedly 'receiving treatment which would make the third degree in a Harlem police station seem like a club dinner',[183] succeeded in protecting Turkey's interests in the issues under consideration, **thereby thwarting in particular the hopes of the French and Italians.** The capitulations were abolished, and no guarantees were made either to those seeking economic concessions or to the (mostly French) bond holders of the Ottoman Public Debt, which was to be divided up amongst the successor states. Greece accepted the principle that Turkey was owed reparations for acts committed by the Greek army in Anatolia, but it was agreed that none would be paid because of Greece's poverty.

The Treaty of Lausanne, incorporating the above provisions, was signed on 24 July 1923, thereby officially ending the war between the Allies and Turkey that had begun almost a decade earlier. The United States and Turkey signed a separate treaty on 6 August. The last allied troops steamed out of Constantinople on 1 October and thus brought to a close an occupation that had lasted longer than the Great War itself. On the 13th the Turkish capital was officially moved from Constantinople, capital of the Ottoman Empire for 470 years and of the Byzantine Empire for 1000 years before that, to **Angora. Later in the month the Turkish Republic was pro-**claimed with Mustapha Kemal as its first president and Ismet Pasha Inönü as its first Prime Minister. The Sultanate was gone, to be followed by the Caliphate in 1924. The definitive end to the Eastern Question, and the decline and dissolution of the Ottoman Empire, keys to European and Eastern politics and diplomacy since the eighteenth century, had finally been reached.

The Treaty of Lausanne is the most successful treaty of the post First World War settlement, and one of the most enduring international documents of the modern era. Apart from changes made in the Straits Convention at Montreux in 1936,[184] it has in all essentials lasted to the present day. That the conference achieved balanced results is reflected by the fact that observers then and now are divided as to whether it marked the ultimate triumph of Nationalist diplomacy or of the statesmanship of Lord Curzon.[185]

Both the British and the Turks achieved their major goals, unlike the French and Italians, who were unable to win the favourable economic and financial provisions they wanted. Curzon overcame his weak position and by February had helped to separate the Soviets and the Turks, to persuade the latter to join the League, and to produce settlements over Thrace, the Straits and Mosul which were in accord with Great Britain's interests. If the relatively strong and defensible Turkey that emerged was neither a goal of Curzon's nor a result of his diplomacy, it was at least an outcome desired by the General Staff. At Lausanne the Turks succeeded in throwing off the fetters of Sèvres. This was accomplished without becoming tied, for the moment at least, to Russia or any other power. The result was an independent, sovereign, largely homogeneous nation-state with prestige in the East. In fact, the Treaty of Lausanne paved the way for the Greco-Turkish rapprochement of 1930 by virtually eliminating the two most important areas of conflict between the two states: minorities and frontiers. Both Ottoman Imperialism and the 'Megali Idea' came to an end. The former had been ruled out in the National Pact while the latter lost its rationale with the return of 1,300,000 Greek Christians to Greece. As a result of this movement the ethnological frontiers of the Greeks generally coincided with the frontiers of the Greek state for the first time in the modern history of Greece. With this mutual end to policies of expansion both Greece and the new Turkey were able to turn their attention to domestic problems.[186]

The Treaty of Lausanne was successful, unlike Sèvres, because it was negotiated, not dictated: it was negotiated with a government that genuinely represented the Turkish people; and it was negotiated not when Turkey was unnaturally weak but after she had recovered. Secondly, Turkey's aims, as enshrined in the National Pact, were realistic in being limited, legitimate and obtainable. Thanks largely to the wisdom of Kemal, the Turks realized that it would be foolhardy to try to preserve the frontiers of the old Empire or to pursue a Pan-Islamic, Pan-Turanian or imperialistic policy. Lastly, there is little doubt that the favourable outcome owed something to the fact that the conference was able to proceed without the baneful influence, machinations and Philhellenic sympathies of the last British Liberal prime minister.

A final few words should be said about the two principal negotiators, both of whom succeeded in obtaining their goals. As the American observer, R.W.Child, commented; 'Curzon and Ismet had about as much in common as a lion tamer and a grower of azaleas'.[187] Curzon had not lost his Viceregal airs, and frequently treated his adversary in a high-handed and impatient manner, with numerous doses of sarcasm, contempt and condescension. 'He treated us like schoolboys but we did not mind', Ismet remarked wryly, 'He treated the French and Italians just the same'.[188] This attitude was accompanied by an exaggerated form of diplomacy. The Foreign Secretary did not hesitate to issue warnings, threats and even what were in effect ultimata.[189] He also frequently and explicitly used the prospect of financial aid to Turkey as an instrument with which to pressure Ismet.[190] It is certainly possible, as has been suggested,[191] that more conciliatory tactics would have been more appropriate and effective, particularly since the Turks were so sensitive about, and insistent upon, their position as an equal. On the other hand, Curzon's tactics did help to produce the desired results.

Ismet's response to Curzon was effective if simple. Since he could not hope to out-argue the former Viceroy, he wore him down through delays, intransigence and obstruction. This war of attrition was effective because of Curzon's notoriously sensitive temperament and impatience. Ismet did, however, know when to compromise, to avoid either rupturing the conference over questions on which Turkey was isolated and had a weak case, or losing credibility in the eyes of Angora, whose relentless pressure not to yield put him in Rumbold's words, 'between the hammer and the anvil'.[192]

Conclusion

Great Britain's policy towards Turkey for four full years after the Armistice contributed to a string of failures: the disastrous Smyrna landing, the abortive Treaty of Sèvres, the end of any semblance of allied cooperation in the Near East, sundry unsuccessful attempts to mediate between the Greeks and the Turks, and the débâcle at Chanak. However, it must be remembered that it was the Greeks rather than the British who paid most of the price for these failures—in lives, in money and in domestic difficulties—and that despite its failures, His Majesty's Government ultimately achieved its major goals at Lausanne without having fired a shot after 1918.

How can we explain Britain's failures? First of all, as discussed above,[193] there were enormous problems in the way of coming to an equitable and just settlement, above all since, as elsewhere, Britain's hands were to a large extent tied by her wartime commitments. Moreover, the period was one in which there were frequent major international crises. Given that the future of great powers such as Germany and Russia was to be considered, the Turkish settlement was relatively unimportant. Hence little time was spent on it by major policy-makers, and that only intermittently. The tardiness of the Turkish peace process ensured that decisions always lagged far behind the changes in circumstances. This tardiness was caused variously by the settlement's low priority, the divisions amongst Britain's top decision-makers, the failure in the middle stages of the process to deal with the real controllers of Turkey, the Nationalists, and by broader factors such as uncertainty about

America's future role, the deterioration of Anglo-French relations, and the Greco-Turkish stalemate in the field.

Secondly, the British government's failures were the result of the personal failures of her statesmen and officials. The man most responsible for policy towards Turkey was Lloyd George, whose post-war tenure of office, significantly enough, coincided with the unsuccessful phases of policy. While he was not the only Philhellenic decision-maker, he was the most important, and he consistently encouraged Greece's extravagant aspirations, in the face of endless accurate warnings about the dangers involved. His misjudgments arose out of his hatred of the Turks, and his inability to appreciate either their military capabilities or the force and determination of their nationalism and loathing for the Greeks, ignited by the Smyrna landing. At the same time he consistently overestimated what the Greeks, and in particular Venizelos, could do. These errors were magnified by his refusal to heed expert (particularly military) advice and that of his representatives on the spot, and by his habit of consulting Venizelos, with his patina of perpetual confidence and optimism. Of course, in the final analysis Lloyd George was fully aware that if the Greeks did not succeed, the price for failure would be directly borne by them, not by their British backers.

Needless to say, the Prime Minister did not blame the complete failure of British and Greek policy by the autumn of 1922 on his own government or his personal miscalculations. Rather, he cited the 'treachery' of his allies, the French and Italians, in supporting and arming the Turks, and, above all, the fall of Venizelos and his replacement by Constantine, whose government, in his view, proceeded to wreck the Greek army.[194] At the cabinet meeting of 7 September 1922 Lloyd George claimed that 'defeat had been engineered by Constantine', while William Tyrrell of the Foreign Office repeated to Curzon later in the month that 'in the Prime Minister's opinion the failure of our Eastern policy is due to the inability of the Greeks to deliver the goods, and therefore nobody is to blame except the wretched Greeks'.[195] While the fall of Lloyd George did not ensure success at Lausanne, it at the very least meant that Curzon could negotiate without the fear that his premier might publicly be urging peace, and privately telling the Greeks not to compromise.

Other policy-makers must share the responsibility for Britain's failure in the Near East from 1918 to 1922, since they either did not or could not act effectively to deter Lloyd George from pursuing his unfortunate policies. There was no cabinet revolt and no resignations. This is particularly open to criticism because ministers had before them the example of Montagu, who successfully persuaded the cabinet to overrule the Prime Minister on the question of Constantinople. The lack of ministerial protest is also inexcusable in view of the enormous amount of perceptive and prophetic criticism of Lloyd George's policies, and the fact that so many key departments of state—the Foreign Office, War Office, India Office and the Colonial Office—came to oppose them.

Looking briefly at the leading figures involved, Winston Churchill, in sharp contrast to his wild schemes for Russia, spoke good sense about Turkey. He did so, however, without any effect, and unwisely came to reverse himself and side with Lloyd George over Chanak. While Montagu did have a direct impact upon policy, his obsession with Indian opinion lessened his credibility and ultimately led to his removal from office.

Given their direct responsibility for foreign policy, the two foreign secretaries of the period must be allocated a major portion of the blame. Because of his age and his lackadaisical attitude, Balfour was generally ineffectual at the peace conference, and in any case he was a pro-Greek who was uncritical of Lloyd George's Near Eastern policies. The same could certainly not be said of Lord Curzon, who was far from lacking as far as plans and incisive criticisms were concerned, and who deserves credit for working diligently to bring about a peace through mediation. He was, however, more a man of words than a man of action. As Churchill has written; 'One of Curzon's characteristic weaknesses was that he thought too much about stating his case, and too little about getting things done'.[196] Moreover, he himself even admitted on one occasion that he felt that his representations were useless.[197] His weakness was clearly shown during the Chanak crisis. While he commendably favoured compromise and worked towards a peaceful solution, his protests against the bellicose policies of Lloyd George and Churchill were little more than gestures. He protested against the communiqué, but was inexcusably absent from London when it was discussed and drawn up; he begged for a delay in delivering the ultimatum, but did nothing—despite his position as Foreign Secretary—when delay was overruled; above all, at no time did he make his disapproval effective by making it public and resigning.

Looking at the problem in its broadest sense, if the Foreign Secretary and Foreign Office had been as strong after the war as they had been before it, Lloyd George would never have been able to determine foreign policy in such a single-handed manner. Although their decline was the product of many complex considerations, the roles assumed by both Balfour and Curzon were partly responsible for that decline. Of course, as far as Turkish policy was concerned, a more powerful Foreign Office might have been a mixed blessing, given the pro-Greek proclivities of Balfour and officials such as Crowe and Nicolson.

The third way in which British fortunes can be explained is in terms of events in the battlefield, where the fate of British policy became dependent upon the performance of the Greek army. Britain's pro-Greek policy ultimately failed with the miltary failure of the Greeks. This failure was hastened, if not made inevitable, by allied limitation of their advance into Anatolia in the summer of 1919, by the withdrawal of financial support and war materials to Greece after the return of Constantine (even though the Turks were still covertly receiving such materials from the French, Italians and Russians), and by the Allies' refusal of August 1922 to let the Greeks occupy Constantinople. In short, Lloyd George's government ended up by supporting the Greeks with little more than words, and letting them suffer the consequences. British policy, therefore, fell between two stools: on the one hand, the Prime Minister encouraged Greece to resolve matters through war, while, on the other, he and his government did not furnish that poor state with the means or opportunities to achieve victory. Paradoxically, failure in the field explains why the Treaty of Lausanne was fair-minded and realistic, since it ensured that it would not be based on dreams of empire.

While in one sense the Greeks were pawns of the British, they were willing pawns, bent on achieving their own goals, despite the ever-increasing risks (of which Venizelos, despite his buoyant façade, was completely aware), and the progressive lessening of concrete support from His Majesty's Government. The Greeks must thus share with the British the blame for the whole Near Eastern tragedy; after all, they did not have to follow Lloyd George's bad advice. Venizelos must be singled out as a major culprit, given his central role alongside the British premier as the originator of the Smyrna policy, which was responsible for so much of the subsequent imbroglio.[198]

Lastly, Britain's mistakes can be seen in the light of the complete failure of most of her policy-makers to understand Turkish nationalism, and the determination, principles and military capacity that accompanied it. The fundamental problem was that the British, especially during Chanak, were victims of a 'war mentality' firmly embedded in the 1914-18 conflict. The Turks were viewed with pre-1918 eyes as corrupt, oppressive and inept people, who, as the High Commissioner in Constantinople tellingly phrased it, were 'under the illusion that they can run their country without foreign help'.[199] To Lloyd George Kemal was simply a bandit, and to Curzon Ismet was a carpet-monger; there was no thought given to the possibility that they might have limited or legitimate goals. Typical is Lloyd George's description for King George V of Bekir Sami, the capable Turkish Nationalist representative at the London conference of March 1921:

A little while ago I had to shake hands with Sami Bey, a ruffian who was missing for the whole of one day, and finally traced to a sodomy house in the East End. He was the representative of Mustapha Kemal, a man who I understand has grown tired of affairs with women and has lately taken up unnatural sexual intercourse. I must confess I do not think there is very much to choose between these persons whom I am forced to meet from time to time in Your Majesty's service.[200]

Kemal himself encapsulated the problem when he astutely observed that: 'The Entente Powers do not realize that the Ottoman Empire has passed into history and is superseded by a new nation and state, determined to obtain their complete independence and sovereignty'.[201] That the Entente Powers were thinking in terms of the past is revealed in a reference by Curzon at Lausanne to treating Turkey 'in a manner different from that accorded to any other beaten nation in the Great War'.[202] Here indeed was the nub of the problem, since the Nationalists did not identify or equate themselves with the Empire beaten in 1918, but with a new nation which had been created by the Smyrna landing, and which had defeated the Greeks and foiled the Allies. After all, Turkey alone of the defeated Central Powers *was* able within a few years to force the abandonment of a harsh peace treaty, and negotiate a very favourable one.

That the British should have maintained their wartime mentality towards Turkey is not without irony. At the same time that they were trying so assiduously to get the French to agree to a hard line against Turkey, they were attempting to persuade their·Entente partner to adopt a more conciliatory policy towards Germany, to recognize, in short, that the war was over and that circumstances had changed. The explanation for this divergence in policies is that Great Britain believed that she would gain nothing by appeasing Turkey, but would increase both her security and her trade by appeasing Germany. She was completely wrong on the first count, as this chapter has shown, and at least partly wrong on the second, as the course of Anglo-German relations during the interwar years was to reveal.

CONCLUSION

We have concentrated on the role and attitudes of top British policy-makers in the peace negotiations. While social and economic considerations did play a part in their deliberations, Prime Minister Lloyd George and his colleagues were primarily concerned with traditional diplomatic and strategic factors, from the balance of power in Europe to the freedom of the seas.

At the same time the possibility did emerge of basing post-war British policy on a new foundation, that of Anglo-American cooperation, alongside American President Woodrow Wilson's envisaged League of Nations, although the institution was never heartily embraced by the British. This possibility, however, evaporated forever when the United States rejected the Treaty of Versailles, a document which, at American insistence, had included the text of the League Covenant.

Nor was there anything new about the insistence of British statesmen such as George Nathaniel Curzon, (the former Viceroy of India and Foreign Secretary from October 1919 to January 1924), upon the need to safeguard Imperial prestige. Ironically enough, however, it was not Curzon but Lloyd George and Winston Churchill, the then Colonial Secretary, who became obsessed with prestige during the ill-fated Chanak crisis of September 1922, an event that helped to make possible the Treaty of Lausanne of July 1923 with Mustapha Kemal's nascent Turkish Republic.

In the wake of the greatest war in history and the Russian Revolution, the British had to contend with seemingly endless pressures. Much of Europe and Asia was in a state of chaos, and subject to the twin influences of 'Bolshevism' and Woodrow Wilson's idealistic vision of a new world order. Britain's diplomatic freedom was severely limited by the depletion of her material and military resources, which after 1919 were stretched to the limit in an attempt to cope with the greatest global responsibilities in her long history as an Imperial power. Her freedom was also curtailed by her unfortunate and often conflicting wartime promises and commitments, such as those made to her Arab allies; by the continuation of her traditional rivalry with her closest wartime ally, France; by the ambitions and lust for the spoils of war of her other allies, such as the Greeks and Rumanians; and by the increasing uncertainty as to America's future role in world affairs. Britain had also to face the rising force of nationalism, a force which—as her unfortunate policies towards the Turks and the Arabs were to show—she was not fully able to comprehend.

There were further peace-making problems of a purely domestic nature. There were quarrels between, and even within, departments of state over their relative jurisdictions and over what Britain should demand. This frequently involved a clash between leading personalities. The long-standing antagonism between Lloyd George and Curzon, for example, was a combination of mutual personal contempt and differing conceptions of authority: Lloyd George felt that as Prime Minister he should be the one to decide major questions of foreign policy in personal meetings with representatives of similar rank from other countries.

Britain's peace-makers also had to contend with often over-heated press and parliamentary critics, who claimed, to some extent justifiably, to represent 'public opinion'. The public, understandably enough, favoured a punitive peace, particularly with Germany, and grew quickly disillusioned with the slowness of de-mobilization and with the meagreness of 'the fruits of victory'.

In view of all these pressures it is scarcely surprising that the British were often overwhelmed by the sheer magnitude of their task. The European settlement, as a result, was a patchwork of compromises between the policies of the United States and of France, powers which had very different views indeed about the kind of post-war world they wanted. While France basically wanted a peace based upon permanent guarantees against a revival of Germany, and the strengthening of her position in Southeast Europe (and the Middle East), the United States favoured — in theory, but not always in practice, as the Fiume dispute and Japan's claim to Shantung were to show — an 'idealistic' settlement based on their President's famous Fourteen Points.

Britain's attempts to play a mediating role between her two major associates in European questions was largely unsuccessful. The chasm between French and American aims could not be bridged, and in any case Britain had her own self-interested goals to pursue. In the end the treaties with Germany and the former Austro-Hungarian Empire satisfied none of the major powers, with appalling consequences for the post-war world.

As for the former Ottoman Empire, the peace settlement brought about the final resolution of the centuries-old Eastern Question, although only at a very high price. The powers partitioned the defeated Empire's Arab lands, including Palestine, and created a configuration of states that closely resembles that of today's Middle East. The Arabs, who had been the recipients of British wartime promises of independence in exchange for military assistance, felt betrayed, a sentiment that fuelled the fires of anti-western, anti-imperialist Arab nationalism. The settlement also enormously increased the conflict between the Arabs and the Jews in Palestine, a consequence that we are still living with today.

As for Turkey itself, British policy was a string of failures. The disastrous allied-backed landing of Greek troops at Smyrna in May 1919 was followed by the abortive Treaty of Sèvres of August 1920, the end of allied cooperation in the Near East, sundry unsuccessful attempts to mediate between the battling Greeks and Turks, and the *débâcle* at Chanak. The Chanak failure, however, perhaps because it was combined with the downfall of the fiercely pro-Greek Lloyd George, paved the way for the Treaty of Lausanne, the only successful post-war settlement.

While Britain's contribution to peace-making has received a great deal of criticism, much of it justified, the enormity of the problems that the British government had to overcome must be fully appreciated. Given the circumstances of the time, there is a certain inevitability to much of Britain's post-war policy. As well as this, it must be remembered that it was not just the treaties themselves, but the way in which they were subsequently interpreted and carried out by an increasingly strained Entente that contributed to the problems of the interwar years.

On balance, from the standpoint of narrow national interests, Great Britain did not do badly out of the peace. She secured a share in reparations from Germany and gained control of most of the Second Reich's colonies. The Kaiser's prized fleet lay beneath the waves at Scapa Flow. Germany herself was confined to less than her pre-1914 frontiers. In the Middle East the Lloyd George government was awarded the mandates for Palestine and Mesopotamia, including oil rich Mosul, mandates the terms of which she herself could determine. And in Turkey, by the Treaty of Lausanne, Britain gained favourable arrangements on the questions she cared most about, the Straits at Constantinople above all.

It had not been the wish of British policy-makers to see the complete dismantling of the Austro-Hungarian empire, despite the strident clamour of a group of Slavophils in Great Britain. British officials were alive to the dangers of the further Balkanization of Southeastern Europe. They hoped for the formation of some kind of federation of these states, without the Habsburgs, or, at the very least, the establishment of a Central European customs union which might eventually lead to political collaboration. The new states were, however, determined to be completely independent, politically and economically, both from their former rulers and from each other. They would not even agree to the limited degree of collaboration implied in a customs union.

Given the refusal of the successor states to fall in with British plans, the British had no alternative but to resign themselves to their territorial aggrandizement, although Lloyd George did intervene to prevent what he regarded as the worst excesses of Polish territorial greed. Britain managed to preserve what few direct interests she had in Central and Eastern Europe in the various peace settlements with her former enemies, but apart from Poland, she usually followed the French lead in this area. French policy looked to the establishment of territorially strong and economically viable states which would, the French hoped, act together as bulwarks against a revived Germany and as a *cordon sanitaire* in the event of the emergence of a Bolshevik-dominated Russia. In the early 1920's the French managed to arrange a series of shaky agreements between Czechoslovakia, Yugoslavia and Rumania—the so-called 'Little Entente'—but this was directed more against a Habsburg restoration in Hungary than against Germany. France also signed a pact with Poland. None of these arrangements compensated France in any real way for the loss of her alliance with Czarist Russia.

Southeast Europe remained unstable and discontented during the interwar years. Many of the successor states claimed territory from one or other of their neighbours. Bulgaria and Hungary were acutely dissatisfied with the treaties imposed on them by the Allies, while Austria, shorn of her former empire, forbidden to unite with Germany and saddled with reparations payments, was unable to survive economically without allied aid. As the British had feared in 1919, once Germany and Bolshevik Russia recovered, Central and Eastern Europe became prime targets for their economic and territorial ambitions.

While the British continued to hope that a liberal Russia would emerge eventually from the ruins of military collapse and civil war, their hopes steadily diminished as the fighting between the rival factions continued in 1919 and as the allied-backed anti-Bolshevik forces demonstrated both their military incompetence and their rejection of Western democratic ideas. Britain and her allies, with varying degrees of enthusiasm, attempted from time to time to secure a negotiated settlement between the various Russian parties, but the bitterness created by the civil war and the Bolshevik conviction that in the long run victory was theirs, made such efforts abortive. At the same time the Allies, from calculations of national interest and detestation of Bolshevism, continued, with waning enthusiasm, their military and financial aid to the anti-Bolshevik forces. The manifest impossibility of squaring this circle led the Allies finally to abandon that strife-torn and divided country to whatever victor finally emerged from the civil war.

The 'favourable' settlement that Britain secured elsewhere in the world was, of course, won at a terrible cost, a cost which had yet to be paid fully by Britain and the other powers. With the possible exception of the United States, all the victors in the 'Great War' were pyrrhic victors. Apart from Turkey, the final treaties, as has been shown above, did not satisfy any of the vanquished, and they even alienated many of Britain's wartime allies, from the Arabs to the French. Italy in particular was bitterly disappointed at what she regarded as her meagre territorial gains, and became an unreliable and uneasy partner of her Entente allies during the interwar period, finally abandoning them altogether in favour of Hitler's Germany. As the remainder of the interwar years were to show beyond any question, the peace settlement after the First World War was a peace without promise.

NOTES

The full titles, places and dates of publication of books cited in the notes are given in the Bibliography.

Chapter One

1 For a detailed account see V. H. Rothwell, *British War Aims and Peace Diplomacy.*
2 War aims and wartime commitments with reference to the Ottoman Empire are dealt with in the introductions to Chapters IV and V, 131-43, 181-6.
3 A. J. P. Taylor, *The Troublemakers,* 156.
4 David Lloyd George, *War Memoirs,* II, 1510-1517.
5 H. W. V. Temperley (ed), *History of the Peace Conference of Paris,* I, 433-4.
6 C. J. Lowe and M. L. Dockrill, *The Mirage of Power,* II, 242.
7 For details of the armistice negotiations see H. R. Rudin, *Armistice 1918.*
8 Temperley, I, 45. On House's activities before and during the conference, see Inga Floto, *Colonel House in Paris.*
9 See Chapter IV, 145-6.
10 Minute by Crowe, 7 Dec 1918, cited in Rothwell, 254.
11 'The Settlement', memorandum by the Political Intelligence Department, 18 Nov 1918, FO 608/435.
12 'Peace Negotiations', memorandum by Lord Hardinge of Penshurst, 10 Oct 1918, Lloyd George Papers, F/3/3/5.
13 For details see Lord Hankey, *The Supreme Control at the Paris Conference,* 21-31, and Stephen Roskill, Hankey, II, 43-67.
14 Borden to Lloyd George, 21 Jan 1919, Lloyd George Papers, C/5/3/1.
15 See Sir James Headlam-Morley, *A Memoir of the Paris Peace Conference,* 57-8.
16 David Lloyd George, *The Truth about the Peace Treaties,* I, 403-16.
17 *ibid.,* 416-20.

Chapter Two

1 See Chapter I.
2 Speech by Woodrow Wilson, 27 Sep 1918, Temperley, I, 400.
3 Speech by Woodrow Wilson, 11 Feb 1918, *ibid.,* I, 409.
4 President Wilson's note of 5 Nov 1918, *ibid.,* I, 415.
5 Seth P. Tillman, *Anglo-American Relations at the Paris Peace Conference,* 24, 71.
6 John Maynard Keynes, *The Economic Consequences of the Peace,* 35-50.

7 War Cabinet, minutes of meeting, 12 noon, 4 Mar 1919, Cabinet Papers, CAB 35/15 no 541A.
8 Memorandum by the General Staff, 2 Jan 1919, FO 608/121.
9 Churchill, War Cabinet meeting, Friday 28 Feb 1919, Cabinet Papers, CAB 23/15 no 538A.
10 Sir Henry Wilson to Eric Drummond, 2 Jan 1919, enclosing memorandum by the General Staff, 2 Jan 1919, FO 608/121.
11 *ibid.*, minute by Headlam-Morley, 16 Jan 1919.
12 Minute by Colonel J. H. M. Cornwall, 11 Mar 1919, FO 608/141.
13 'Notes of a discussion with M. Tardieu and Dr Mazes, 11-12 Mar 1919', Philip Kerr, 12 Mar 1919, FO 608/142.
14 Derby to Curzon, 7 Mar 1919, Curzon Papers, F/6/2(f).
15 Minute by Balfour, 18 Mar 1919, FO 608/141.
16 Minute by Headlam-Morley, 28 Feb 1919, FO 608/2 Pt 1.
17 Memorandum by Headlam-Morley, 25 Mar 1919; Minute by Crowe, 25 Mar 1919, *ibid.*
18 Minute by Balfour, Apr 1919, *ibid.*
19 Minute by Kerr, May 1919, FO 608/241; Minute by Balfour, May 1919, FO 608/121.
20 Lloyd George to Kerr, 12 Feb 1919, Lloyd George Papers, F/89/2/8.
21 'Notes on the Military Peace Proposals', A. J. Balfour, 5 Mar 1919; Sir Henry Wilson to Lloyd George, 6 Mar 1919, Lloyd George Papers, F/3/4/15 and F/47/8/9.
22 This section is based on the excellent account by Ronald E. Bunselmeyer, *The Cost of the War 1914-1918.*
23 *ibid.*, 88.
24 *ibid.*, 89.
25 *ibid.*, 143.
26 For a different view see Marc Trachtenberg, 'Reparation at the Paris Peace Conference', *JMH*, 1979, 24-55.
27 Temperley, I, 415.
28 Leo Amery, Dec 1918, in Bunselmeyer, 176.
29 Hankey to Hughes, 9 Jan 1919, Lloyd George Papers, F/23/4/2.
30 In 1920 France and Britain agreed on a 52:22 division of the proceeds. The rest went to the lesser allies.
31 Hankey to Lloyd George, 21 Feb 1919, Lloyd George Papers, F/23/4/19.
32 Montagu to Lloyd George, 21 Feb 1919, *ibid.*
33 Montagu to Lloyd George, 12 Mar 1919, Lloyd George Papers, F/40/2/21.
34 'Some Considerations for the Peace Conference before they finally Draft their terms', 25 Mar 1919, Lloyd George, *The Truth,* I, 404-5.
35 'Reparations', a report by Hughes, Sumner and Cunliffe, 18 Mar 1919, Lloyd George Papers, F/213/2/1.
36 Lloyd George to Bonar Law, 30 Mar 1918, Lloyd George Papers, F/30/3/40.
37 Cecil to Lloyd George, 4 Apr 1919, Lloyd George Papers, F/6/6/25.
38 Derby to Curzon, 5 Apr 1919, Curzon Papers, P/6/2(f).

39 'Meeting of the Dominions representatives at the Rue Nitot at 9 a.m. 11 April 1919, Minutes', Lloyd George Papers, F/28/3/24.

40 Hughes to Lloyd George, 11 Apr 1919, Lloyd George Papers, F/28/3/26.

41 This section is based on George W. Egerton's *Great Britain and the Creation of the League of Nations*.

42 *ibid.*, 61.

43 *ibid.*, 65-69.

44 *ibid.*, 99.

45 Hughes to Ferguson, 17 Jan 1919, quoted in W. Roger Louis, *Great Britain and Germany's Lost Colonies 1914-1919*, 129.

46 For details see Arthur J. Marder, *The Royal Navy in the Fisher Era 1904-1918*, V, 224-36.

47 Temperley, I, 433.

48 *ibid.*, II, 114.

49 For a more comprehensive account, on which this section is based, see W. R. Louis, *passim*.

50 For the German side see Alma Luckau, *The German Delegation at the Paris Peace Conference*.

51 Sir Henry Wilson to Lloyd George, 16 June 1919, Cabinet Papers, CAB 24/75.

52 Jere Clemens King, *Foch versus Clemenceau*, 107-10.

53 The full correspondence is in *Selections from the Smuts Papers*, ed W. K. Hancock and Jean van der Pohl, IV, 148ff.

54 Botha to Lloyd George, 15 May 1919; Barnes to Lloyd George, 16 May 1919; Churchill to Lloyd George, 20 May 1919; H. A. L. Fisher to Lloyd George, 28 May 1919; Cecil to Lloyd George, 27 May 1919, Lloyd George Papers, F/5/5/9, F/4/3/15, F/8/3/55, F/16/7/39, F/6/6/47. Also 'Negotiations for the Peace Treaty', Churchill, 21 May 1919, Cabinet Papers, CAB 29/25/825.

55 Bonar Law to Lloyd George, 31 May 1919, Lloyd George Papers, F/30/3/71.

56 Meetings of the British Empire delegation, Friday 30 May 1919, 3.30 p.m. and Sunday 1 June 1919, 11 a.m. and 5 p.m., Cabinet Papers, CAB 29/28/32, 33 and 34.

57 Meeting of the British Empire delegation, Sunday 1 June 1919 at 5 p.m., Cabinet Papers, CAB 29/28/34.

58 Barnes to Lloyd George, 2 June 1919, Lloyd George Papers, F/4/3/19.

59 Lloyd George to Barnes, 3 June 1919, *ibid.*, F/4/3/20.

60 Smuts to Lloyd George, 2 June 1919; Lloyd George to Smuts, 3 June 1919; Smuts to Lloyd George, 5 June 1919, *ibid.*, F/45/9/39 and 40, and F/7/2/32.

61 Howard Elcock, *Portrait of a Decision*, 270-86.

62 Meeting of the British Empire delegation, Tuesday 10 June 1919 at 3.00 p.m., Cabinet Papers, CAB 29/28 no. 35.

63 Luckau, 90-111.

64 Lloyd George to Curzon, 10 Dec 1919, Curzon Papers, F/12/2/11.

65 *ibid.*

66 For details see Egerton, 170ff.
67 *ibid.*, 175.
68 *ibid.*, 176.
69 Hurst to Hardinge, 5 Nov 1919, Lloyd George Papers, F/12/2/3.
70 Hardinge to Wingate, 28 Nov 1918, Hardinge Papers, vol 39.
71 Trachtenburg, *op cit.*

Chapter Three

1 For details see Kenneth J. Calder, *Britain and the Origins of the New Europe, (passim)*.
2 *ibid.*, 143.
3 D. Perman, *The Shaping of the Czechoslovak State*, 105.
4 Temperley, IV, 132.
5 'The settlement', Political Intelligence Department, Nov. 1918, FO 608/435.
6 Minute by Hardinge, Apr. 1919, FO 608/7.
7 Spicer (for Curzon) to Balfour desp 1473, 18 Mar. 1919, FO 608/6.
8 Minute by Hardinge, 12 Apr. 1919, FO 608/18.
9 Minute by Cecil, Apr. 1919, FO 608/9.
10 'The Mission to Austria-Hungary', report by General Smuts, 9 Apr 1919, FO 608/16.
11 Minute by Hardinge, 12 Apr 1919, FO 608/18.
12 'Note by Mr Balfour on the Report of the Czecho-Slovak Committee', 1 Apr 1919, FO 608/5.
13 Minute by Crowe, 15 Mar 1919, FO 608/45.
14 Minute by Hardinge, June 1919, FO 608/13.
15 Churchill to Lloyd George, 29 Jan 1919, Lloyd George Papers, F/8/3/9.
16 Perman, 123.
17 For a full discussion of the relationship between Britain and Greece, see Chapter V.
18 DBFP, I, 590.
19 Temperley, V, 305-58.
20 Venizelos, 3 Feb 1919, FRUS, III, 866.
21 DBFP, I, 262-3.
22 General Baird, *ibid.*, 316.
23 General Staff memorandum, 'The Situation in S.E. Europe and Turkey in Asia', FO 608/161. Minute by Crowe, 18 Apr 1919, FO 608/32.
24 Minute by Nicolson, 7 July 1919, FO 608/52. Kerr to Lloyd George, 9 Aug 1919, Lloyd George Papers, F/89/4/2.
25 Balfour to Bryce, 15 Aug 1919, Balfour MSS 49749.
26 Minute by Nicolson, 15 July 1919, FO 608/55.
27 Sir H. Lamb (Sofia) to Curzon, 14 Apr 1919, FO 608/31.
28 D.H. Miller, *My Diary at the Conference of Paris*, X, 298-9.
29 Minute by Crowe, 16 July 1919, FO 608/55.
30 On the subsequent fate of Eastern Thrace, see below, Chapter V.
31 Pichon, 5 Sept 1919, DBFP, I, 634.

32 See, for example, Leeper minute, 25 Jan 1919, FO 608/48.
33 Balfour, 3 Sept 1919, DBFP, I, 615.
34 Crowe, 1 Nov 1919, DBFP, II, 141.
35 Balfour, 1 Aug 1919, DBFP, I, 282.
36 Crowe, 11 July 1919, FO 608/55.
37 Nicolson, 18 June 1919, FO 608/225.
38 Note of 4 June 1919, FO 608/225. This view is reflected in article 121 of the treaty.
39 Crowe, 1 Nov 1919, DBFP, II, 151-2.
40 Introduction to Part IV, the military clauses of the treaty.
41 For an account of Rumania at the peace conference see Sherman David Spector, *Rumania at the Paris Peace Conference*. For Hungary see Francis Deák, *Hungary at the Paris Peace Conference*.
42 Spector, 116.
43 *ibid.*, 144.
44 'Memorandum by the British Delegation (Political Section). Recommendations submitted by the British technical delegates.' 8 Feb 1919, FO 608/142.
45 Minute by Hardinge, end Mar 1919, FO 608/11.
46 General Smuts' Report, FO 608/16.
47 Minute by Crowe, 30 May 1919, 9 April 1919, FO 608/11.
48 For details see René Albrecht-Carrié, *Italy at the Paris Peace Conference*; Ivo J. Lederer, *Yugoslavia at the Paris Peace Conference: A Study in Frontier Making*; C. J. Lowe and F. Mazari, *Italian Foreign Policy 1870-1940*, Chapters 7 and 8.
49 Lederer, 61.
50 Minutes by Crowe, 16 and 19 June 1919, FO 608/16 and 39; Minutes by Hardinge, May and June 1919, FO 608/8 and 225.
51 Memorandum by the Director of Military Operations, 15 Jan 1919, FO 608/5.
52 Admiralty to Foreign Office, 15 Jan 1919, FO 371/3507.
53 Minute by Crowe, 16 Jan 1919, FO 608/15.
54 FRUS, V, 81.
55 Nicolson to Kerr, 14 Apr 1919, FO 608/15.
56 Hardinge to Rodd, 19 May 1919, FO 608/6.
57 For a detailed account see Perman and Deák, (*passim*).
58 Minute by Crowe, 24 May 1919, FO 608/6.
59 Minute by Hardinge, Apr 1919, *ibid.*
60 Perman, 171-2.
61 For details see Karl S. Stadtler, *The Birth of the Austrian Republic, 1918-1921*.
62 Minute by Headlam-Morley, 18 Mar 1919, FO 608/9.
63 T. Komarnicki, *Rebirth of the Polish Republic*, 275.
64 FRUS, IV, 316.
65 Drummond to Kerr, 18 Jan 1919, Lothian MSS, GD 40/17/15.
66 Memorandum by G. W. Prothero, 20 Feb 1919, FO 608/141.
67 'Note on West Prussia and Danzig', by Headlam-Morley, 25 Feb 1919, FO 608/141.

68 FRUS, IV, 414-9.
69 Minute by Paton, 12 Jan 1919, FO 608/63.
70 Minute by Balfour, Apr 1919, FO 608/69.
71 Minute by Balfour, Apr 1919, *ibid.*
72 Minute by Paton, 15 May 1919, FO 608/62.
73 For details see Stanley W. Page, *The Formation of the Baltic States.*
74 Minute by Paton, 16 Mar 1919, FO 608/183.
75 Minute by Hardinge, Mar 1919, *ibid.*
76 Hardinge to Balfour, 26 Apr 1919, FO 608/203.
77 Minute by Paton, 28 Mar 1919, FO 608/198.
78 Minute by Esmé Howard, 30 May 1919, *ibid.*
79 Carr to Tufton, 5 Sept 1919, FO 608/193.
80 This section is largely based on John M. Thompson's excellent *Russia, Bolshevism and the Versailles Peace.*
81 Lloyd George to Churchill (two telegrams), 16 Feb 1919, FO 608/177.
82 At the Council of Four, 29 Mar 1919, cited in Thompson, 207.
83 Minutes by Carr, 28 May 1919, and Hardinge, May 1919, FO 608/178.
84 Minute by Esmé Howard, 24 Apr 1919, FO 608/230.
85 Crowe to Hardinge, 15 Nov 1919, FO 608/208.
86 On 7 April 1920, Deák, 175 footnote 2.
87 For details of the complex negotiation see Lowe and Mazari, 172-80.

Chapter Four

1 This conflict began well before 1914. See Neville J. Mandel, *The Arabs and Zionism Before World War I.*
2 See A. S. Klieman, 'Britain's War Aims in the Middle East in 1915', *JCH*, 1968.
3 J. D. Goold, 'Lord Hardinge and the Mesopotamia Expedition', *HJ*, 1976, 930-31.
4 J. Nevakivi, *Britain, France and the Arab Middle East*, 8-9.
5 E. Kedourie, 'Cairo and Khartoum on the Arab Question, 1915-1918', *HJ*, 1964.
6 Letter of 14 Oct 1915, Cmd 5957 (1939).
7 Minute, 27 Oct 1915, I.O. L/P&S/10/523.
8 A. Nicolson to Hardinge, 11 Nov 1915, Hardinge Papers, 94.
9 Minute by A. Hirtzel, 2 Nov 1915, I.O. L/P&S/10/523.
10 C. M. Andrew and A. S. Kanya-Forstner, 'The French Colonial Party', *HJ*, 1974.
11 'French Draft of a Proposed New Anglo-French Agreement on Syria', c 6 Feb 1919, FO 608/107.
12 DBFP, IV, 245-7.
13 Leonard Stein, *The Balfour Declaration*, frontispiece.
14 Lloyd George, *The Truth*, II, 1138-9; Drummond note for Balfour, 24 Apr 1917, FO 371/3054.
15 Lloyd George, *The Truth*, II, 1129-30.
16 Nevakivi, 264.

17 A. T. Wilson, *Mesopotamia 1917-1920,* 103-4.

18 Minute of 8 Nov 1915, I.O. L/P&S/10/524.

19 Memorandum of 8 Nov 1915, 'Negotiations with Grand Shareef', *ibid.*

20 Minute of 23 Mar 1916, I.O. L/P&S/10/525.

21 E. Monroe, *Britain's Moment in the Middle East,* 32-7.

22 FO 608/107.

23 DBFP, IV, 343.

24 E. Kedourie, *In the Anglo-Arab Labyrinth.*

25 Z. N. Zeine, *The Struggle for Arab Independence,* 46.

26 Minute by Hardinge, undated, on Cambon communication of 18 Nov 1918, FO 371/3385.

27 Lloyd George, *The Truth,* II, 1038. According to the Sykes-Picot agreeement, Mosul was within France's sphere, while Palestine was to be internationalized.

28 Zeine, 59.

29 Nevakivi, 89-93.

30 *ibid.,* 100-101.

31 'The Strategic Importance of Syria to the British Empire', FO 608/107.

32 Nevakivi, 99-100.

33 Lloyd George, *The Truth,* II, 1153.

34 *ibid.,* II, 1150.

35 *ibid.,* II, 1153-4, 1151.

36 Article 6. Quoted in P. C. Helmreich, *From Paris to Sèvres,* 27.

37 Nevakivi, 102-3.

38 FRUS, III, 889-94. Praise from Hardinge in Hardinge to Chirol, 8 Feb 1919, Hardinge Papers, 40. See also 'Memo by the Emir Feisal', 1 Jan 1919, and Foreign Office minutes praising it, FO 608/80.

39 'Comments by the Foreign Office Section on the French Memo', 6 Feb 1919, FO 608/107. 'Statement of British Policy in the Middle East for Submission to the Peace Conference (If Required)', 18 Feb 1919, FO 608/83.

40 Letter of 23 Jan 1919, FO 608/107.

41 Minute by Louis Mallet, 4 Feb 1919, Lothian Papers, GD 40/17/37. Minute by Gertrude Bell, representing her views and those of T. E. Lawrence, 14 Mar 1919, FO 608/105.

42 'English Translation of the French Draft of a Proposed New Anglo-French Agreement over Syria', undated, FO 608/107.

43 Nevakivi, 117-9; Helmreich, 29-31.

44 Minute of 30 Jan 1919, FO 608/107.

45 Note of 5 Mar 1919, *ibid.* For an interesting and caustic reply to French complaints, see Curzon to Cambon, 19 Mar 1919, *ibid.*

46 *ibid.*

47 See below, 156.

48 Milner to Lloyd George, 8 Mar 1919, Lloyd George Papers, F/39/1/10. See also Kerr to Lloyd George, 11 and 12 Feb 1919, *ibid.,* F/89/2/7 and 9.

49 FRUS, V, 1-14.

50 Miller, *My Diary,* VII, 169-90. H. W. Steed, *Through Thirty Years,* 300.

51 Clemenceau to Faisal, 17 Apr 1919 (never sent); Faisal to Clemenceau,

undated, FO 406/41 or DBFP, IV, 251-3.

52 Zeine, 86.

53 FRUS, V, 760-6, 807-12. Quote from C. E. Callwell, *Field Marshal Sir Henry Wilson,* II, 194.

54 FRUS, V, 812.

55 See DBFP, IV, 1089 ff. Marion Kent, *Oil and Empire,* Appendix IV.

56 DBFP, IV, 1089 ff; Lloyd George to Clemenceau, 12 June 1919, Lloyd George Papers, F/12/1/25(a). Lloyd George in FRUS, V, 809-10. For Anglo-French oil negotiations during 1919-20, see Kent, 137-57.

57 FRUS, IV, 161-70.

58 L. Mallet, 'Memo on Dr Weizmann's Account of his Interview with President Wilson, the 14th January 1919', FO 608/98.

59 Balfour to Lloyd George, 19 Feb 1919, Lloyd George Papers, F/3/4/12.

60 Balfour memo of 23 Mar 1919, Balfour MSS 49751.

61 Minute by W. Ormsby-Gore, 21 Jan 1919, FO 608/98.

62 See, for example, Ormsby-Gore memos of 22 and 23 Jan 1919; Ormsby-Gore to Sokolov, 24 Jan; Mallet minute of 30 Jan, *ibid.*

63 Agreement of 16 Jan 1919, *ibid.*

64 Letter of 1 Mar 1919, *ibid.*, and in R. Meinertzhagen, *Middle East Diary,* 15-6, who says that the letter was drafted by Faisal, T. E. Lawrence, Weizmann, Frankfurter and himself.

65 Balfour MSS, 49687.

66 Letter of 3 Apr 1919, *ibid.*

67 Letter of 9 Apr 1919, *ibid.*

68 Minutes by Toynbee of 18 Jan and by Ormsby-Gore of 21 Jan 1919, FO 608/98.

69 Telegram no 259 of 31 Dec 1918 and minute by Curzon of 10 Jan 1919, *ibid.*

70 Minute by Curzon of 26 Jan 1919, FO 608/99.

71 Curzon to Balfour, 26 Jan 1919, Curzon Papers, F/2/2.

72 Curzon to Balfour, 16 Jan 1919, Lloyd George Papers, F/3/4/4.

73 Curzon to Balfour, 25 Mar 1919, Curzon Papers, F/2/2.

74 DBFP, IV, 259.

75 *ibid.,* 345.

76 *ibid.*

77 Allenby, *ibid.,* 256. Minute by H. Wilson, 5 June 1919, FO 608/107.

78 FRUS, XII, 751-63.

79 Minutes by Adam, 13 Aug 1919, by Balfour, undated, FO 608/107.

80 Hardinge to Hohler (Constantinople), 30 June 1919, Hardinge Papers, 40. Minute by Vansittart, undated, FO 608/107.

81 Lloyd George Papers, F/89/4/13.

82 H. Wilson, 2 Sep 1919, Callwell, II, 211. Curzon to Lloyd George, 2 Sep 1919: 'You might as well attempt to take Deauville [in northern France where Lloyd George was staying] by landing a force at Marseilles'. Lloyd George Papers, F/12/1/39.

83 DBFP, I, 700-1.

84 DBFP, IV, 384-5; DBFP, I, 690-3.

85 Monroe, *Britain's Moment in the Middle East,* 64-6, 71, cf. Nevakivi, 191,

who refers to the *aide-mémoire* as 'a frank and realistic programme'.
86 DBFP, IV, 401.
87 Kerr to Lloyd George, 8 Nov 1919, Lloyd George Papers, F/89/4/20.
88 Balfour memo, 9 Sep 1919, Balfour MSS, 49752.
89 23 Sep 1919, DBFP, IV, 418.
90 19 Sep 1919, *ibid.*, 403. See also Derby to Curzon, 25 Oct 1919, Curzon Papers, F/6/2.
91 1 Jan 1920, DBFP, IV, 588.
92 24 Dec 1919, *ibid.*, 592.
93 *ibid.*, 625-7.
94 20 Dec 1919, *ibid.*, 592.
95 Memo of 9 Sep 1919, Balfour Papers, 49752.
96 DBFP, IV, 623.
97 14 Jan 1920, *ibid.*, 630.
98 21 Dec 1919, *ibid.*, 1114. Also in Kent, app IV.
99 DBFP, XIII, 226.
100 But not Mesopotamia, with which he had no legitimate connection, and which in the 1918-19 inquiry had emphatically pronounced against a Sherifian ruler.
101 DBFP, XIII, 231, 233-4.
102 Quoted in Helmreich, 274.
103 DBFP, VIII, 9-10, 144-5.
104 18 Feb 1920, DBFP, VII, 116.
105 DBFP, VIII, 175.
106 Callwell, II, 235..
107 Kedourie, *England and the Middle East,* 147.
108 Nevakivi, 197.

Chapter Five

1 Above, 132
2 Above, *ibid*
3 J. Hurewitz (ed), *Diplomacy in the Near and Middle East,* II, 11.
4 Wilson's Twelfth Point, quoted in Helmreich, 8; Lloyd George's speech of 5 Jan 1918 in Lloyd George, *The Truth,* II, 1254.
5 Lothian Papers, GD/40/17/38.
6 M. Gilbert, *Sir Horace Rumbold,* 165.
7 For a good review of British policy towards the Straits, see Harold Nicolson's memo of 15 Nov 1922, DBFP, XVIII, 974-83.
8 H. Nicolson, *Curzon: The Last Phase,* 76-7.
9 *ibid.*, 77-8; M. Llewellyn Smith, *Ionian Vision,* 65; and see J. B. Gidney, *A Mandate for Armenia,* 126: 'Prior to May 15, 1919 the Turks were prepared to accept a harsh peace'.
10 Meetings of departmental missions, 30 and 31 Jan, FO 374/20 or FO 608/109.
11 30 Jan, FRUS, III, 788. Cf, however, Kerr to Lloyd George, 26 Feb, Lloyd George Papers, F/89/2/33.

12 FRUS, III, 859-66, 868-75.

13 Hardinge to Rodd, 6 Feb, Hardinge Papers, 40; Balfour to Rodd, 14 Mar, Balfour Papers, 49745; Balfour to Curzon, Curzon Papers, F/2/2.

15 Crowe, 10 and 13 Mar, FO 608/103; Nicolson, 15 and 21 Mar, FO 608/37 and 103.

16 Miller, X (2), 291.

17 FO 608/102.

18 12 Apr, Lloyd George Papers, F/24/2/25.

19 Curzon 'Note of Warning', 25 Mar, Cab Paper G.T. 7037; Curzon to Balfour, 25 Mar, Curzon Papers, F/2/2.

20 Harold Nicolson, *Peacemaking 1919,* 312; memo of 14 Apr with minutes, FO 608/110.

21 Mantoux, *Les Délibérations,* I, 455-6. Cf. FRUS, V, 412-3, 422.

22 FRUS, V, 466-7.

23 *ibid.,* 484.

24 *ibid.,* 570.

25 Nicolson, 6 May, *Peacemaking,* 327.

26 FRUS, V, 432.

27 Smith, 79.

28 13 May, FRUS, V, 582.

29 17 Nov, 1920, Lloyd George Papers, F/55/1/41.

30 M. G. Fry, *Lloyd George and Foreign Policy,* I, 257.

31 Quoted in Smith, 80.

32 *ibid.,* 83.

33 *ibid.,* 79.

34 Winston Churchill, *The World Crisis: The Aftermath,* 389. Cf. A. J. Toynbee, *The Western Question in Greece and Turkey,* xxi.

35 Minute of 7 May, Lothian Papers, GD 40/17/38.

36 Rodd to Balfour, 12 May, Curzon Papers, F/3/1.

37 Callwell, II, 190.

38 Helmreich, 101.

39 B. C. Busch, *Mudros to Lausanne,* 91.

40 Nicolson, *Peacemaking,* 326-7, 331.

41 Quoted in Smith, 89-90.

42 FRUS, V, 690-701.

43 Nicolson, *Curzon,* 99-103; D. Waley, *Edwin Montagu,* 239.

44 21 May, FRUS, V, 756.

45 Balfour memo of 16 May, *ibid.,* 669-72, or FO 608/110.

46 21 May, FRUS, V, 756.

47 25 June, FRUS, VI, 675.

48 DBFP, IV, 655 and 895. See also Calthorpe to Balfour, 1 July, FO 608/89.

49 Helmreich, 162-5.

50 DBFP, I, 879-80.

51 Smith, 111.

52 FRUS, IX, 47, 69, 71 and 72.

53 *ibid.,* 80.

54   *ibid.*, 43.
55   Callwell, II, 213.
56   DBFP, II, 295-6.
57   *ibid.*, 352-3.
58   B. Lewis, *The Emergence of Modern Turkey*, 237.
59   *ibid.*, 285; Lord Kinross, *Ataturk*, 503. For a more theoretical approach
     to Kemal's career, see D. A. Rustow, 'Atatürk as Founder of a State',
     Daedalus, summer, 1968, 793-828.
60   Pact in Temperley, VI, 605-6, as adopted by the Constantinople parliament
     on 28 Jan 1920.
61   See above, 164 ff.
62   Lloyd George Papers, F/89/4/23.
63   DBFP, II, 727-8.
64   *ibid.*, 728-33; DBFP, IV, 938 ff; A. L. Macfie, 'The British Decision
     Regarding the Future of Constantinople, November 1918-January 1920',
     HJ, 1975, 391-400.
65   Montagu, 18 Dec 1919 and 1 Jan 1920, Cabinet Papers, CAB 24/326 and
     382. Montagu to Lloyd George, 5 Jan 1920, Lloyd George Papers,
     F/40/3/1.
66   DBFP, IV, 992-1000.
67   Nicolson, *Curzon*, 112-3, and see above, 185.
68   Meeting of 5 Jan, 1920, CAB 23/20, CAB I, appendix I.
69   Cmd 964 (1920).
70   H. N. Howard, *Turkey, the Straits and United States Policy*, 100-101.
71   DBFP, VII, 164-73. 'I said [to the Italians] that frankly the Tripartite
     Agreement was not a very pretty looking document . . .'. Vansittart to
     Curzon, 11 May 1920, FO 608/278.
72   DBFP, VII, 56; Busch, 198-9.
73   Gidney, 21-3; R. G. Hovannisian, *Armenia on the Road to Independence,
     1918*, 243.
74   DBFP, VIII, 54-64. Cf General Staff memo of 1 Apr 1920, CAB 24/1014.
75   DBFP, VIII, 61.
76   DBFP, XIII, 18.
77   Curzon to Kerr, 12 Mar 1920, Curzon Papers, F/3/3. See also Curzon to
     Lloyd George, 9 Apr, *ibid.* Curzon to Lloyd George, 18 Mar, warns of
     Greek exaggeration, Lloyd George Papers, F/12/3/19.
78   General Staff memos of 1 and 7 Apr 1920, CAB 24/1014 and 1027.
     Counter memo by Kerr, 7 Apr, Lloyd George Papers, F/90/1/4.
79   Letter of 9 Apr 1920, *ibid.*, F/12/3/24.
80   DBFP, VIII, 61, 56.
81   DBFP, VII, 302.
82   *ibid.*, 377-9.
83   *ibid.*, 416.
84   DBFP, VIII, 92.
85   DBFP, VII, 412.
86   Helmreich, 285.
87   A. E. Montgomery, 'The Making of the Treaty of Sèvres of 10 August
     1920', *HJ*, December, 1972, 785.

88   Curzon to de Robeck, 18 May 1920: 'It [the Treaty] was conditioned by promises given (as I think, most unwisely) to Venizelos in Paris last year'. Curzon Papers, F/3/3.

89   *Sunday Times*, 30 May 1920, quoted in E. G. Mears, *Modern Turkey*, 516. Cf Churchill, 20 Mar 1922, CAB 23/29/22: 'The signature of the Treaty of Sèvres had been one of the most unfortunate events in the history of the world'.

90   Callwell II, 244.

91   Smith, 123-6.

92   House of Commons Debates, fifth series, vol 132, cols 478-9. Venizelos thanks Lloyd George, letter of 23 July, Lloyd George Papers, F/55/1/32.

93   House of Commons Debates, 22 Dec 1920, fifth series, vol 136, cols 1893-1901.

94   DBFP, XII, 533; VIII, 840-1, 864.

95   Minute by D. G. Osborne, 29 Dec 1920, FO 371/5181.

96   S. R. Sonyel, *Turkish Diplomacy, 1918-1923*, Chapter 3.

97   Conference of ministers, 18 Feb 1921, CAB 23/24/14.

98   Churchill, *The World Crisis: The Aftermath*, 418-9.

99   War Office memo, 19 Feb 1921, CAB 24/2608.

100   DBFP, XV, 150. See also 'The Greek Army in Asia Minor', enclosed in Rangabe to Kerr, 25 Feb 1921, Lloyd George Papers, F/55/2/4.

101   Calogeropoulos (London) to Minister of Foreign Affairs (Athens), 1 Mar 1921, Curzon Papers, F/1/7.

102   Calogeropoulos to Minister of Foreign Affairs, 19 Mar 1921, *ibid.*

103   Churchill, *The World Crisis: The Aftermath*, 417.

104   Callwell, II, 281.

105   See FO memo of 22 Apr 1921, 'The Supply of War Material to Greece', and the Greek response: Greek legation to Lloyd George, 1 May 1921, Lloyd George Papers, F/13/2/18 and F/55/2/9.

106   Notes by the General Staff and Harrington, 20 and 25 May, CAB 24/2981. Busch, 313. Also see Roskill, *Hankey, Man of Secrets*, II, 230.

107   Callwell, II, 294.

108   Smith, 205.

109   Quoted in *ibid.*, 226.

110   House of Commons Debates, 16 Aug 1921, fifth series, vol 146, col 1235.

111   Churchill, *The World Crisis: The Aftermath*, 424.

112   Curzon to Hardinge, 20 Sep 1921, Hardinge Papers, 44.

113   DBFP, XVII, 564-9.

114   Curzon to Hardinge, 10 Nov 1921, Hardinge Papers, 44.

115   For typical British opinions on Poincaré, see Viscount d'Abernon, *An Ambassador of Peace*, I, 317-8; Cecil to Balfour, 11 July 1922, Cecil Papers, 51095; Crewe to Curzon, 28 Dec 1922, Curzon Papers, F/7/3.

116   DBFP, XVII, 579-80. Curzon-Poincaré conversation of 16 Jan 1922, also in CAB 24/3640.

117   Letter of 26 Jan 1922, Hardinge Papers (Kent), U. 927/029/99.

118   DBFP, XVII, 572.

119   Letter in House of Lords Debates, fifth series, vol 52, cols 338-40.

120 Curzon reply of 6 Mar 1922, *ibid.*, cols 342-3.
121 DBFP, XVII, 621.
122 *ibid.*, 634.
123 *ibid.*, 645.
124 *ibid.*, 749-54.
125 Memo of 22 Dec 1921, CAB 24/3576. Montagu to Curzon, 2 Feb 1922, Curzon Papers, F/5.
126 Telegram of 1 Mar 1922, CAB 24/133, CP 3794.
127 Letter of 6 Mar 1922, Curzon Papers, F/5.
128 Quoted in Waley, 272-3.
129 Lloyd George to Curzon, 9 Mar 1922, Lloyd George Papers, F/13/3/11.
130 Waley, 277-9; Busch, *Mudros to Lausanne*, 333.
131 Quoted in Smith, 248; DBFP, XVII, 641-2.
132 Lloyd George Papers, F/86/2/3.
133 House of Commons Debates, fifth series, vol 157, cols 1997 ff.
134 DBFP, XVII, 919.
135 *ibid.*, 919; Curzon to Hardinge, 19 Aug 1922, Hardinge Papers, 45.
136 Kinross, 311.
137 Smith, 302.
138 Kinross, 326.
139 Gilbert, 263.
140 Churchill, *The World Crisis: The Aftermath*, 444-5.
141 Cabinet meeting of 7 Sep 1922, CAB 23/31/48.
142 Martin Gilbert, *Winston S. Churchill*, IV, 820.
143 Busch, *Britain, India and the Arabs*, 350.
144 DBFP, XVIII, 22.
145 Busch, *Britain, India and the Arabs*, 345.
146 For the Balkans, see Nicolson memo of 14 Sep, and Lloyd George to Curzon, 15 Sep, Lloyd George Papers, F/13/3/32 and 33.
147 Text in Churchill, *The World Crisis: The Aftermath*, 452-4. For criticism of the communiqué, see William Tyrrell to Curzon, 22 Sep, Curzon Papers, F/5, and Lord Grey in *The Times*, 20 Sep.
148 DBFP, XVIII, 32-4.
149 Curzon's two meetings of 20 Sep, *ibid.*, 38-61 (quote from 52-3). Also in CAB 24/4201 and 4202.
150 DBFP, XVIII, 66-85; also in CAB 24/4213.
151 DBFP, XVIII, 78.
152 Nicolson, *Curzon*, 274.
153 Hardinge, *Old Diplomacy*, 272.
154 DBFP, XVIII, 84-5, 88-96. *The Times*, 25 Sep 1922, 10.
155 DBFP, XVIII, 104.
156 Roskill, II, 289.
157 DBFP, XVIII, 118.
158 Gilbert, *Churchill*, IV, 850.
159 Roskill, II, 291.
160 Gilbert, *Rumbold*, 269.
161 Curzon to Hardinge, 1 Oct, Hardinge Papers, 45.
162 Hardinge to Curzon, 2 Oct, *ibid.*

163 Alice Keppel to Rumbold, 12 Oct, quoted in Gilbert, *Rumbold*, 274.
164 Curzon Papers, F/5.
165 Curzon to Hardinge, 15 Nov, Hardinge Papers, 45.
166 Nicolson, *Curzon*, 282.
167 For the details of the negotiations, see Cmd 1814 (1923), 'Records of Proceedings of the Lausanne Conference on Near Eastern Affairs 1922-1923, and Draft Terms of Peace'; DBFP, XVIII, Chapters II-IV; and Cmd 1929 (1923) for the treaty itself.
168 DBFP, XVIII, 399.
169 *ibid.*, 436.
170 Cmd 1814, 219.
171 H. J. Psomiades, *The Eastern Question: The Last Phase*, 68.
172 Cmd 1814, 215.
173 Gilbert, *Rumbold*, 276.
174 DBFP, XVIII, 400.
175 *ibid.*, 415-6.
176 J. C. Grew, *Turbulent Era, A Diplomatic Record of Forty Years, 1904-1945*, I, 524.
177 Earl of Ronaldshay, *The Life of Lord Curzon*, III, 332.
178 Bonar Law to Curzon, 8 Jan 1923, *ibid.*, 333; R. Blake, *The Unknown Prime Minister: The Life and Times of Andrew Bonar Law*, 486-90.
179 '. . . I believe Barrère to be fairly straight, thanks probably to his having been educated at Eton'. Hardinge to Curzon, 10 Nov 1922, Hardinge Papers, 45.
180 DBFP, XVIII, 460, 467.
181 Quoted in Busch, *Mudros*, 383.
182 The conference resumed on 23 Apr 1923. For a full account see Sonyel, 215-26.
183 Grew, I, 584.
184 Howard, Chapter V and appendix III.
185 For the former view, see *ibid.*, 113 and 123; Sonyel, 225; R. H. Davison, 'Middle East Nationalism: Lausanne Thirty Years After', *The Middle East Journal*, Summer, 1953, 344; and Grew, I, 569, who claims that Ismet's victory 'was probably the greatest diplomatic victory in history . . .'.
     For the view that Lausanne was a victory for Curzon, see Nicolson, *Curzon*, 282; Ronaldshay, III, 341-3; Roskill, II, 326; Blake, 390. For Curzon's own assessment, see DBFP, XVIII, ix.
186 Psomiades, 106-9. There was, however, to be great trouble over Cyprus, which was not an issue at Lausanne, where both Turkey and Greece recognized Britain's annexation of November 1914.
187 Grew, I, 536.
188 Nevile Henderson, *Water under the Bridges*, 116.
189 See, for example, DBFP, XVIII, 336, 387, 398 and 465.
190 *ibid.*, 338, 448, 523.
191 Grew, 525-6.
192 Gilbert *Rumbold*, 292.
193 See above 185-6.

194 Lloyd George, *The Truth*, II, 1342 ff.
195 CAB 23/31/48; Tyrrell to Curzon, 23 Sep, Curzon Papers, F/5. Cf Lloyd George to Curzon, 15 Sep 1922, Lloyd George Papers, F/13/3/33: 'From the moment Greece threw over Venizelos and placed its destinies in the hands of Constantine I realized that a pro-Greek policy in Anatolia was doomed . . .'
196 W. S. Churchill, *Great Contemporaries*, 281.
197 Curzon to Balfour, 20 June 1919, FO 608/110.
198 Toynbee, 61, 72-3.
199 Gilbert, *Rumbold*, 275.
200 Frances Stevenson, *Lloyd George: A Diary by Frances Stevenson*, 241.
201 Sonyel, 209.
202 DBFP, XVIII, 504. Cf Grew, I, 492, 515.

BIBLIOGRAPHY

Documents and Papers

OFFICIAL PAPERS   Public Record Office
Foreign Office Political Series   FO 371 series
Foreign Office Confidential Prints   FO 406 series
India Office Political Department   L/P & S/10 series
The Paris Peace Conference 1919   FO 608 series
War Cabinet Minutes 1919   CAB 23 series
Cabinet Minutes 1919-1922   CAB 23 series
Cabinet Memoranda   CAB 24 series
War Cabinet papers   G.T. 1-8412
Cabinet papers, post November 1919   C.P. 1-4379

PRIVATE MANUSCRIPT MATERIAL

Balfour, A. J.   British Museum and Public Record Office (FO 800
                         series)
Curzon, Lord   India Office Library and Public Record Office
                         (FO 800 series)
Hardinge, Lord   Cambridge University Library
Lloyd George, David   House of Lords Record Office
Lothian, Lord   National Library of Scotland
  (Philip Kerr)

PUBLISHED DOCUMENTS

Documents on British Foreign Policy, 1919-1939, First Series,
ed. Woodward, E. L. and Butler, R. (London, 1947-   ).
Diplomacy in the Near and Middle East: A Documentary Record, Vol II, 1914-1956
ed. Hurewitz, J. C. (New York, 1956).
Mantoux, Paul *Paris Peace Conference, 1919: Proceedings of the Council of Four,
March 24th-April 18th* (Geneva, 1964)
             Les Délibérations du Conseil des Quatre: Notes de l'Officier Interprète,
2 vols (Paris 1955)

*Papers relating to the foreign relations of the United States. The Paris Peace Conference,
1919.* United States Department of State, Washington 1924-47.
Parliamentary Command Papers.
Parliamentary Debates, House of Commons Debates, fifth series.
Parliamentary Debates, House of Lords Debates, fifth series.

Books

Albrecht-Carrié, R. *Italy at the Paris Peace Conference* (New York, 1938)

Alostos, D. *Venizelos: Patriot, Statesman, Revolutionary* (London, 1942)

Blake, R. *The Unknown Prime Minister: The Life and Times of Andrew Bonar Law, 1858-1923* (London, 1955)

Bunselmeyer, Ronald E. *The Cost of the War, 1914-1919: British Economic War Aims and the Origins of Reparation* (Hamden, Conn., 1975)

Busch, B. C. *Britain, India and the Arabs, 1914-1921* (Berkeley, 1971)
  Mudros to Lausanne: Britain's Frontier in West Asia, 1918-1923 (Albany, N.Y., 1976)

Butler, J. R. M. *Lord Lothian, Philip Kerr: 1882-1940* (London, 1960)

Calder, Kenneth J. *Britain and the Origins of the New Europe, 1914-1918* (Cambridge, 1976)

Callwell, Major-Gen. Sir C. E. *Field-Marshal Sir Henry Wilson: His Life and Diaries*, 2 vols (London, 1927)

Churchill, Winston S. *The World Crisis: Vol 5, The Aftermath, 1918-1928* (New York, 1929)
  Great Contemporaries (London, 1938)

Cohen, S. A. *British Policy in Mesopotamia, 1903-14* (London, 1976)

Craig, G. A. and Gilbert, F. *The Diplomats: 1919-1939*, 2 vols (New York, 1965)

D'Abernon, Viscount *An Ambassador of Peace: Pages from the Diary of Viscount D'Abernon (Berlin 1920-26)*, 3 vols (London, 1929-30)

Deák, Francis *Hungary at the Paris Peace Conference: The Diplomatic History of the Treaty of Trianon* (New York, 1942)

Egerton, George W. *Great Britain and the Creation of the League of Nations: Strategy, Politics and International Organization 1914-1919* (London, 1979)

Elcock, Howard *Portrait of a Decision: The Council of Four and the Treaty of Versailles* (London, 1972)

Floto, I. *Colonel House in Paris: A Study of American Policy at the Paris Peace Conference, 1919* (Aarhus, 1973)

Fry, Michael G. *Lloyd George and Foreign Policy, Vol One: The Education of a Statesman, 1890-1916* (London, 1977)

Gelfand, Lawrence E. *The Inquiry: American Preparations for Peace, 1917-1919* (New Haven and London, 1963)

Genov, G. P. *Bulgaria and the Treaty of Neuilly* (Sofia, 1935)

Gidney, J. B. *A Mandate for Armenia* (Kent, Ohio, 1967)

Gilbert, Martin *Winston S. Churchill*, Vol IV, *1917-1922* (London, 1975)
  Sir Horace Rumbold: Portrait of A Diplomat, 1869-1941 (London, 1973)

Grew, J. C. *Turbulent Era: A Diplomatic Record of Forty Years, 1904-1945*, 2 vols (Boston, 1952)

Hancock, W. K. *Smuts: The Sanguine Years 1907-1919* (Cambridge, 1962)

Hancock W. K. and van der Pohl, Jean (eds) *Selections from the Smuts Papers, 1886-1950*, 7 vols (Cambridge, 1966-73)

Hankey, Lord *The Supreme Control at the Paris Peace Conference, 1919: A Commentary* (London, 1963)

Hardinge, Lord *Old Diplomacy: The Reminiscences of Lord Hardinge of Penshurst* (London, 1947)

Headlam-Morley, Sir James (ed. Agnes Headlam-Morley) *A Memoir of the Paris Peace Conference, 1919* (London, 1972)

Helmreich, P. C. *From Paris to Sèvres: The Partition of the Ottoman Empire at the Peace Conference of 1919-1920* (Columbus, Ohio, 1974)

Henderson, Nevile *Water under the Bridges* (London, 1945)

Hovannisian, R. G. *Armenia on the Road to Independence, 1918* (Berkeley, 1967)

The Republic of Armenia, Vol I, *The First Year, 1918-1919* (Berkeley, 1971)

Howard, H. N. *Turkey, the Straits and United States Policy* (Baltimore and London, 1974)

Kedourie, E. *England and the Middle East: The Destruction of the Ottoman Empire, 1914-1921* (London, 1956)

In the Anglo-Arab Labyrinth: The McMahon-Husayn Correspondence and its Interpretations, 1914-1919 (London, 1976)

The Chatham House Version and other Middle-Eastern Studies (London, 1970)

Kent, Marion *Oil and Empire: British Policy and Mesopotamian Oil, 1900-1920* (London, 1976)

Keynes, John Maynard *The Economic Consequences of the Peace* (London, 1919)

King, Jere Clemens *Foch versus Clemenceau: France and German Dismemberment 1918-1919* (Cambridge, Mass, 1960)

Kinross, Lord *Atatürk: A Biography of Mustafa Kemal, Father of Modern Turkey* (New York, 1965)

Komarnicki, T. *Rebirth of the Polish Republic: A Study in the Diplomatic History of Europe 1914-1920* (London, 1957)

Lederer, Ivo J. *Yugoslavia at the Paris Peace Conference: A Study in Frontiermaking* (New Haven, 1963)

Lewis, B. *The Emergence of Modern Turkey* (London, 1961)

Lloyd George, David *The Truth about the Peace Treaties*, 2 vols (London, 1938)

The Truth about Reparations and War Debt (London, 1932)

War Memoirs, 2 vols (London, 1936)

Louis, W. Roger *Great Britain and Germany's Lost Colonies 1914-1919* (Oxford, 1967)

Lowe, C. J. and Dockrill, M. L. *The Mirage of Power: British Foreign Policy 1902-1922*, 3 vols (London, 1972)

Lowe, C. J. and Mazari, F. *Italian Foreign Policy 1870-1940* (London, 1975)

Luckau, Alma *The German Delegation at the Paris Peace Conference* (New York, 1941)

Macartney, C. A. *Hungary: A Short History* (Edinburgh, 1962)

Macartney, C. A. and Palmer, A. W. *Independent Eastern Europe: A History* (London, 1962)

Mandel, Neville J. *The Arabs and Zionism before World War I* (Berkeley and Los Angeles, 1977)

Mayer, Arno J. *Political Origins of the New Diplomacy, 1917-1918* (New Haven, 1959)

Politics and Diplomacy of Peacemaking: Containment and Counterrevolution at Versailles 1918-1919 (London, 1968)

Marder, Arthur J. *From the Dreadnought to Scapa Flow: The Royal Navy in the*

Fisher Era: 1904-1919, Vol V, *Victory and Aftermath, January 1918-June 1919* (London, 1970)

Meinertzhagen, R. *Middle East Diary, 1917-1956* (New York, 1960)

Miller, D. H. *My Diary at the Conference of Paris, with Documents*, 21 vols (New York, 1928)

Monroe, E. *Britain's Moment in the Middle East, 1914-1956* (London, 1963)

Nelson, Harold I. *Land and Power: British and Allied Policy on Germany's Frontiers, 1916-19* (London, 1963)

Néré, Jacques *The Foreign Policy of France from 1919 to 1945* (London, 1975)

Nevakivi, J. *Britain, France and the Arab Middle East, 1914-1920* (London, 1969)

Nicolson, Harold *Curzon: The Last Phase, 1919-1925. A Study in Post-War Diplomacy* (London, 1934)

Peacemaking 1919 (London, 1964)

Northedge, F. S. *The Troubled Giant: Britain among the Great Powers 1916-1939* (London, 1966)

Page, Stanley W. *The Formation of the Baltic States: A Study of the Effects of Great Power Politics upon the Emergence of Lithuania, Latvia and Estonia* (New York, 1970)

Perman, D. *The Shaping of the Czechoslovak State: A Diplomatic History of the Boundaries of Czechoslovakia 1914-1920* (Leiden, 1962)

Psomiades, H. J. *The Eastern Question: The Last Phase. A Study in Greek-Turkish Diplomacy* (Thessalonika, 1968)

Ronaldshay, Earl of *The Life of Lord Curzon, Being the Authorized Biography of . . .*, 3 vols (London, 1928)

Roskill, Stephen *Hankey: Man of Secrets*, 3 vols (London, 1970-74)

Rothwell, V. H. *British War Aims and Peace Diplomacy, 1914-1918* (Oxford, 1971)

Rudin, H. R. *Armistice 1918* (New Haven, 1944)

Smith, M. Llewellyn *Ionian Vision: Greece in Asia Minor, 1919-1922* (London, 1973)

Sonyel, S. R. *Turkish Diplomacy, 1918-1923: Mustafa Kemal and the Turkish National Movement* (Beverly Hills, 1975)

Spector, Sherman David *Rumania at the peace conference: A study of the diplomacy of Ioan I. C. Brátianu* (New York, 1962)

Stadler, Karl S. *The Birth of the Austrian Republic 1918-1921* (Leyden, 1968)

Steed, H. Wickham *Through Thirty Years, 1892-1922, A Personal Narrative*, Vol II (London, 1924)

Stein, Leonard *The Balfour Declaration* (New York, 1961)

Stevenson, Frances *Lloyd George: A Diary by Frances Stevenson* ed. by A. J. P. Taylor (London, 1971)

Taylor, A. J. P. *The Troublemakers: Dissent over Foreign Policy 1792-1939* (London, 1954)

Temperley, H. W. V. (ed) *A History of the Peace Conference of Paris*, 6 vols (London, 1920-1924)

Thompson, John M. *Russia, Bolshevism, and the Versailles Peace* (Princeton, 1966)

Tillman, Seth P. *Anglo-American Relations at the Paris Peace Conference of 1919* (Princeton, 1961)

Toynbee, A. J. *The Western Question in Greece and Turkey: A Study in the Contact of Civilisations* (London, 1923)

Troeller, Gary *The Birth of Saudi Arabia: Britain and the Rise of the House of Sa'ud* (London, 1976)

Trumpener, U. *Germany and the Ottoman Empire, 1914-1918* (Princeton, 1968)

Walder, David *The Chanak Affair* (London, 1969)

Waley, S. D. *Edwin Montagu: A Memoir and an Account of His Visits to India* (New York, 1964)

Wilson, A. T. *Mesopotamia 1917-1920: A Clash of Loyalties: A Personal and Historical Record* (London, 1931)

Zeine, Z. N. *The Struggle for Arab Independence: Western Diplomacy and the Rise and Fall of Faisal's Kingdom in Syria* (Beirut, 1960)

Articles

Andrew, C. M. and Kanya-Forstner, A. S. 'The French Colonial Party and French Colonial War Aims, 1914-1918', *HJ*, 1974

Davison, R. H. 'Middle East Nationalism: Lausanne Thirty Years After', *The Middle East Journal*, 1953

Dockrill, M. L. and Steiner, Zara 'The Foreign Office at the Paris Peace Conference 1919', *International History Review*, 1980

Egerton, G. W. 'Britain and the "Great Betrayal": Anglo-American Relations and the Struggle for United States Ratification of the Treaty of Versailles, 1919-1920', *HJ*, 1978

'The Lloyd George Government and the Creation of the League of Nations', *American Historical Review*, 1974

Friedman, I. 'The McMahon-Hussein Correspondence and the Question of Palestine', *JCH*, 1970

Goold, J. D. 'Lord Hardinge and the Mesopotamia Expedition and Inquiry, 1914-1917', *HJ*, 1976

'Lord Hardinge as Ambassador to France, and the Anglo-French Dilemma over Germany and the Near East, 1920-1922', *HJ*, 1978

Kedourie, E. 'Cairo and Khartoum on the Arab Question, 1915-1918', *HJ*, 1964

Klieman, A. S. 'Britain's War Aims in the Middle East in 1915', *JCH*, 1968

Lowe, C. J. 'Britain and Italian Intervention, 1914-15', *HJ*, 1969

'The Failure of British Diplomacy in the Balkans, 1914-1916', *Canadian Journal of History*, 1969

Macfie A. L. 'The British Decision Regarding the Future of Constantinople, November 1918-January 1920', *HJ*, 1975

Montgomery, A. E. 'The Making of the Treaty of Sèvres of 10 August 1920', *HJ*, 1972

Robbins, K. 'British Diplomacy and Bulgaria, 1914-1915', *Slavonic and East European Review*, 1971

Rustow, D. A. 'Atatürk as Founder of a State', *Daedalus*, 1968

Sharp, A. J. 'The Foreign Office in Eclipse, 1919-22', *History*, 1976

Toynbee, A. J. 'The McMahon-Hussein Correspondence: Comments and a Reply', *JCH*, 1970

Trachtenburg, Marc 'Reparation at the Paris Peace Conference', *JMH*, 1979

Troeller, Gary 'Ibn Sa'ud and Sherif Husain: A Comparison in Importance in the Early Years of the First World War', *HJ*, 1971

Warman, Roberta M. 'The Erosion of Foreign Office Influence in the Making of Foreign Policy, 1916-18', *HJ*, 1972

INDEX

Abdullah Ibn Hussein, Emir (Emir of Transjordan, 1921-46), 172

Adam, Forbes (Foreign Office official), 164

Albania, 106, 128

Alexander (King of Greece, 1917-20), 215

Allenby, General Sir Edmund (Commander-in-Chief Egyptian Expeditionary Force, 1917-19; High Commissioner for Egypt and the Sudan, 1920-25), 143, 144, 156, 158, 162, 168, 172-3, 237

Alsace-Lorraine, 19, 24, 29, 32, 34-5, 40

Anglo-American Guarantee to France, 28, 35, 37-8, 70, 85, 205

Angora, 221, 225, 228, 231, 232, 238, 244, 247

Arabia, 131, 148, 149, 176

Armenia, 65, 148, 149, 150, 153, 156, 159, 165, 166, 175, 181, 183, 184, 185, 187, 195, 198, 202, 209, 211, 214, 216, 228, 239

Asquith, Herbert Henry (Prime Minister, 1908-16), 17, 20-1, 48, 52, 133

Australia, 64

Austria-Hungary (Dual Monarchy), 17, 19, 87-113, 129, 188, 207, 255-6

Austria (Republic 1918-38), 91, 103, 104, 110, 111-3, 197, 257

Balfour, A. J. (Foreign Secretary 1916-19; Lord President of the Council 1919-22), 24, 27, 40, 80-1, 83, 94; and Anglo-American co-operation, 23; on Franco-German relations, 37; supports Belgian claims, 42; on future size of German army, 45; and Central Europe, 91-2, 95, 97-9, 103-4, 117; and Italy, 106-7; and Austria, 113, 175; the Balfour Declaration, 138-9, 175; and The Middle East, 142, 148, 159, 160-1, 162-4, 167, 169; and Turkey, 183, 188, 190, 197-8, 206, 217, 249-50

Barnes, George Nicholl (Member of the War Cabinet 1917-19; Minister without Portfolio 1917-20), 70, 72, 75, 76, 79

Belgium, 19, 32, 34, 111; claims at Peace Conference, 39-43; and reparations, 48-9, 57; secures Ruanda-Urandi, 67

Berthelot, Philippe, 170-1, 212

Birkenhead, Lord (F. E. Smith) (Attorney-General 1915-19; Lord Chancellor 1919-22), 72, 229, 236

Bohemia (see Czechoslovakia)

Bolshevism, 28-9, 93, 102-3, 114, 116, 118, 119, 120-4, 139, 154, 184, 186, 195, 205-6, 209, 217, 253, 257, 258

Borden, Sir Robert Laird (Canadian Prime Minister 1911-20; Chief Canadian Delegate at Paris Peace Conference 1919; Member of Imperial War Cabinet, 1917-19), 26

Botha, Louis (South African Prime Minister), 55, 66, 70

Bratianu, Ion (Rumanian Prime Minister), 98, 102-5

Brest-Litovsk, Treaty of, 18

Brian, Aristide (French Prime Minister and Foreign Minister 1921-2), 221-2

Bulgaria, 81, 93-101, 181, 187, 257

Bullitt, William C. (Member of American delegation), 122

Bunsen, Sir Maurice de (British diplomat), chairs Committee on war aims for Asiatic Turkey, 133, 134, 137

Cambon, Paul (French Ambassador to Great Britain), 172, 212

Carr, E. H. (Foreign Office official), 26, 120, 124

Cecil, Lord Robert (Minister of Blockade 1916-18; British delegate to the Paris Peace Conference 1919), 62-3, 71, 147; and war aims, 19; and reparations, 53-4; and the League, 57-8; on League Commission, 60-1; and the 'Cecil Plan', 59; and Central Europe, 90

Chamberlain, Sir Austen (Secretary of State for India 1915-17; Minister without Portfolio 1918-19; Chancellor of the Exchequer 1919-21; Lord Privy Seal 1921-22), 72, 136, 141, 234

Chanak, 228-36, 242, 247, 250, 251, 253, 255

Chicherin, G. V. (Soviet Commissar for Foreign Affairs 1918-30), 239

China, 67-8, 207

Churchill, Winston S. (Secretary of State for War 1918-20; Colonial Secretary 1920-22), 71, 93, 121, 123; and Greece and Turkey, 186, 195-6, 206, 212, 217, 219, 229, 231, 233-6, 249, 250, 253

Clemenceau, Georges (French Prime Minister 1917-20), 35, 40, 42, 45, 66, 81, 166, 173, 175, 177; and Fourteen Points, 22; visits London Dec 1918, 23, 145; assassination attempt, 27; and Fontainebleau Memorandum, 28-9; and Rhineland, 38; supports Japan's China claims, 68; refuses changes in Versailles treaty, 77-9; and Russia, 121; and Central Europe, 103, 105, 109, 113, 117, 125, 126; and Turkey, 147, 150, 155-8, 171, 194, 195, 201, 205

Clerk, Sir George (British diplomat), 125

Constantine (King of Greece 1913-17, 1920-22), 94, 97, 182, 187, 212, 213 215-6, 225, 227, 233, 248, 250

Constantinople [and the Straits], 181-7, 197-8, 202, 204-8, 212-3, 215, 218-20, 224, 227-30, 232-3, 235-9, 242, 244, 245, 249-50, 256

Council of Four (Prime Ministers), 27, 38, 39, 42, 53, 55, 69, 73, 77-9, 90, 95, 104, 108, 111, 112, 115, 120, 124, 155, 190, 191, 197-9

Council of Five (Foreign Ministers), 27, 95, 119, 120

Council of Ten, 26, 40, 44-5, 66, 88, 93, 102, 114, 115, 122, 150, 158, 187

Crane, Charles R. (US Commissioner to Middle East), 158, 162-4, 167, 177, 178

Crowe, Sir Eyre (AUS Foreign Office 1912-19; PUS 1920-5), 26, 32; and France, 23; and Belgian demands, 42; attacked by Lloyd George, 80-1; and Italy, 108; and Austria, 113; and Russia, 125; and Central Europe, 93, 95, 97-100, 104; and Turkey, 188, 190, 199, 201, 250

Cunliffe, Lord (Member of Imperial War Cabinet; Committee on Indemnity Nov-Dec 1918; British delegate on Peace Conference Commission on Reparation 1919), 47, 48, 51, 52, 55-6, 72

Curzon, George Nathaniel (Marquess of Kedleston) (Lord President of the Council, and member of War Cabinet 1916-18; Foreign Secretary 1919-24), 80, 148, 253, 254; war aims (territorial), 21; replaces Balfour, 81; and Central Europe, 90; and Russia, 121; and Zionism, 139; and Middle East, 144, 146, 161-2, 168, 170-1, 172, 173-4; and Greece and Turkey, 183, 185, 188-9, 193, 196, 199, 204, 205-8, 210-1, 216, 222-6, 228, 230-2, 234, 251; and Lausanne, 237-43, 245, 246-7, 248-9, 250, 252

Czechoslovakia, 26, 69-70, 87, 91-2, 103, 110-1, 118, 122, 127, 129, 257

Daniels, Josephus (US Secretary of the Navy), 62

d'Annunzio, Gabriele (Italian poet), 471

Danzig, 27, 70, 72, 91-2, 114-7

Denmark, 40

Derby, Earl of (British Ambassador to France 1918-20); on Franco-German relations, 36; on reparations, 54; on Syria, 169

Dmowski, Roman (Polish delegate at Paris Peace Conference), 115

Drummond, Eric (Foreign Office official), 114

Egypt, 93, 132, 137, 141, 147, 148, 151, 154, 165, 217

Estonia, 118-20

Faisal, Ibn Hussein (King of Syria 1920; King of Mesopotamia 1920-33), 144, 146, 150-1, 154-7, 159, 160-2, 167, 169, 170, 173-8, 240

Finland, 124

Fisher, H. A. L. (President of the Board of Education 1916-22), 71

Fiume, 68, 106-10, 128, 188, 191, 192, 194, 196, 255

Foch, Ferdinand (Marshal of France 1918; Commander of Allied Forces, France 1918), 102, 104, 123, 145, 209-11; and the Rhineland, 23, 24, 37-8, 79; and German disarmament, 44-5; and Allied military weakness, 69-70

Fontainebleau Memorandum, March 1919, 28-9, 51, 52, 61, 69

Foster, Sir George (Canadian Finance Minister), 47

France (see also Rhineland, Saar and
    Reparations), 17, 19, 23, 26, 29, 31-9,
    69-70, 74, 76, 85, 119, 248, 254, 255, 257,
    258; and Belgium, 39-43; and German
    disarmament, 43-5; and the League,
    60; and German colonies, 67; and
    Central Europe, 88, 91-2, 94, 95, 101,
    102-5, 127, 129; and Italy, 107-9, 128;
    and Czechoslovakia, 110-1; and
    Austria, 111-3; and Poland, 113-8; and
    Russia, 121-5; and the Middle East,
    131-79; Sykes-Picot Agreement, 137-8;
    and Turkey, 182-246, 250
Franklin-Bouillon, Henri (French
    politician), 221
George V, 251, 252
Germany (see also Rhineland and
    Reparations), 81, 88, 90, 145, 154, 189,
    195, 198, 205, 247, 252, 254-5, 257-8;
    March offensive, 21; and ex-colonies,
    19-21, 29, 33, 64-8, 84, 256; armistice
    appeal, 22; and German fleet, 33, 44,
    84; and disarmament, 34, 37, 43-5; and
    Belgian claims, 39-43; and North
    Schleswig, 40; and Versailles Treaty,
    69, 71-80; and Central Europe, 87, 91,
    96, 111; and Austria, 111-2; and
    Poland, 114-7; and Baltic Provinces,
    118-21; and Russia, 122-4, 197
Gladstone, W. E., 181
Gounaris (Greek Prime Minister), 220,
    223-4, 225, 226
Greece, 26, 94, 95-101, 106, 107, 165,
    182-229, 237, 244-5, 247-9, 250-2, 254-5
Grey, Sir Edward (Viscount Grey of
    Fallodon) (Foreign Secretary 1905-16),
    134, 135, 136, 141, 182; and entry into
    the war 1914, 17; Special Mission to the
    United States 1919-20, 83
Habsburg Empire (see Austria-
    Hungary)
Haig, Sir Douglas (Commander-in-
    Chief British Expeditionary Force
    1913-18), 22
Hankey, Maurice (Secretary, Committee
    of Imperial Defence, 1912-38;
    Secretary, War Cabinet, 1916-18, and to
    the Cabinet, 1919-38), 83, 189, 195, 233,
    234; Paris Peace Conference 1919, 25;
    Secretary to Council of Four, 28; and
    reparations, 49-50
Hardinge, Sir Charles (Baron Hardinge
    of Penshurst) (Viceroy of India

1910-16; PUS Foreign Office 1916-20;
    British Ambassador to France
    1920-23), 25, 32, 42, 83-4, 119-20, 124,
    133, 165; and war aims, 20; at Peace
    Conference, 25; and Central Europe,
    90-1, 93, 103; and Fiume, 108-10; and
    Turkey, 186-8, 190, 222-3, 231-4
Harington, General Sir Charles (GOC
    Allied Forces of Occupation, Turkey
    1920-23), 219-20, 230, 233-5
Haskins, Dr Charles H. (US Delegation
    Adviser), 117
Headlam-Morley, Sir James (Foreign
    Office official), and Danzig and Saar
    disputes, 27; and German
    constitutional changes, 32; and the
    Rhineland, 35; and the Saar, 39; and
    Belgian demands, 40-2; and Austria,
    111, 112, 113; and Danzig, 115, 116
Hirtzel, Sir Arthur (AUS for India
    1917-21), 136, 140, 153-5
Holland, 34, 39-43, 57
Hoover, Herbert, 209
House, Colonel Edward M. (Aide to
    President Wilson), 27, 38, 109, 111;
    and Fourteen Points, 22; and US naval
    programme, 62; and Russia 122; and
    Armenia, 209
Howard, Sir Esmé (Foreign Office
    official), 26, 114, 119, 120, 124
Hughes, William Morris (Australian
    Prime Minister 1915-23), on
    reparations, 46-56, 71-3, 75; on
    League, 59, 61; on racial equality, 63;
    on German colonies, 66
Hungary, 81, 88, 91, 110, 112, 257;
    territorial losses, 101-5;
    Bolshevik regime, 102-5, 123; and
    Rumania, 125; Peace Treaty, 126-7
Hurst, Cecil (Foreign Office Legal
    Adviser), 60, 83
Hussein (Sherif of Mecca 1908-16; King
    of the Hejaz 1916-24), 133, 135, 136,
    139, 140, 142, 148, 150, 151, 167, 168,
    176, 178
Hymans, Paul (Belgian Foreign
    Minister), 40
India, 71, 132, 141, 165, 184, 197, 198, 205,
    206, 217, 226
Iran (see Persia)
Iraq (see Mesopotamia)
Ismet Pasha Inönü (Turkish delegate at
    Lausanne 1923 and Turkish Prime

Minister and Foreign Minister
1922-24), 237-47, 251
Israel, 131
Italy, 26, 32, 48, 67, 68, 69, 145, 165,
177, 258; Treaty of London, 17, 105-6;
and Central Europe, 88, 90, 93, 95, 96,
98-102, 127; and Fiume, 105-10, 128;
and Austria, 111, 146, 148; and Turkey,
182-246, 248, 250
Japan, 26, 27, 95, 122; claims in
Shantung, Kioachow and Tsingtao,
17, 64-68, 255; racial equality, 63;
secures North Pacific islands, 67
Jordan, 131
Kemal, Mustapha (Ataturk) (President of
Turkey), 168, 185, 195, 202-4, 206, 208,
212, 214, 216, 218-21, 224, 228-31, 233-4,
241, 244, 246, 251-3
Kerr, Philip Henry (Secretary to Lloyd
George 1916-21), 79, 81, 83, 114, 165;
and Fontainebleau Memorandum, 28;
and the Rhineland, 35-6; and Belgian
demands, 42; and reparations, 50, 55;
and Turkey, 183, 204-5, 218
Keynes, John Maynard (Treasury
official), 27, 33, 50, 52-3, 84, 189
Khan, Aga (Head of Ismaili Muslims),
197
Kidston, George (Foreign Office official),
169
King, H. C. (US Commissioner to Middle
East), 158, 162-4, 167, 177, 178
Kitchener of Khartoum, Field-Marshal
Lord (Consul-General in Egypt
1911-14; Secretary of State for War
1914-16), 133, 135, 137
Klagenfurt, 112
Klotz, Louis (French Minister of
Finance), 53-4
Kolchak, Admiral A. V. (White Russian
Admiral), 123, 125
Kun, Bela (Soviet Prime Minister of
Hungary Mar-Aug 1919), 102-5, 123
Lansdowne, Marquess of (Minister
without Portfolio 1916), 20-21
Lansing, Robert (US Secretary of State
1915-20), 22, 83, 88, 103, 118
Latvia, 118-20
Lausanne Conference, 101, 236-47, 249,
251, 253, 255, 256
Law, Andrew Bonar (Chancellor of the
Exchequer 1916-19; Lord Privy Seal
1919-21; Prime Minister 1922-3), and

French demands, 33; and reparations,
53, 55, 56; and the Versailles Treaty,
71; and Turkey, 241-2
Lawrence, T. E., 144, 214
League of Nations, 19, 24, 25, 27, 28, 31,
34, 36, 39, 57, 70, 71, 73, 74, 82, 83, 90,
111-3, 115, 127, 142, 148, 163, 173-4,
185, 187, 205, 208-9, 240, 243, 245; and
the Peace Conference, 56-63; and arms
limitation, 61, 63; Covenant, 63; and
mandates, 65-7, 76, 79, 131, 151, 178,
198-9, 205
Lebanon, 131, 146, 155, 169, 172, 173, 174
Leeper, Allen (Foreign Office official), 26
Lenin, V. I., 122
Lindley, Sir Francis (British Minister to
Athens 1922-23), 224, 227, 228
Lithuania, 117, 118-20
Lloyd George, David (British Prime
Minister 1916-22), 26, 27-9, 35, 40, 61-2,
82, 84, 93, 111, 253-4; and war aims,
18-20, 57, 64; freedom of the seas, 22;
1918 election, 23; organization of Peace
Conference, 25-6; and Rhineland, 36;
and German disarmament, 44-5; and
reparations, 46-56; and League, 57-63;
82; and German colonies, 64-8;
Shantung, 68; and Versailles Treaty,
69-75; and Eyre Crowe, 80-1; and
Central Europe, 89, 103, 104, 125-7;
and Italy, 107, 109; and Poland, 114-8,
256-7; and Russia, 121-4; and the
Middle East, 139-40, 144-5, 148, 153,
157-9, 165-7, 168, 171-5, 177, 179; and
Turkey, 183, 185, 189, 191-6, 201, 203,
205, 207-20, 223, 225-8, 231, 233, 235-6,
246, 248-51, 255
Long, Walter Hume (Viscount)
(Colonial Secretary 1916-19; First
Lord of the Admiralty 1919-21), 158,
171; on Committee on Indemnity
Nov-Dec 1918, 47; on reparations, 53
Lord, Dr Robert H. (US Adviser on
Poland), 114
Luxemburg, 34, 39-43
Macedonia, 97, 101
Mallet, Sir Louis (Chairman, Foreign
Office Committee on War Aims 1916),
20, 153
Malta, 202, 237
Massey, William Ferguson (New Zealand
Prime Minister 1912-25; Member of
Imperial War Cabinet 1917-18; New

Zealand Representative at Peace
Conference 1919), 55, 66, 73, 75
Max, Prince of Baden (German
Chancellor 1918), 22
McMahon, Sir Henry (High
Commissioner in Egypt 1914-16), 135,
136-9, 140, 141, 142, 166, 168, 176-7
Mesopotamia, 131-8, 144-5, 148-51, 154,
156, 165-6, 169-78, 217, 224, 238-40,
242-3, 256
Mezes, Sidney E. (Member of the US
Delegation at Paris 1919), 35, 36
Miller, David Hunter (Member of US
Delegation at Paris 1919), 60
Millerand, Alexandre (French Prime
Minister 1920), 126, 173, 207, 215
Milne, General Sir George (Allied
Commander-in-Chief Asiatic Turkey),
200, 215
Milner, Alfred (Viscount) (Secretary of
State for War 1918; for Colonies
1919-21; Member of War Cabinet
1916-19), and war aims (economic), 21;
and reparations, 71; and Russia, 121;
and The Middle East, 155, 157
Monroe Doctrine, and the League, 61-3
Montagu, Edwin (Secretary of State for
India 1917-22), and reparations, 50-1;
and Turkey, 184, 196-8, 204-7, 225-6,
249
Montenegro, 93, 106, 108
Morison, Samuel E. (Member of US
Delegation at Paris 1919), 119
Mussolini, Benito, 237
New Zealand, claim to Samoa, 64, 66-7,
231
Nicolson, Harold (Foreign Office
official), 26, 99, 108, 188, 190, 192, 196-7,
232, 250
Nitti, Francesco (Italian Prime Minister
1919-20), 109, 126, 207, 212
Northcliffe, Lord (Newspaper magnate),
52
Orlando, Vittorio Emanuele (Italian
Prime Minister 1917-19), and
Fourteen Points, 22; on Council of
Four, 27; and Fiume, 106, 107, 108, 109;
and Turkey, 187, 191, 192
Ottoman Empire (see Turkey)
Palestine, 131, 134, 138-9, 143, 144, 145,
147, 148, 149, 150, 152, 155, 156, 158-9,
160, 161, 162, 163, 164, 170, 171, 172, 174,
175,176, 177, 178, 255, 256

Parker, Alwyn (Foreign Office
Librarian), 24-5
Paton, H. J. (Admiralty official at Paris
Peace Conference), 116, 117, 119
Percy, Lord Eustace (Foreign Office
official), and the League, 59; on League
Commission, 60
Persia, 132, 133, 171, 175
Phillimore, Sir Walter (Committee on
the League 1918), 58
Pichon, Stephen (French Foreign
Minister 1917-20), 27, 54
Picot, François Georges (French
diplomat), 137, 139, 141, 142, 145, 146,
149, 150, 151, 152, 154, 155, 166, 168, 171,
177, 178, 182
Poincaré, Raymond (President of France
1913-20; French Prime Minister and
Foreign Minister 1920-24), 38, 222-3,
225, 231, 232, 237, 241
Poland, 19, 29, 32, 41, 69-70, 72, 74, 87, 89,
91, 119-20, 124, 129; frontiers of, 113-8,
121, 198, 257
Political Intelligence Department
Foreign Office, 89, 23-4
Polk, Frank (US Delegate to the Peace
Conference), 83, 201
Portugal, 67
Prothero, G. W. (Foreign Office official),
115
Reparations, 19, 22-3, 26, 27, 28, 32, 33, 34,
40, 241, 244, 257; at the Peace
Conference, 45-56, 61, 71-4, 75, 76, 77,
85, 124, 256; Central Europe, 99-100,
112-3, 127
Rhineland, 23, 28, 29, 34-8, 42, 61, 70,
73-4, 76, 77, 79, 145, 213
Robeck, Admiral Sir John de
(Commander-in-Chief
Mediterranean Fleet and High
Commissioner at Constantinople
1919-20), 199, 210, 211-2
Roberts, General Sir William (Chief of
the Imperial General Staff 1915-18), 21
Rodd, Sir Rennell (Baron Rennell)
(Ambassador to Italy 1908-19), 188, 195
Rumania, 17, 26, 32, 48, 88, 89, 94, 97, 98,
124, 127, 129, 230, 254, 257; and
Hungary, 101-5; occupation of
Hungary, 105, 125, 127
Ruhr, 241, 242
Rumbold, Sir Horace (High
Commissioner at Constantinople

1920-24), 228-9, 230, 233, 234, 241, 243-4, 247

Russia, 19, 27, 32, 70, 81, 85, 86, 90, 114, 116, 117, 119, 120-4, 129, 132-4, 140, 145, 181, 182, 186, 187, 203, 215, 228, 235, 237, 239, 240, 245, 247, 249, 250, 253-4, 257, 258

Saar, 27, 29, 38-9, 40, 42, 73

Sami Bey (Turkish Nationalist representative at London Conference 1921), 251-2

Samuel, Sir Herbert (High Commissioner for Palestine 1920-25), 161

San Remo, 97, 146, 172, 173-4, 175, 177, 179, 207

Saud, Ibn, 141, 148, 167, 176

Serbia (see Yugoslavia)

Sèvres, Treaty of, 101, 178, 207, 213, 214, 215, 216, 218, 223, 226, 229, 230, 236, 242 245, 246, 247, 255

Sforza, Count Carlo (Italian Foreign Minister 1920-21), 215, 231

Shantung, 64-8, 255

Smith Llewellyn (Board of Trade official at Paris), 189, 197

Smuts, General Jan Christian (Member of the War Cabinet 1917-19; South African Minister of Defence 1910-20; Prime Minister of South Africa 1919-24), 48, 49, 53, 55; and war aims, 19; and Peace Conference organization, 25; and the League, 57, 148-9; and German colonies, 65-6; protests severity of Versailles Treaty, 69-75, 76, 77; mission to Hungary, 90-1, 104

Smyrna, 182-3, 185, 186, 187, 188, 189, 190, 191, 192, 193, 194, 195, 196, 197, 198, 199, 200, 201, 202, 203, 205, 207, 208, 209, 210, 212, 215, 217, 218, 220, 223, 225, 227, 228, 247, 248, 251, 252, 255

Sonnino, Baron Sydney (Italian Foreign Minister 1914-19), 106, 187, 192

South Africa, 64-7

Sumner, Lord (Lord of Appeal; British delegate on the Peace Commission on Reparation 1919), 48-56, 72; Bulgaria, 99; Austria, 113

Straits (see Constantinople)

Switzerland, 111, 112

Sykes, Sir Mark (M. P. and Assistant Secretary, War Cabinet Secretariat

1916-19), 137, 139, 141, 142, 145, 146, 149, 150-1, 152, 154, 155, 166, 168, 171, 174, 177, 178, 182

Syria, 131, 134, 135, 136-8, 143, 144, 146, 147, 149, 151, 152, 153, 154, 155, 156, 157, 163, 164-5, 166, 167, 168, 169, 170, 171, 172, 173, 174, 175, 176, 177, 178, 179, 195

Tardieu, André (French Delegate to Paris Peace Conference 1919), 35, 117, 157

Teschen, 118

Thrace, 96-101, 187, 205, 208 209, 210, 212, 218, 223, 224, 227, 229, 232, 233, 234, 235, 238, 245

Thwaites, General Sir William (Director of Military Intelligence 1918-22), 186

Tittoni, Tommaso (Italian Foreign Minister 1919-20), 109, 200

Toynbee, Arnold (Foreign Office official), 26, 190

Turkey, 19, 71, 81, 93, 95, 96, 254, 255, 258; future of, 131-252

Tyrrell, Sir William (Foreign Office official), 26, 87, 248

United States of America, 20, 26, 29, 31, 49-50, 61-3, 75, 82-4, 95-9, 102, 105-6, 110, 127, 145, 147, 148, 150, 153-6, 163-4, 166, 177-9, 184, 186-9, 192, 194, 205, 208-9, 213, 237, 244, 248, 253, 255, 258

Vansittart, Robert (Foreign Office official), 165, 189

Venizelos, Eleutherios (Greek Prime Minister 1910-15, 1917-21), 94, 97, 151; and Smyrna, 182, 183, 187, 188, 189, 190, 191, 192, 193, 194, 196, 200, 201, 202, 204, 208, 210, 211, 212, 213, 214, 215, 220, 227, 233, 248

Versailles, Treaty of, 83, 85, 124, 205, 214, 253; China's refusal to sign, 68; Draft presented to Germany, 69; British efforts to ameliorate, 69-80; signature, 79-80, 81-2

Weizmann, Dr Chaim (Director Admiralty Laboratories 1916-19; President of the World Zionist Organization 1921-31), 158-9, 160, 161

William II (German Emperor 1888-1918), 40, 47, 182, 256

Wilson, A. T. (Indian Political Department official; Civil Commissioner in Mesopotamia), 134, 139, 148

Wilson, General Sir Henry (Chief of the

Imperial General Staff 1918-22), 92-3, 157, 174, 201, 206, 219, 220; and Fontainebleau Memorandum, 28; and the Rhineland, 34; and the German army, 45; and the occupation of Germany, 69

Wilson, Woodrow (President of the United States 1913-21), 24, 27, 31, 45, 76, 111, 122, 128, 139, 150-2, 155-7, 164, 177-8, 205; and war aims, 17, 89; Fourteen Points, 19, 31-2, 44, 48-9, 63, 183, 203, 255; visits London, 23, 49, 59; and Council of Four, 27; character, 33; and Rhineland, 35-8; reparations, 48-56; and League, 57-9, 60, 84-5, 253; and Senate, 61, 81; and German colonies, 64-5; Shantung, 67-8; and Central Europe, 103, 104; and Italy, 106; and Poland, 113-6; and Turkey, 185, 187, 189, 191, 194, 199, 209

Yudenich, General N. N. (White Russian General; Commander of Baltic army 1919), 120

Yugoslavia, 19, 26, 32, 48, 87, 88, 93, 95, 97-9, 101, 102, 106-10, 112, 124, 127, 128, 230, 257

Zimmern, Alfred (Foreign Office official), 59

Zionism, 138-9, 147, 158-60, 162-3, 164, 171, 172, 176